MORAL DISAGREEMENT

Widespread moral disagreement raises ethical, epistemological, political, and metaethical questions. Is the best explanation of our widespread moral disagreements that there are no objective moral facts and that moral relativism is correct? Or should we think that just as there is widespread disagreement about whether we have free will but there is still an objective fact about whether we have it, similarly, moral disagreement has no bearing on whether morality is objective? More practically, is it arrogant to stick to our guns in the face of moral disagreement? Must we suspend belief about the morality of controversial actions such as eating meat and having an abortion? And does moral disagreement affect the laws that we should have? For instance, does disagreement about the justice of heavily redistributive taxation affect whether such taxation is legitimate?

In this thorough and clearly written introduction to moral disagreement and its philosophical and practical implications, Rach Cosker-Rowland examines and assesses the following topics and questions:

- How does moral disagreement affect what we should do and believe in our day-to-day lives?
- Epistemic peerhood and moral disagreements with our epistemic peers.
- Metaethics and moral disagreement.
- Relativism, moral objectivity, moral realism, and non-cognitivism.
- Moral disagreement and normative ethics.
- Liberalism, democracy, and disagreement.
- Moral compromise.
- Moral uncertainty.

Combining clear philosophical analysis with summaries of the latest research and suggestions for further reading, *Moral Disagreement* is ideal for students of ethics, metaethics, political philosophy, and philosophical topics that are closely related, such as relativism and scepticism. It will also be of interest to those in related disciplines such as public policy and philosophy of law.

Rach Cosker-Rowland is a Lecturer in the School of Philosophy, Religion, and History of Science at the University of Leeds, UK. They are the author of *The Normative and the Evaluative*, and the co-editor of *Companions in Guilt Arguments in Metaethics* (Routledge, 2019).

NEW PROBLEMS OF PHILOSOPHY

SERIES EDITOR: JOSÉ LUIS BERMÚDEZ

"*New Problems of Philosophy* is developing a most impressive line-up of topical volumes aimed at graduate and upper-level undergraduate students in philosophy and at others with interests in cutting edge philosophical work. Series authors are players in their respective fields and notably adept at synthesizing and explaining intricate topics fairly and comprehensively."

– John Heil, Monash University, Australia, and Washington University in St. Louis, USA

"This is an outstanding collection of volumes. The topics are well chosen and the authors are outstanding. They will be fine texts in a wide range of courses."

– Stephen Stich, Rutgers University, USA

The *New Problems of Philosophy* series provides accessible and engaging surveys of the most important problems in contemporary philosophy. Each book examines either a topic or theme that has emerged on the philosophical landscape in recent years, or a longstanding problem refreshed in light of recent work in philosophy and related disciplines. Clearly explaining the nature of the problem at hand and assessing attempts to answer it, books in the series are excellent starting points for undergraduate and graduate students wishing to study a single topic in depth. They will also be essential reading for professional philosophers. Additional features include chapter summaries, further reading and a glossary of technical terms.

Disjunctivism
Matthew Soteriou

The Metaphysics of Identity
André Gallois

Consciousness
Rocco J. Gennaro

Abstract Entities
Sam Cowling

Embodied Cognition, Second Edition
Lawrence Shapiro

Self-Deception
Eric Funkhouser

Relativism
Maria Baghramian and Annalisa Coliva

Empathy
Heidi Maibom

Moral Disagreement
Rach Cosker-Rowland

For more information about this series, please visit: https://www.routledge.com/New-Problems-of-Philosophy/book-series/NPOP

MORAL DISAGREEMENT

Rach Cosker-Rowland

Routledge
Taylor & Francis Group

LONDON AND NEW YORK

First published 2021
by Routledge
2 Park Square, Milton Park, Abingdon, Oxon OX14 4RN

and by Routledge
52 Vanderbilt Avenue, New York, NY 10017

Routledge is an imprint of the Taylor & Francis Group, an informa business

© 2021 Rach Cosker-Rowland

British Library Cataloguing in Publication Data
A catalogue record for this book is available from the British Library

Library of Congress Cataloging-in-Publication Data
Names: Rowland, Richard (Writer on ethics), author.
Title: Moral disagreement / Rach Cosker-Rowland.
Description: New York City : Routledge, 2021. | Series: New problems of
philosophy | Includes bibliographical references and index. | Identifiers:
LCCN 2020027106 | ISBN 9781138589841 (hbk) | ISBN
9781138589858 (pbk) | ISBN 9780429491375 (ebk)
Subjects: LCSH: Ethics.
Classification: LCC BJ1012 .R69 2021 | DDC 170–dc23
LC record available at https://lccn.loc.gov/2020027106

ISBN: 978-1-138-58984-1 (hbk)
ISBN: 978-1-138-58985-8 (pbk)
ISBN: 978-0-429-49137-5 (ebk)

DOI: 10.4324/9780429491375

For Zoë, with whom I disagree both more and less than anyone else

CONTENTS

ILLUSTRATIONS

FIGURES

TABLES

ACKNOWLEDGMENTS

I would like to thank Tony Bruce and Adam Johnson at Routledge for all the work and encouragement throughout this project and for finding several great referees who made this book a lot better. One of these was Michael Klenk who read the whole of the manuscript and contributed many extremely helpful comments. One of several great referees on the initial proposal that helped shape the direction of this project was Klemens Kappel. Steph Collins gave extremely helpful comments on chapter 9. Zoë Cosker gave extremely helpful comments on chapters 1-2. Audiences at Leeds, Reading Cambridge, and Mancept gave extremely useful feedback on the material that turned into chapter 7. Discussions with David Killoren greatly helped chapters 1 and 11. Steve Finlay helped me think about chapter 3. I would like to thank my graduate class on moral disagreement in Oxford in 2015 who helped me think in more detail about different facets of moral disagreement, especially Simon-Pierre Chevarie-Cossette and Tanya Goodchild. And, once again, thanks to Phil and Carol for granting me use of their dining table for gratuitous amounts of time as I finished this book in lockdown in the wonderful Lincolnshire countryside.

PREFACE

I grew up in a very politically involved working class household. I was surrounded by trade unionists and left-wing activists canvassing for the Labour party. We lived in Nottinghamshire, on the edge of the north of England, a Labour stronghold.[1] When I was 10 we moved to a village near Bude, a seaside town in Cornwall at the other end of the country. Cornwall was much more conservative than Nottinghamshire. I'd never found myself in a political disagreement before I moved. But now I frequently would. My local MP in Nottinghamshire was strongly anti-hunting: he'd been proposing a ban on fox-hunting for years. And Labour eventually got a ban on fox-hunting through parliament. But I now lived in a rural farming community. On my school bus teenagers would chastise the Labour government for not understanding their way of life, and for banning something they said was integral to the functioning of local farms.

In Bude, one of the first disagreements that I found myself in was with my new best friend. We were in a tiny rural school. We were both doing well academically, and we also liked the same video games, films, and were both big into football. One afternoon he said that his parents supported the right-wing Conservative (Tory) party. He asked me which political party my parents supported (by which he meant, which party was my family's). I said it was Labour. I still remember his response: 'Oh, what do you know anyway?' he exclaimed, before walking away. I remember this response because it struck me as both right and wrong. Yeah, of course, the fact that he and his parents were Tories didn't make me change my view at all, so I wouldn't expect the fact that my parents and I disagreed with him to make much difference to him either. And there wouldn't be too much point in us talking about it. Other things were more interesting to talk about anyway! But at the same time I did know things. He didn't really know about how politically engaged I'd been in Nottinghamshire: that doesn't come up when you have *Mario Kart* and *The Matrix* to discuss instead! But even if he'd have known all that, it's not clear that it would or should have mattered. My political upbringing was in a cosy echo-chamber that intensified the opinions I inherited from my parents. But then that was the same for him.

We often find ourselves in moral and political disagreements where we know a lot about those with whom we disagree because they are our friends, family members, colleagues, classmates, members of our clubs or societies, or because they are in the public eye (politicians, public intellectuals, celebrities, academics). We find ourselves in such disagreements about immigration policy, freedom of speech, taxing the rich, supporting the poor, what it's okay to do in a relationship, whether certain kinds of relationships are okay, eating meat, drinking milk, testing on animals, euthanasia, whether torture is ever permissible, affirmative action, the death penalty, abortion, gun control, our charitable obligations, whether certain kinds of police responses are permissible, and whether particular international sanctions and military actions are right or just. We disagree about whether it is just to penalise recipients of social security or unemployment benefits for failing to apply for a certain job when they are out of work; some think such welfare conditionality is just and that we do not use enough of it, others think that we shouldn't have any such conditionality at all. We disagree about the permissibility of certain activist tactics such as no-platforming, road blocks, locking on, and sabotage. And, as I finish this book in the middle of the COVID-19 pandemic, we disagree about whether it is right to continue lockdowns that are crippling our economies and destroying millions of peoples' lives for the sake of saving (tens of) thousands of lives.

For at least some of these issues, we often think that those with whom we disagree are our *epistemic equals* on the topics about which we disagree; that is, that they're as sensitive to the issues relevant to this topic and as likely to be right about it as we are. Another's being your epistemic equal or peer about a matter involves their having something like approximately equal epistemic credentials about it: their having capacities for assessing the evidence about the matter that are as good as your own, their being equally likely to get the right answer about that matter, or having as good evidence as you have about it. When we morally disagree with others whom we believe to be our epistemic equals about a particular topic, we think that they know about as much as we do about it, have thought about it about as much as we have, and have arguments for their views. We just disagree about how to interpret some idea, we have different moral intuitions or inclinations, or they have some evidence or data that we don't have, and we have some that they don't have.

It can be worrying to think that we are in moral disagreements with our epistemic equals about issues that we have strong and relatively settled moral convictions about. How can we reasonably stick with our own views given that our epistemic equals disagree with us? It can seem very arrogant to do so. Doing so seems like illegitimately privileging our thought and reasoning above theirs. And it seems odd to think that this is okay. But even more worrying, if we can't reasonably maintain our moral views, how can we reasonably and justifiably act on them? Normally if you can't reasonably believe something, you shouldn't act on it: if I don't know whether the supermarket will be open past 5 p.m., I shouldn't act as if it will be open past 5! So, disagreements with our epistemic equals about morality may have implications for what we ought to do, as well as what we can reasonably believe and know. Part II of this book focuses squarely on the implications of moral disagreement for what we can reasonably believe and do.

Where Part II of the book focuses on the consequences of moral disagreement for what we can be justified in believing and doing, Part I focuses on the descriptive implications of moral disagreement for how we should understand what morality is like. These descriptive implications don't depend on whether the moral disagreements that we find ourselves in are with our epistemic equals or not. In the US, over 5 million NRA members and close to half of 18–29-year-olds believe that we have rights to own guns; most Europeans disagree (BBC 2019). A significant proportion of the 41 million Yoruba people in Nigeria believe that it is permissible to scarify their young children's faces to identify their heritage or for the purpose of beatification; many others disagree. How do we explain moral disagreements like these? If you think that these millions of parents and gun owners are very wrong about guns and scarification (respectively), how so? How come you have access to the moral truth and they don't? A natural thought is that it's not that you are hooked up to the moral truth in a way that they're not, but rather that our differing moral views are just a product of our different cultures. There is a strong gun-owning culture in the US but not in Europe, and there is a strong cultural practice of scarification in Nigeria but not elsewhere. And this explains why people in these different places have different moral views. (I was brought up in a left-wing environment, my friend was brought up in a more right-wing environment, and that explains why we held different political views.) But if our moral views are just a product of our cultures, then what these views are about cannot be entirely independent of our cultures. In this case, some argue that whether an action is right or wrong isn't a matter that there is an objective truth about: morality is rather just relative to us or our cultures.

However, the idea that there are no objective moral truths seems to clash with our everyday moral practice. If we didn't think that there was an objective truth about the morality of abortion, vegetarianism, gun control, euthanasia, and legitimate warfare, then why would we make arguments for different views about these things and disagree with one another about them; if there were no objective moral truths about these things, then there would be nothing to disagree about and to make arguments for, only different preferences and ways of life to express. But when we disagree and argue morally we seem to do more than express our preferences or our ways of life. To express a preference or way of life we do not need to make a complicated argument. Pro-choicers and pro-lifers seem to make inconsistent claims. But when we express preferences or ways of life we do not make inconsistent claims. If I say that I like my family's practice of going on holidays to small islands, bird watching, and playing board games, and you say that you prefer your family's metropolitan lifestyle of going to the ballet and having expensive dinners, we don't disagree or express inconsistent propositions: the fact that A likes X, or A's way of life is X, is consistent with the fact that B likes Y, or B's way of life is Y. But the claim that abortion is wrong is inconsistent with the claim that it's permissible. Furthermore, we treat many moral claims, such as that gender and racial equality are right and that homosexuality is morally permissible, as though they are objective truths: we do not think that those who disagree with us about these matters just have different tastes or preferences from us but rather that they're making a fundamental mistake. Part I of this book discusses the implications of moral disagreement for debates about the objectivity of morality and whether moral judgments are just expressions of preferences, that is, for metaethics.

The final area that this book focuses on is political philosophy. A long liberal tradition in political philosophy has sought to find legitimate ways to accommodate the many moral disagreements that we find within particular societies and nations. Even if Catholicism is the true religion and the Pope has a direct connection to the moral truth, it would seem wrong for a state to force all of its non-Catholic citizens to conform with the dictates of Catholicism. But in holding this view aren't we just holding another view about the moral truth? (That it's wrong for a state to impose its moral views on others.) Some argue that the answer is no. Many political liberals hold that in order for a law to be legitimate it must be possible to justify it to all of those whom it coerces, where to justify a law to someone is to give them a reason that fits with their current values. These liberals seek to find principles for the legitimacy of a state and its laws that take very seriously the moral disagreements in pluralistic societies. Part III of the book focuses on the political upshot, or lack thereof, of moral disagreement, on the implications of moral disagreement for the laws and states that are legitimate as well as for how we ought to act, reason, and compromise when discussing and making policy decisions.

The main aim of the book is to provide a thorough introduction to the topic of moral disagreement that puts readers in a position to understand and evaluate contemporary work about the significance of moral disagreement for moral and political philosophy. The book also has two further aims. First, it aims to show that moral disagreement makes a difference to the metaethical theories we should accept as well as to what we should believe and do. Part of the way in which the book does this may illustrate the value of philosophy. For it shows that abstract philosophical work on moral disagreement makes a difference to what we should think and do in our everyday lives. Second, the book aims to link discussions of moral disagreement in different domains (e.g. moral epistemology and political philosophy) together and to link discussions of moral disagreement to other relevant work in moral philosophy to reveal unexplored features of the significance of moral philosophy and its limits. Accordingly, all chapters of the book summarise and introduce work on the significance of moral disagreement. But some parts of it, particularly Chapters 2, 6, 7, and 8 (and the final sections of Chapters 4 and 10), go beyond this literature in evaluating arguments that have yet to be evaluated, drawing out the implications of particular discussions of moral disagreement, and bringing discussions in different areas together.

This book is an introduction to contemporary work on moral disagreement that aims to be as comprehensive as possible. But it deals with several very different and large areas of philosophy including moral metaphysics, epistemology, and semantics, as well as applied ethics, normative ethics, political philosophy, and applied moral epistemology. Because of this, there are limits to how comprehensive it can be. For instance, this book cannot at all claim to comprehensively deal with issues about how moral disagreement is or may be important in political philosophy and political theory; that would be a book in itself. And because it is a general introduction aimed at anyone with a philosophical interest in moral disagreement that could not be even longer than it already is, some discussions are slightly more simplified and more cursory than they could have been. For instance, Chapter 3 discusses moral semantics very briefly and in a somewhat simplified way. But I still hope that this discussion can be of use to those with some metaethical knowledge as well as those with next to none.

NOTE

1 At the time; alas it is no more.

1

INTRODUCTION

This book focusses on moral disagreements that are fundamentally the result of differences of moral views rather than differences of judgments about empirical facts. I will refer to such disagreements as disagreements in moral principles or values. §1.1 explains what these moral disagreements are. §1.2 shows that many moral disagreements are disagreements in moral principles or values.

1.1. WHAT ARE DISAGREEMENTS IN MORAL PRINCIPLES OR VALUES?

Suppose that Alice disagrees with Becky and Christina about whether their government should tax the rich heavily (e.g. by taxing earnings at a rate of 75% above £50,000). Alice believes that their government morally should adopt such a heavily redistributive taxation policy and that it would be wrong and unjust for her government to fail to do so. In contrast, Becky and Christina judge that their government should not adopt such a heavily redistributive taxation policy and that it would be wrong and unjust for their government to do so. But the reasons why Becky and Christina believe this are different.

Becky believes that it would be wrong and unjust for the government to adopt this tax because she believes that it would be very bad for the least well-off. She believes that if this tax were adopted, most of the most productive and creative industries, highest payers of taxes and providers of jobs, would leave the country. The country's currency would become devalued and costs of living would spiral because the country would become dependent on

DOI: 10.4324/9780429491375-1

foreign imports and would have to pay more for them due to its devalued currency. There would be less jobs. And the economy would tank leading to a vicious cycle of negative consequences for the least well-off.

Alice disagrees with Becky about these consequences. She believes that their country has enough cultural attractions to prevent the big companies leaving and that even if some did they can rely on many of their own products and would still have their own goods to sell to those abroad if the big companies left. She thinks that everyone always scaremongers about the awful con-sequences of heavily redistributive taxation. But we have no evidence that the consequences of such taxation would be so bad other than the claims of those who have an interest in our government not adopting such taxes—and so whose views on this matter should be taken with a pinch of salt.

Becky and Alice agree that their government should pursue the taxation policy that benefits the least well-off. They just disagree about the empirical facts relevant to figuring out which policy is in fact best for the least well-off. So, Alice and Becky's disagreement is not fundamentally a moral disagree-ment; it's not a moral disagreement at all at heart, it's a disagreement about the non-moral empirical facts.

Now, in contrast, Christina agrees with Alice that strongly redistributive taxation would be better for the least well-off but she nevertheless judges that implementing such a strongly redistributive taxation policy would be wrong and unjust because she (libertarian that she is) judges that such strongly redistributive taxation would contravene the self-ownership rights of those who would be taxed; such taxation, she believes, would be akin to forced labour.[1] Alice's disagreement with Christina is fundamentally a moral dis-agreement. This is because it does not boil down to a disagreement about empirical economic or sociological facts, such as about which policies would make things go better for some group.

We can distinguish two types of such fundamentally moral disagreements. The broadest type of such disagreements are disagreements in moral princi-ples or values. What distinguishes Alice's disagreement with Christina from Alice's disagreement with Becky is that Alice and Christina hold different moral principles or values: Alice accepts the principle that justice requires that we make the poor better off; Christina does not accept this principle. In contrast, Alice and Becky do not have different moral values or accept dif-ferent moral principles; they both accept that justice requires that we make the poor better off.

Some disagreements in moral principles or values are disagreements that are the result of religious disagreements. For instance, many disagreements about the moral status of abortion are disagreements in moral principles or values that are the result of religious disagreements. Some people believe that it is wrong to abort foetuses because they hold religious beliefs according to which human life begins at conception and it is always wrong to end a human life. Similarly, many moral disagreements about the permissibility of euthanasia, homosexuality, and polygamous relationships are disagreements in moral principles or values that are the result of religious disagreements.

Some disagreements in moral principles or values are *not* the result of religious or other philosophical disagreements. We can call these disagreements *pure* moral disagreements. Alice and Christina's moral disagreement may well be a pure moral disagreement. Suppose that Alice and Christina are both atheists and neither have really studied or thought about philosophical claims, neither have particularly strong views about causation, free will or any other potentially relevant matter. In this case, their disagreement about whether we should tax the rich is just due to their holding different moral principles, and not the result of their holding different religious views or different (non-moral/political) philosophical claims such as different metaphysical or epistemological views. In contrast, moral disagreements about euthanasia, homosexuality, abortion, and polygamy that are the result of the parties to these disagreements holding different religious views are not pure moral disagreements.

Perhaps the most clear-cut case of a pure moral disagreement is the disagreement about what we ought to do in trolley cases. In the switch trolley case, there is a runaway trolley (a tram, if you're British or Australian). And if it keeps on going on the track that it's on, it will run over and kill five innocent people who are tied to the track. Suppose that you're stood next to the track. There's a lever that you can pull. If you pull the lever, you will switch the trolley so that instead of carrying on going on the track that it's on it will go down a sidetrack. There is only one innocent person tied to the sidetrack. So, if you pull the lever and turn the trolley onto the sidetrack, it will only kill one person rather than five. The majority of people think that it's right or permissible to pull the switch in this case, to save the five lives at the cost of one, though a significant minority think that it would not be wrong to do this.[2]

Figure 1.1 The switch trolley case.

In the footbridge trolley case, most things are the same: there's a runaway trolley and if it keeps on going on the track that it's on, it will run over and kill five innocent people who have been tied to the track. But in this case, there's no switch and no sidetrack. Instead, there's a bridge above the track. You are on the bridge. Next to you is a very heavy innocent man, leaning over the bridge. The man is just heavy enough that if you pushed him off the bridge and onto the track, he and his weight would stop the trolley in its tracks, the trolley would come to a halt, and the lives of the 5 who are tied to the track would be saved. (You know that your bodyweight on its own would not be enough to stop the trolley.) However, if you pushed the heavy man off the bridge and onto the track, the heavy man would die in the process. What is it morally permissible, right, and wrong to do in this case?

People frequently want to add in further details to the footbridge trolley case. We can explicitly rule all of these out: suppose that all the lives involved are equally good, all the people are equally good people, and that you have no special relationship to any of them. Suppose that you will forget about what you did either way and that no one will find out what you did. So, there are no reasons to hold that pushing or refraining from pushing is good or bad outside of the conditions stipulated in the case, namely that pushing would involve pushing one person to their death in front of a trolley in order to stop the trolley from killing five people.

People disagree about whether we should push the heavy man off the bridge. A majority of people judge that it would be wrong to do so. Others judge that it wouldn't be wrong to push, that it is permissible to push, or even that, if we are in this situation, we are morally required to push the one off the bridge so that five people's lives are saved. They argue that it is arbitrary to hold that we should pull the switch in the switch case but that we should not push in footbridge. Since all the relevant features of these two cases are the same: in both cases we can save 5 lives at the cost of 1 other, with no other additional bad consequences.[3]

Figure 1.2 The footbridge case.

These disagreements about what we should do in trolley cases are disagreements in moral principles or values for they survive when any grounds for differences in empirical judgments are explicitly stipulated away. But many disagreements about what we should do in trolley cases are also pure moral disagreements. Some may believe that we should not push the heavy man in the footbridge case because of their religious views and disagree with those who believe it is permissible to push the heavy man because of the different religious views they hold. But many atheists and people with the same religious views also disagree about whether we should push the heavy man off the bridge. They disagree about what we morally ought to do not because they hold different religious views or different views about metaphysics or epistemology more broadly; rather they disagree because they have different moral intuitions about this case or because they accept different moral principles. Those who hold that it's wrong to push hold principles such as that it is always wrong to intentionally kill a person, to kill a person with your hands, to breach someone's rights by seriously harming or killing them, or to kill one person to save 5 lives (rather than to, for instance, save 2 billion lives). Those who think that we should push disagree, believe that we should reject these principles and/or hold that we should do whatever will promote the most lives being saved in trolley cases.

So, some moral disagreements are just due to disagreements about the empirical consequences of actions and policies (e.g. Alice and Becky's). These are, *in a sense*, not really moral disagreements at all; they are disagreements about other things such as economics. These disagreements are not disagreements in moral principles or values. Other disagreements are disagreements in which the parties disagree because they hold different moral principles. Even if a disagreement about vegetarianism or abortion is a result of one of the parties to this disagreement being a devout Christian of a certain denomination and the other being an atheist, they still hold different moral principles. These disagreements *are* disagreements in moral principles or values but *are not* pure moral disagreements. Finally, some moral disagreements are entirely moral. They bottom out in moral disagreements such as those about the trolley problem. These moral disagreements are not disagreements due to disagreements about metaphysics, epistemology, religious claims, or the empirical consequence of actions or policies. They are disagreements in moral principles or values that *are also* pure moral disagreements.[4]

Much of the time pure moral disagreements and disagreements in moral principles and values are disagreements that would survive even if parties to these disagreements agreed on all the relevant non-moral facts and information. So, a good heuristic for thinking about whether a disagreement is a disagreement in moral principles of values is to ask whether that disagreement would survive agreement about all the relevant non-moral facts such as all the economic, psychological, sociological, facts. If this disagreement would

survive such non-moral agreement, then it is a disagreement in moral principles or values.[5]

Some moral disagreements are only partially disagreements in moral principles or values or only partially pure moral disagreements. For instance,
suppose that you disagree with someone about whether abortion if permissible partially because you hold different views about when a foetus can survive outside of the womb and partially because you hold different moral
principles. This disagreement is (only) partially a disagreement in moral
principles or values. (Note that we can be in a disagreement in moral principles or values without explicitly or implicitly holding a particular moral
principle. I just use this name because it is clearer than any alternative.)[6]

1.2. HOW MUCH DISAGREEMENT IN MORAL PRINCIPLES OR VALUES IS THERE?

There is clearly a lot of moral disagreement. Surveys seem to show that U.S.
opinion splits close to 50/50 on the morality of abortion, the death penalty,
same-sex relationships, and physician-assisted suicide (McCarthy, 2014). There
is inter- and intra-cultural disagreement about whether it's sometimes justifiable
to torture people in order to do good for others/society at large: in the United
States around 45% of people believe it is sometimes justifiable; 53% believe it is
not. 74% of people in China and India believe that torture is sometimes justified; while 81% of people in Spain believe that torture is never justified
(McCarthy, 2017). When I began writing this book in the first quarter of 2019
in Melbourne, Australia, the middle of the city was awash with vegan protestors shutting down the public transport system. Animal activists, in Melbourne
but also in Queensland, were invading farms on mass to liberate animals and
to show the world both how animals are treated in Aussie farms and how
wrong they believe this treatment of animals to be. A majority of people do not
agree with vegans that our practice of farming animals is morally wrong.[7] At
the same time, in London, Extinction Rebellion (XR) protestors were shutting
down major roads to protest a lack of political action on climate change. Many
politicians, police chiefs, newspaper owners, and members of the public did not,
and still do not, think that the issue is as pressing as XR protestors think it is,
and believe that there are moral problems with XR's tactics. There is also
clearly disagreement about the taxation policies that our governments should
adopt and about whether, and which, gun control laws and restrictions on
immigration our governments should adopt as well as about freedom of speech,
what it's okay to do in a relationship, affirmative action, the death penalty, our
charitable obligations, and whether certain kinds of sanctions on other countries or military action in other countries' territory are right or just. But how
much of this disagreement about what we ought to do, what's good, and what
justice requires is disagreement in moral principles or values?

We have quite a lot of anecdotal evidence that many moral disagreements are disagreements in moral principles or values. Although we do not know exactly how much disagreement about abortion is disagreement in moral principles and/or values, it seems safe to say that quite a large amount of it is, since quite a large number of these disagreements are the result of religious differences. Although some people are vegan for environmental or health reasons many are vegan because they believe that it is, other things equal, wrong to kill beings that are capable of feeling pleasure and pain—regardless of whether there are further bad consequences to doing so. And many people disagree with them about this. It's not entirely clear how much of the disagreement about the morality and justice of the death penalty is disagreement in moral principles or values. However, many people are in favour of the death penalty not just because of the deterrent benefits that it brings but rather because they believe that murderers deserve it.[8] Similarly, although we do not know how many of the disagreements about the justice of redistributive taxation are disagreements in moral principles or values (like Alice and Christina's disagreement in §1.1), we know that at least some of them are: libertarians are in disagreements in moral principles or values with liberal egalitarians and socialists for instance.[9]

A well-known body of work on moral disagreements within Western societies stems from Jesse Graham, Jonathan Haidt, and Brian Nosek's Moral Foundations Survey. The survey aims to ascertain the moral principles or values of those who take it. It also asks respondents questions about how they self-identify politically. Over two hundred thousand responses to the survey have been recorded. The authors argue that the results show that conservatives view the extent to which an action involves disrespect for an authority figure or the traditions of their society, disloyalty, or doing something disgusting, impure, 'unnatural', or degrading as more morally important in determining the moral status of that action than liberals do.[10] And the authors take this disagreement to be one that boils down to a conflict in moral values. It is not entirely clear from the Moral Foundations Survey data whether this disagreement between liberals and conservatives is an instance of disagreement in moral principles or values or not. It could be that many conservatives think that a society is stronger, happier, and safer if people are loyal, respect authority, and don't do things that others regard as disgusting, unnatural, or degrading; this is a traditional conservative thought.[11] And the survey does not differentiate between people who think that loyalty and authority are important for those reasons alone and those who believe they are important for other reasons too. But it seems relatively safe to presume that not all conservatives believe that it is just the good consequences of loyalty and respect for authority that give us reasons to be loyal and respect authority: some people think that a society without family loyalty and respect for elders and traditions would be bad in itself even if such a society would not lead to worse economic consequences than one with such respect and loyalty.[12] If this is right, then at least a portion of the moral disagreements that Graham, Haidt, and Nosek point to between social conservatives and liberals are disagreements in moral principles or values.[13]

As we discussed in §1.1, all disagreements among those who in fact understand the switch and footbridge trolley cases are disagreements in moral principles or values and many of these disagreements will be pure moral disagreements too. Several studies have found a lot of disagreement about these cases. For instance, in some studies people split 60/40 about whether it is permissible to push the heavy man off the bridge in the footbridge trolley case.[14]

Disagreements about trolley cases may seem irrelevant to real life. But trolley cases are, in fact, very similar to several real-life cases. In World War II the British government found themselves in a situation in which they could feed misleading information to the Nazis which would lead them to bomb areas of London that were less densely populated than those that were currently being bombed. But in directing bombs to less densely populated areas, the government would be redirecting a threat from killing a greater number of innocent people to killing a smaller number of innocent people, just as we would be doing if we pulled the switch in the switch trolley case. As Edmonds (2010) documents, the government were divided over whether it was permissible to redirect the Nazi bombs.

Some utilitarians argue that we shouldn't worry so much about trolley cases because we often sanction the building of new roads, railways, or sports stadiums in full knowledge that building these things will lead to a number of deaths that would not have occurred otherwise (either by those using the roads or the construction workers building these amenities). But nonetheless we accept the cost of these predictable deaths as a reasonable cost for the general well-being promoted by better roads, railways, and sports facilities. If the happiness of a greater number can outweigh the deaths of a few unknown people, then redirecting a threat away from the many towards the few is at least permissible.[15]

Somewhat similar debates also occurred in Western countries during the lockdowns that aimed to slow the spread of COVID-19 in 2020. Some argued that we should not prioritise the saving of thousands of lives that the lockdowns were aimed at saving over the severe costs to millions that would inevitably result from the dire economic consequences of these lockdowns. Others argued that saving tens of thousands of lives should take priority over the economy—even given the predictable negative consequences to many of an economic crash. Given that disagreements about trolley cases are pure moral disagreements, many of these disagreements may be pure moral disagreements too.

Some philosophers who hold that moral disagreement has significant implications for moral philosophy have done in-depth empirical work to shed light on whether salient moral disagreements are (i) disagreements in moral principles or values, (ii) pure moral disagreements, or neither. (This work will be important in the next chapter.) The first such empirical investigation by a philosopher interested in the significance of moral disagreement that I know of is Richard Brandt's. In 1954 Brandt turned anthropologist to investigate the ethics of the Hopi, a Native American Tribe in Arizona, in an attempt to ascertain the extent to which any moral disagreements that we have with them are disagreements in moral principles or values or pure moral disagreements. Brandt found that (many of) the Hopi did not seem to believe there to be anything wrong with playing with birds in a way that we would see as torturing them. As Brandt (1954, p. 213) puts it:

> [Hopi c]hildren sometimes catch birds and make 'pets' of them. They may be tied to a string, to be taken out and 'played' with. This play is rough, and birds seldom survive long. [According to one informant:] 'Sometimes they get tired and die. Nobody objects to this.'[16]

In contrast to (many of the) Hopi, most of us (now) believe that it's wrong to make birds suffer just for fun. Brandt (1954, p. 103) tried to figure out whether this disagreement was due to differences in empirical or religious beliefs or whether it was a pure moral disagreement. He could find no non-pure moral disagreement: the Hopi didn't have any relevant false non-moral beliefs such as that birds don't feel pain or that animals are rewarded for martyrdom in the afterlife. Neither did the Hopi regard birds as pure machines; rather, according to Brandt, they regarded animals as 'closer to the human species than does the average [American]' (Brandt, 1954, p. 245). So, it seems that most Americans find themselves in a pure moral disagreement with the Hopi about the permissibility, badness, or objectionable status of causing animals to suffer for fun.[17]

In their 1996 book, Richard Nisbett and Dov Cohen showed that: (a) white males in the south of the US are much more likely than white males in other regions of the US to be involved in homicides resulting from arguments; (b) white Southerners are more likely than Northerners to believe that violence would be extremely justified in response to a variety of affronts and to believe that if a man fails to respond violently to such provocation, he is 'not much of a man'; (c) southern states allow greater freedom to use violence in defence of both oneself and one's property than do northern states; (d) southern employers were more sympathetic to job applications from a prospective employee who had killed another in a barroom brawl after the person they killed had boasted of sleeping with the applicant's fiancée and asked the applicant to step outside (Nisbett & Cohen, 1996). John Doris and Alexandra Plakias (2008a, pp. 315–318) argue that this data shows that Northerners and Southerners disagree about the permissibility of interpersonal violence, and that it is very unlikely that this disagreement between them is the result of a disagreement about the non-moral facts. This is because all the data in Nisbett and Cohen's work seems to indicate that both Northerners and Southerners agree about all the relevant non-moral facts.[18] So, the disagreement between Northerners and Southerners appears to be a pure moral disagreement. (Perhaps this disagreement is due to a disagreement in religious beliefs. In this case it would be a disagreement in moral principles or values rather than a pure moral disagreement. But it is hard to see what religious differences could lead to such differences in views about the permissibility of interpersonal violence.)[19]

Many people think that it is morally worse to actively kill than to let someone die by refraining to help them; for instance, that it is morally worse to poison someone than to refrain from sending money to starving children in a faraway country and thereby let these children die. If actively killing is morally worse than letting die, then there is a moral difference between what ethicists call actions and omissions. Fraser and Hauser (2010, pp. 551–552) discuss data that reveals that British, American, and Canadian people accept that there is a moral difference between actions and omissions (e.g. that it is morally worse to harm someone than to pass by while they come to harm). But rural Mayans do not judge that there is a moral difference between actions and omissions. They argue that this disagreement is very likely to be a pure moral disagreement because Mayans do not have views about causation that are different from Westerners and Mayans do not have different religious and supernatural beliefs that bear on the actions and omissions that they were asked about.

1.3. THE STRUCTURE OF THE BOOK

So many moral disagreements are disagreements in moral principles or values. This book asks whether disagreements in moral principles or values make a difference to what moral principles or values we should accept, what we should do in our everyday lives, what political institutions may legitimately do, as well as how we should understand what morality itself is like. It is divided into three parts. Part II discusses how disagreements in moral principles or values can make a difference to what we ought to believe and do in our everyday lives. It discusses how abstract philosophical principles about the significance of disagreement are extremely practically relevant. Part III discusses the relevance of disagreement in moral principles or values for political philosophy and political decision-making.

Parts II and III of the book focus on the first-order *normative* work that moral disagreement might do in ethics and applied ethics, political philosophy, and applied epistemology. Part I is *descriptive*. It is about how we can best explain and interpret moral disagreement. Metaethical theories are descriptive theories. They aim to give descriptive accounts of our moral judgments, moral thought, and moral language: they aim to give accounts that fit well with what our actual moral judgments, thought, and language is like. For instance, in metaethics there is a debate between cognitivists and non-cognitivists. Cognitivists hold that moral judgments are beliefs, they aim to represent or fit the way the world is. Non-cognitivists hold that moral judgments are not belief-like states but are desire-like states such as intentions, plans, or approvals or disapprovals. This debate is about which view of the nature of our moral judgments most accurately describes our moral judgments and the features that they have. For instance, non-cognitivists argue that it is impossible to sincerely judge that you're morally required to take some action without being motivated to take that action: if you think you have a duty to go on strike, you must be to some extent motivated to strike; moral judgments always come with a degree of motivational force. If this description of moral judgments is correct, it counts in favour of non-cognitivism, which holds that moral judgments are constituted by motivational states such as intentions, plans, or desires. Chapters 2–4 discuss how descriptive facts about the amount and types of disagreements in moral principles and values that we find have philosophical implications.

Objectivists about morality hold that there are objective moral facts and truths that outstrip what we or our societies currently think is morally right and wrong. Chapters 2 and 4 discuss arguments from moral disagreement against objectivism. According to these arguments, in order to best explain or interpret the moral disagreements that we find within and across different countries and cultures we must reject objectivism. However, non-objectivist views about the nature of morality also face problems with their ability to make sense of disagreements: objectivists argue that these views struggle to accommodate the fact that we do in fact engage in moral disagreements. Chapter 3 discusses whether if we are non-objectivists, we can adequately describe ourselves as engaging in moral disagreements.

Part II of the book focuses on *personal justification:* what we are justified in believing and doing as individuals and how moral disagreement can impact on this. Chapter 5 discusses a general issue in epistemology: whether finding ourselves in a disagreement about an issue with a cognitive equal should lead us to change our beliefs about that issue or can alter what we can justifiably believe or know about that issue. According to an interesting set of views, finding ourselves in such disagreements does alter what we can be justified in believing. Chapter 6 discusses the implications of these views for what we can know and should believe about a variety of controversial moral issues including distributive justice, animal rights, and abortion. This chapter is about *applied epistemology:* the implications that particular epistemological principles have for what we should believe and can know about particular topics. Chapter 7 discusses how moral disagreement can have implications for what we ought to do. Sometimes what we can reasonably do depends on what we can reasonably believe. If I cannot reasonably believe that a substance in a jar is sugar rather than arsenic, then I cannot reasonably put that substance into a cake that I'm making. Does this mean that if moral disagreement with our cognitive equals makes it the case that we cannot reasonably believe that taxing the rich is permissible, then we cannot reasonably tax the rich? This chapter discusses how the epistemic impact of moral disagreement can have practical implications for what we ought to do.

The focus of Part II is extremely practical: it is about whether and how moral disagreement makes a difference to what we should believe and what we should do in our everyday lives. But it is also on the practical relevance of quite abstract philosophical principles about the epistemology of moral disagreement, moral obligations, and moral uncertainty for whether we should give to charity, eat animal products, vote for egalitarian political parties, or have an abortion, and whether we can believe that it is right or permissible to do these things. For instance, Chapter 5 discusses the view, sometimes known as conciliationism, that if we believe that p, and a significant number of our cognitive equals about a proposition p disagree with us about whether p, then we should lower our confidence or suspend belief about whether p. Chapter 6 discusses the implications of conciliationism for a wide range of moral topics (e.g. eating animals, gender and marriage equality, abortion) and for a wide range of the circumstances that we find ourselves in with regards to these particular topics. Chapter 7 discusses whether the epistemic impact of moral disagreement discussed in Chapter 6 has implications for what we personally ought to do: for whether we should give more to charity, stop eating meat, and refrain from having an abortion for instance. The aim of these chapters is to provide you, the reader, with resources to think about what the epistemology of moral disagreement means for your moral views: whether you can be justified in holding them given disagreement about them, and whether this has implications for how you should act. (We might therefore also think of this part of the book as showing the practical value of philosophy, that is, the value of philosophy for thinking about everyday life.)

Part III of this book focuses on *interpersonal political justification*, that is, on how moral disagreements can impact on the justification of actions and policy decisions at the level of state and group political decision-making. Chapter 8 discusses how moral disagreement can impact on what we ought to do as members of a collective making political or other group decisions. Does moral disagreement show that we should adopt compromise policies or decisions, and if so when? Many political liberals hold that in order for political power to be legitimate it must be justifiable to everyone over whom power is exercised, where to justify a law to someone is to give them a reason that fits with their current values.[20]Chapter 9 discusses whether we should hold this view and whether it implies that only particular kinds of states (e.g. heavily redistributive states or conversely libertarian minimal states) are justified. Democracy might seem like a fair way of mediating moral disagreements. Sometimes there is no policy that is morally neutral: if we tax the rich, the libertarians will say that's wrong; if we don't, the socialists will say that justice requires that we tax them. Democracy tries to find a way past entrenched moral disagreements by giving everyone an equal vote in determining the laws that our state adopts. Some argue that in light of moral disagreement a state that isn't democratic isn't legitimate. Others argue that other alternative voting and decision-making mechanisms are just as good if not better at fairly mediating moral disagreement. Chapter 10 discusses these arguments.

Parts II and III of the book discuss how moral disagreement can have implications for what we are individually and collectively justified in doing. Chapter 11 (Part III) of the book discusses how moral disagreements' justificatory implications may in fact have descriptive metaethical consequences beyond those discussed in the first part of the book. One aim of this book is to link the debates about the epistemological, metaethical, and political philosophical implications of moral disagreement together in the way that Chapter 11 does. But Chapters 8, 9, and 10 also contain some discussion of links between debates about disagreement in epistemology and political philosophy.

I hope that readers of this book will come from a variety of different backgrounds and have a variety of different interests. But some readers may not be interested in particular topics that this book covers in depth or may prefer to focus in on particular areas that this book discusses. The book focuses first on metaethics because the metaethical issues concerning moral disagreement focus on perhaps the most striking fact about moral disagreement, which we have discussed in this chapter, namely that there is widespread disagreement in moral principles and values. The epistemic consequences of disagreement relate to perhaps less striking, and more controversial, features of moral disagreement; though features of moral disagreement that can be of greater concern to us in figuring out how to go about our lives. But if you're not interested in metaethics, you should skip Chapters 2–4 of this book and focus on Parts II–III of this book which focus on more practical issues about the implications of moral disagreement.

NOTES

1 See Nozick (1974, pp. 169–174).

2 See note 14.

3 Those who disagree contest that there is no relevant difference between the cases: some argue, for instance, that the trolley's hitting the one is not part of our plan if we switch the lever, but must be part of our plan if we push the heavy man.

4 The notion of a 'pure moral disagreement' is due to Bennigson (1996, p. 422) and McGrath (2011).

5 However, although this is a useful heuristic, we should not think of pure moral disagreements and moral disagreements in principles and values as those which would survive non-moral agreement. To see this take pure moral disagreements. Suppose that A and B disagree about whether homosexuality is permissible. A believes it is not because she believes that her God outlaws it; B disagrees because she believes that (i) A's God does not exist and (ii) if they did exist, their outlawing homosexuality wouldn't make a difference to its moral status. This disagreement is in part a pure moral disagreement—that is, it is in part purely the result of differences in moral judgments and nothing else—in virtue of being in part about (ii). Now suppose that if B were to change her view about (i) and convert to A's religion, then A would also simultaneously change her view about (ii) and so change her pure moral views. If pure moral disagreements are those which would survive non-moral agreement, then A and B's disagreement is not in part a pure moral disagreement. But this is the wrong result. A and B's disagreement is in part a pure one since (ii) is a purely moral issue.

6 So, if, like particularists, you're sceptical of moral principles, or think that we do not make moral judgments on the basis of them, you needn't be sceptical of the idea that there are disagreements in moral principles or values.

7 See Morgan (2016) and McCarthy (2018) for statistics regarding how few people are vegan; although, in 2020, this does seem to be changing quickly.

8 For a different research project I recruited a random sample of 196 people from Amazon's Mechanical Turk platform and asked them about a case in which there was no beneficial effects to punishing someone rather than monitoring them. 39% of participants said that they thought it was right to punish rather than monitor.

9 Cf. Stich's (2007) argument that data concerning different small communities responses to the ultimatum game show that different small communities have different views about fairness; it is unclear that this data reveals disagreement in moral principles or values, however.

10 See Graham et al. (2009, pp. 1031–1033), Haidt (2012), and Kim et al. (2012).

11 See, for instance, Robin (2011).

12 I was not entirely sure that this was the case. So, I recruited a random sample of 105 people from Amazon's Mechanical Turk Platform. I asked them about several cases in which if respect for authority and loyalty matter, they must matter for their own sake rather than because of the good personal or social consequences of being loyal or obeying an authority. Those who respond to these cases by holding that we should respect authority/be loyal are in a disagreement in moral principles or values with those who respond to these cases by claiming that we need not respect authority/be loyal in these cases. In a case involving parental authority 71% of participants thought it was wrong for the subject of the case to disobey their parents' orders—even though no short or long term bad consequences would ensue and the subject was stipulated to know this. In an analogous case involving a boss figure, 55% thought it was wrong to disobey. In two analogous cases involving group and family loyalty—and knowledge of no short- or long-term consequences—38% and 39% thought it was wrong to be disloyal.

13 It is an interesting question how much of this disagreement is disagreement in moral principles or values. A survey along the lines of that discussed in note 12 but with a representative sample of the US/UK would shed light on this question.

14 See Weijers, Unger, and Sytsma (2019) and Rowland and Killoren (2020); on the latter see also §11.2.2 See also Hauser et al. (2007), Kelman and Kreps (2014), and Wiegmann and Meyer (2015). Doris and Plakias (2008a, pp. 322–325) discuss a study about a similar case. They argue that it showed that many American and Chinese people are in a disagreement in moral principles or values about certain trolley-style cases.

15 For discussion see Fried (2012).

16 See also Doris and Plakias (2008a, p. 314).

17 For discussion see Doris and Plakias (2008a, pp. 313–316).

18 Doris and Plakias (2008a, pp. 320–321) argue that the disagreement between Northerners and Southerners is not the result of self-interest biasing the views of either party either. Since there is no reason to think that, for instance, southerners' economic interests are served by 'being quick on the draw' rather than 'turning the other cheek'.

19 Cf. Fraser and Hauser (2010, pp. 546–551).

20 This is Lister's (2016, pp. 12–13) gloss.

PART I

METAETHICS
THE DESCRIPTIVE CONSEQUENCES OF MORAL DISAGREEMENT

2

EXPLAINING MORAL DISAGREEMENT

Some things call for explanation. And when something calls for explanation we offer different theories of what explains it. Take one example. Tyler Gillett and his wife are driving home from a party. He starts singing a song that has gotten stuck in his head. His wife asks him what the song is. Tyler is alarmed: 'You don't know this song? This was like a huge thing in the '90s! I can't believe you don't know this song.' He pulls out his phone and googles its lyrics. But he can't find it anywhere. This surprises him because the lyrics are really specific; one of them is 'better than a sultan for a bride'. Tyler stays up for hours that night and the next. The song is driving him crazy. He keeps on remembering more lyrics. But it's no use, he can't find it on Google or anywhere else. Tyler's sure that the song wasn't obscure. He was a kid in the '90s and he only listened to mainstream music he heard on the radio. What explains how Tyler could have heard the song a million times on Arizona radio 20 years ago but now the song is nowhere to be found? It's like it's been erased: deleted without a trace.

First explanation. It's a regional hit that didn't make it out of Arizona.

But this explanation doesn't hold up for very long. Eventually Tyler finds one reference to the song online. It's in an internet forum posted by someone from Trinidad and Tobago. So, evidence that the song wasn't just a regional Arizonan hit.

Tyler phones up one of the producers of the show *Reply All*, PJ Vogt, to ask for help figuring out what the song he couldn't get out of his head is. Tyler has an incredible memory of the song. He's no musician. But by this

DOI: 10.4324/9780429491375-3

point he's recorded a multi-tracked version of the song in which he sings the rhythm, lead, and bass guitar parts as well as *all* of the lyrics to the song. PJ manages to get some musicians together to record a full band version of the song directed by Tyler using his detailed memory of it. PJ then uses the recording to ask people who know a lot about the music industry in the '90s if they know the song. PJ calls up six critics at *Rolling Stone* and plays them the track. They've never heard it. He calls up the ex-editor of *Pitchfork* and *MTV News*. She's never heard it. He calls up a radio programme director from the '90s. He's never heard it. The song sounds like the most famous Bare Naked Ladies song, 'One Week'. So, PJ phones the former frontman of the Bare Naked Ladies. He doesn't recognise it. He calls up Susan Rogers, who was one of the producers who produced all the records for bands who sounded a bit like the Bare Naked Ladies in the '90s. She's never heard it.

So, not only had Tyler heard the song a million times on the radio in the '90s and there's now next to no trace of the song on the internet, but none of a wide assortment of music industry producers, musicians, and critics have heard the track either. But though none of them had heard it they do propose several explanations of how this could have happened.

> **Second explanation.** The critics at *Rolling Stone* think that the fact that they've never heard it means that the song probably doesn't exist. They think that Tyler is probably lying, that the whole thing is a hoax.
>
> **Third explanation.** This one's from the ex-frontman of the Bare Naked Ladies. 1997–2002 was the music industry boom. The industry was signing loads of bands. They would trial the songs of bands they'd signed in particular areas. And if no one responded positively to the song, they would the pull the record or it would come out without promotion. So sometimes a song would seem like it was a hit to you because it was on the radio all the time where you were. But in reality you were only hearing it because it was being tested in your market.
>
> **Fourth explanation.** Susan Rogers thinks that Tyler has probably created this song himself. She says that when she was as producer this happened all the time. She remembered Prince playing something on the piano and not knowing whether it was something he'd just written or not. She remembered Crosby, Stills, and Nash producing a song that they thought was their own but which was actually all over the radio at the time. Even professional musicians sometimes mistake whether they are writing or recalling a song.

Are any of these explanations the right one?

One problem with both the second and fourth explanation is that neither of them can explain the post about the song from Trinidad and Tobago. Only the third explanation can explain this. So, PJ goes back to looking at the forum post from Trinidad and Tobago. It mentions that the full lyrics to the song have been posted on Facebook. So, PJ trawls Facebook. Eventually he finds the post. At the very bottom, the post references the writer of the song. It was Evan Scott Olson. The second and fourth explanations were wrong. And, as it turns out, explanation three was right. Olson was signed by Universal Records. But Universal didn't put any funding into his record because the lead single off the album—which Tyler heard—flopped in the markets it was tested in. The release of Olson's record was buried by the label and he was dropped quickly after.[1]

The fact that Tyler Gillett recalled a full song from 20 years ago that he'd heard a lot on the radio in that time but that had now completely disappeared and couldn't be found on the internet called for explanation. According to some philosophers working in metaethics, the wide-ranging disagreements about morality that we discussed in the last chapter similarly call for explanation. And the theory that best explains these disagreements is a particular theory about the nature of morality, namely a kind of relativism about the nature of morality which holds that there are no universal moral truths and no moral facts that outstrip our or our communities' sensibilities. In this chapter we'll look at why we might think that widespread moral disagreement calls out for explanation. As we'll discuss, there are many ways widespread moral disagreement might be explained, just as there were many possible explanations of how Tyler seemed to remember a song from the '90s that had now been completely lost. We'll discuss how the view that morality is not objective, and is rather relative, does seem to provide a particularly good explanation of widespread moral disagreement, which like explanation 3 of Tyler's inability to find the song, has particular virtues that other explanations do not have. Objectivists argue that they can provide explanations of widespread moral disagreement that are just as good as those provided by relativists. We'll assess whether objectivists are right about this. But before discussing whether the view that morality is relative best explains widespread moral disagreement, we need to know bit more about objectivist and relativist theories of morality.

2.1. THEORIES OF THE NATURE OF MORALITY: A BRIEF PRIMER

First-order normative ethical theories give accounts of which actions are right, wrong, just, unjust, good, and bad, and what makes these actions right, wrong, good, and bad. For instance, utilitarianism gives an account of which actions are right and wrong. According to utilitarians, it is right to tell a white lie or break a promise when doing so would lead to better consequences than not doing so. Utilitarians argue that what makes this the case is that it is right to take whatever action would promote the best consequences and wrong to take actions that do not promote the best consequences. Deontologists disagree. Some hold that it is always wrong to break promises or to lie. Others hold that it is not always wrong to lie or break a promise but disagree with utilitarianism because it holds that we should kill one person when our doing so is the only way in which we can save five people (such as in the trolley cases discussed in Chapter 1). Deontologists also give accounts of what makes actions wrong; for instance, Kantians hold that wrongful actions are wrong because they are actions that involve treating others as mere means to your end (or others' ends).

Metaethical theories of the nature of morality give accounts of what first-order theories in normative ethics are about. For instance, suppose that Kantians are right and that for someone to do something morally wrong is for them to treat another as a mere means to their or others' ends. What makes it the case that wrongful actions are those that involve treating others as mere means to others' ends? Or suppose that egalitarians are right and that it is unjust for some people (like Donald Trump and Michael Bloomberg) to have vast amounts of wealth and power while others—through no fault of their own—live off of next to nothing and have next to no power. Supposing that egalitarians are right. What makes it the case that they're right?

Let's start by contrasting two metaethical theories that give answers to these questions. *Constructivists* say that the correct moral and political theories are made correct by being the outcome of our best moral and political reasoning. Suppose that we knew all the relevant non-moral empirical facts and we were free from distorting biases, and we then engaged in the best moral reasoning process we could engage in (considering cases and principles, modifying the principles in line with the cases and *vice versa*, making our theories consistent with the best economic, philosophical, psychological, and sociological theories).[2] Whatever theories of justice and wrongness we would accept at the end of such a reasoning process are the correct theories. But according to constructivists, when we engage in this reasoning process and come to the right conclusion we are not latching on to *reasoning-independent* moral truths, that is, right answers about what's just and what's right and wrong that exist independently of our reasoning and that our reasoning can help us to discover. Rather facts about what's right, wrong, just, and unjust are *constituted by* the views about rightness, wrongness, and justice that we would come to if we engaged in the best reasoning process about these topics.[3]

In contrast, *robust realists* believe that there are reasoning-independent moral truths, which we can come to discover and know by engaging in a good moral reasoning process. These moral truths extend beyond our reasoning about morality: what's right and wrong is not constituted by our best reasoning about morality. And for any reasoning process that we could actually or even hypothetically engage in, we could still fall short of accessing the moral truths when we engage in that process. So, according to constructivists, morality is essentially dependent on human reasoning in a way that it is not according to robust realists. For realists, morality is entirely *mind-independent* in the way that facts about physics and the external world more generally are:

even if there were no humans reasoning about physics and the external world there would still be laws of physics and facts in the external world. For constructivists, morality is not like this: if there were no moral reasoning process, there would be no morality. So, suppose that utilitarianism is correct. Constructivists say that it is correct because if we reasoned ideally about morality, we would accept it; robust realists say that it is a mind-independent fact that utilitarianism is correct, just as it is a mind-independent fact that when the temperature drops below 0° Celsius water freezes and turns into ice and just as it is a mind-independent fact that dinosaurs once roamed the earth.

For X to ground Y is for X to make Y the case. For instance, facts about whether you are a criminal are grounded by facts about whether a judge or jury have ever convicted you of a crime. And facts about who the most popular artist in the world is right now are grounded by facts about who everyone in the world likes best. According to constructivism, facts about our ideal moral reasoning process ground facts about morality. According to robust realism, facts about morality ground what the best reasoning about morality will look like: it will involve more closely approximating moral truths than other forms of reasoning. To get especially clear on the relationship between constructivism and robust realism let's, for a second, assume that utilitarianism is true, that is, that for an action to be right is for it to promote the best consequences (out of the available options). Figure 2.1 depicts the difference between constructivism and robust realism.

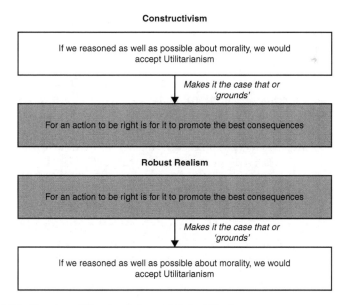

Figure 2.1 The Structure of Constructivism and Robust Realism.

Forget about problems that you might foresee with these views for the time being. Instead let's look at some other theories that contrast with contructivism and robust realism. *Indvidualist relativists* say that if you believe that utilitarianism is correct, and you're right about this, this just amounts to your approving of actions that promote the best consequences out of available options and disapproving of actions that do not promote the best consequences out of available options.

Like constructivism—and unlike robust realism—individualist relativism says that facts about *us* ground moral facts. But individualist relativism is more relativistic than constructivism. Constructivism says that there are universal moral truths constituted by the result of our best reasoning about morality; individualist relativism says that facts about right and wrong are not universal in this way because the only facts about right and wrong are facts that depend on, and are grounded in, our attitudes.

Cultural relativism is less individualistic than individualist relativism but is still more relativistic than constructivism. According to cultural relativism, the attitudes of our societies ground what's right, wrong, just, and unjust. Cultural relativists say that moral truths are constituted by the attitudes of our societies. For utilitarianism to be correct (relative to our society), would be for it to best explain the attitudes of our society. On this view, the attitudes of (the majority in) our society determine what's right and wrong.

Cultural relativism and individualist relativism share several features. They both hold that moral facts are *mind-dependent*: there are no moral facts that are not grounded in the moral views that some individual or group would believe or accept; this is a feature of cultural relativism and individualist relativism that is shared by constructivism. But unlike both constructivism and robust realism, cultural and individualist relativism hold that there are no correct moral claims, true moral principles, or moral facts that outstrip the attitudes of particular individuals or communities. There are facts about what's right relative to us and our society, but no objective moral facts beyond this. We can say that these views hold that there are *no fully objective moral facts*. For according to these views, the only moral facts that there are, are facts that are grounded in particular individuals' or communities' attitudes. So, cultural and individualist relativism are species of *non-objectivism* or *relativism*. In contrast, realism and constructivism are species of *objectivism*. In this chapter, I'll focus on non-objectivist or relativist views in general: individualist and cultural relativism are just two among many non-objectivist views that we might hold about the nature of morality; they are simplified or toy versions of contemporary non-objectivist and relativist metaethical theories. It helps in our context to discuss such simplified versions of non-objectivism; we'll get

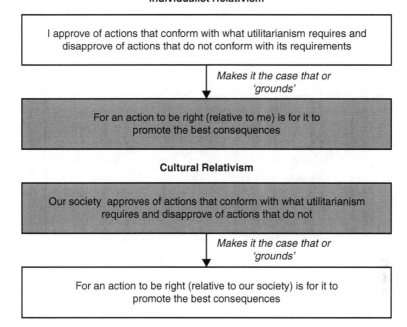

Individualist Relativism

I approve of actions that conform with what utilitarianism requires and disapprove of actions that do not conform with its requirements

Makes it the case that or 'grounds'

For an action to be right (relative to me) is for it to promote the best consequences

Cultural Relativism

Our society approves of actions that conform with what utilitarianism requires and disapprove of actions that do not

Makes it the case that or 'grounds'

For an action to be right (relative to our society) is for it to promote the best consequences

Figure 2.2 The Structure of Relativism

clearer on non-toy versions of these views in the next chapter. But for the time being, think of non-objectivism as the view that there are no objective, moral facts out there in the world beyond those relative to our or our cultures moral framework(s).

Objectivism seems to many to fit well with how we think and talk about moral matters. We think that people in the past were mistaken about the moral status of slavery and homosexuality. But this can seem hard to square with non-objectivist views such as individualist relativism and cultural relativism, for many people and cultures approve(d) of slavery and disapprove(d) of homosexuality. Objectivists aim to show that we're right in how we think and talk about morality. They are motivated to preserve our ordinary moral practice of holding that certain horrific actions of people and cultures quite different from our own in the past were morally wrong.[4] Because of this, objectivists do not just hold that there are moral facts that are not grounded in our or our culture's attitudes; they also hold that we have some knowledge of these moral facts. This is because we say that we know that racism, sexism, and homophobia are wrong. And objectivism is motivated in part as an attempt to maintain the moral appearances, to vindicate our moral thought and talk. Although it's possible that objectivism could be correct even though we have no moral knowledge or justified moral beliefs, this would not be an attractive view. For according to such a view there are moral facts, but we're completely disconnected from them. There are no actions that we can know or even justifiably believe, or claim, to be right or wrong. This kind of view would not fit with the motivations of objectivism to maintain and preserve our everyday moral practice. This kind of view would be like a view about free will that held that we do have free will but we have absolutely no idea when we are exercising it; we do sometimes exercise it but in no way close to the pattern in which we think we do. So, objectivists hold that we have quite a bit of moral knowledge.

2.2. THE EXPLAINING DISAGREEMENT ARGUMENT

The most famous argument involving moral disagreement in metaethics aims to establish that relativism/non-objectivism can explain widespread moral disagreement better than objectivism can.

2.2.1. MACKIE'S ARGUMENT

The most well-known presentation of this argument from disagreement is due to J. L. Mackie. He says that this argument

> has as its premiss the well-known variation in moral codes from one society to another and from one period to another, and also the differences in moral beliefs between different groups and classes within a complex community. Such variation is in itself merely a truth of descriptive morality, a fact of anthropology which entails neither first order nor second order ethical views. Yet it may indirectly support second order [relativism]: radical differences between first order moral judgments make it difficult to treat those judgments as apprehensions of objective truths.
>
> (Mackie, 1977, p. 36)

Mackie recognised that disagreement by itself does not undermine objectivism because there is disagreement about historical and scientific matters; but we should accept that there are objective facts about history and science: water freezes at zero regardless of what we or anyone else thinks; dinosaurs once roamed the earth, and this would be true even if no one believed it. But according to Mackie,

> scientific disagreement results from speculative inferences or explanatory hypotheses based on inadequate evidence, and it is hardly plausible to interpret moral disagreement in the same way. Disagreement about moral codes seems to reflect people's adherence to and participation in different ways of life. The causal connection seems to be mainly that way round: it is that people approve of monogamy

because they participate in a monogamous way of life rather than that they participate in a monogamous way of life because they approve of monogamy ... In short,
the [explanatory] argument from [disagreement] has some force simply because the
actual variations in the moral codes are more readily explained by the hypothesis
that they reflect ways of life than by the hypothesis that they express perceptions,
most of them seriously inadequate and badly distorted, of objective values.

(Mackie, 1977, pp. 36–37)

There are several different ways of interpreting this argument of Mackie's.
One way of understanding it, which is somewhat faithful to what Mackie
says, is to understand him as arguing that objectivism *simply cannot* explain
the wide-ranging disagreements that we find about moral issues, but non-
objectivism/relativism can, so we should accept relativism rather than objectivism. But this is not a plausible argument. There are objectivist explanations
of this disagreement: that many people are just mistaken about what's right
and wrong for instance. The question is: how plausible and powerful are these
explanations in comparison to non-objectivist relativist explanations of disagreement? In general it is easy for a theory to (merely) explain something.
For example, suppose that I theorise that every cat has a hat on top of its
head. How can this theory explain why no one has seen these hats? Simple:
the hats are un-observable. This explains the lack of observations. The problem is that this is not a good explanation of the lack of observations. (As we
will see in §2.3, objectivists have explanations of widespread disagreement
that are a lot better than this.)

An alternative way of interpreting Mackie's argument is to understand it as
holding that *non-objectivism provides a better explanation of widespread disagreement than objectivism*—or that non-objectivism provides the best explanation of such disagreement. Even objectivist critics of Mackie's argument
from disagreement, such as David Enoch (2009, p. 21), agree that there is an
intuitive thought here that, 'it is harder for the [objectivist] to explain moral
disagreement than it is for those rejecting [objectivism]. Assuming some version of subjectivism, or relativism ... such disagreement is just what one
would expect ...' This is because if relativism is correct, then our moral
judgments are not apprehensions of an objective moral reality, but are rather
a function of our own desires, wants, plans, or intentions, or the rules, or
mores of our society. Non-objectivism/relativism predicts widespread moral
disagreement. If people have different ways of life that conflict in various
ways, are in a fight for various resources, and have different inclinations about
what to do in certain circumstances, then, so long as relativism is true, we will
get widespread moral disagreement. This is because moral properties do not
extend beyond these conflicting ways of life, conflicting desires, and divergent
inclinations: according to relativism/non-objectivism, our moral beliefs and
opinions just reflect different perspectives, cultures, and ways of life because

this is all that moral properties consist in. In contrast, objectivism does not predict widespread moral disagreement. According to objectivism, our moral beliefs and opinions reflect (with differing success) a moral reality that outstrips our and our society's moral views.

There are, however, two issues about this understanding of Mackie's argument:

1 Why think that widespread moral disagreement calls for explanation?
2 Why can't objectivists explain widespread moral disagreement in the same way that relativists/non-objectivists explain it, that is, by appeal to the different perspectives and ways of life that we lead and the conflicting desires we have.

I'll explore what the answers to these two questions are before discussing objectivist responses to Mackie's argument.

2.2.2. WHY DOES WIDESPREAD MORAL DISAGREEMENT CALL FOR EXPLANATION?

What is it about widespread moral disagreement that makes it call for explanation in the same way that Tyler Gillett's seeming to recall the entirety of all the musical parts of a chart hit from the '90s that had seemingly been erased from existence called for explanation?[5]

One idea is that there is just more moral disagreement than disagreement about objective matters such as about science and mathematics. Non-objectivism/relativism explains why this is, why the level of disagreement about morality is similar to the level of disagreement about non-objective matters such as aesthetics and matters of taste rather than the level of disagreement about objective matters such as physics: morality is not objective (like taste but unlike physics); objectivism cannot explain this in the same way.

There is at least one shortcoming of this account of why moral disagreement calls for explanation. It seems to require empirical evidence of how much disagreement there is about objective matters and how much there is about non-objective matters. For we might think, for instance, that there is quite a lot of disagreement about whether there is a God, whether there is free will, and how old the earth is, yet there are objective facts of the matter about whether there is a God, whether we have free will, and how old the earth is. So, it is not the case that there is more disagreement about morality than about any objective matter.[6]

An alternative view about why widespread moral disagreement calls for explanation is inspired by Mackie's focus on the connection between people's participation in a way of life (e.g. monogamy) and their moral beliefs matching that way of life (e.g. their disapproving of polygamy). We might understand widespread moral disagreement as calling for explanation because not only is there widespread moral disagreement but there is a striking correlation between the views that parties to these moral disagreements hold and their ways of life.

In general, if there is a striking correlation between X and Y, then that correlation demands explanation, and we should, other things equal, accept theories that explain this correlation over those which do not. To see this take two examples. First, suppose that there is a striking correlation between socio-economic status and voting: those who are socio-economically worse-off tend to (not exclusively but on the whole) vote for one party, while those who are socio-economically better-off vote for another party. If this is the case, then it seems that this calls for explanation. And indeed there are explanations readily available: the first party has policies (or rhetoric) that appeal to the worse-off and the second party has policies (or rhetoric) that appeals to the better-off (be that by catering to the better/worse-off's interests, perceived interests, desires, fears, or ideas). Second, suppose that I make lots of claims about the people who live on an island in the South Pacific. I say that the number of people who live on this island is 246, that they got the internet on 3 December 2013, that their preferred dish is (surprisingly) passion fruit yoghurt, and so on. Suppose further that many of these claims are true. Now, if there were no explanation of why all my claims about the people on this island were true, this would be very puzzling. If it weren't the case that I know someone from the island, that someone told me about this island, that I've been to the island, or watched or read something about the island, it would be extremely puzzling that all my claims about the island are correct; if I had never had any even indirect contact with anyone from this island, then it would seem miraculous (like a form of clairvoyance) if all my specific claims about the island were true.[7] So, similarly, this striking correlation requires explanation.

Now we might think that there is a striking correlation between different people's different moral views and their different perspectives, cultures, and ways of life and that this striking correlation calls for explanation. As Mackie puts it, people whose way of life involves monogamy and not polygamy tend to think monogamy is morally right and polygamy is wrong. Those who practice polygamy in contrast tend to believe that it is permissible. People whose way of life involves eating meat tend to think it is morally permissible. Those of us (most of us) whose way of life doesn't involve giving a large amount to charity tend to think this is morally okay. People whose way of life involves scarifying or genitally mutilating their children tend to think that this is morally permissible or right. Those whose way of life does not involve scarification or genital mutilation tend to think that these actions are wrong. This correlation between our ways of life and our moral views is not a necessary correlation: some people think that it's wrong to eat meat even though their traditions and family's way of life involves eating meat, just as any correlation between socio-economic status and voting is not a necessary one: some people vote in ways that most of those of their socio-economic status do not. Nonetheless there does seem to be a striking correlation between our moral views and our ways of life. And striking correlations call for explanation.

Non-objectivism/relativism seems to provide a better explanation of the striking correlation between different people's (different) moral views and their different perspectives, cultures, and ways of life than objectivism. How exactly does it do this? Well, according to non-objectivism/relativism, our moral beliefs and opinions reflect different perspectives, cultures, and ways of life; according to objectivism, our moral beliefs and opinions reflect (with differing success) a moral reality that outstrips our and our society's moral views. In this case, we would expect there to be a striking correlation between people's moral beliefs and opinions and their different ways of life if relativism holds. But we would not expect this if objectivism holds. So, on this view, widespread moral disagreement calls for explanation because there is a striking correlation between the side of a moral disagreement that people are on and their ways of life.[8]

2.2.3. WHY DOES OBJECTIVISM STRUGGLE TO EXPLAIN WIDESPREAD DISAGREEMENT?

So, there is a good case that widespread moral disagreement calls for explanation. But why can't objectivists explain widespread moral disagreement in the same way that relativists explain it, that is, by appeal to the different perspectives and ways of life that we lead and the conflicting desires we have.

Remember that at the end of §2.1 I explained that objectivists want to preserve our moral thought and talk because this is a key motivation for objectivism. As I explained, because of this objectivists want to hold, not just that there are moral facts and truths that outstrip our attitudes, but also that we know some of these moral facts and truths and have justified beliefs about them. For we think that we know that slavery is wrong and that we are justified in believing that homosexuality is permissible. Objectivists might try to explain widespread disagreement in the way that non-objectivists do: by holding that the different perspectives and ways of life that we have and the conflicting desires we have lead to the widespread moral disagreements that we have. However, if objectivists can only explain widespread moral disagreement in this way, this might undermine the idea that we have any moral knowledge or justified moral beliefs. To see this consider the following principle:

> *Disconnection.* If our different moral beliefs are just the product of our different perspectives and desires but moral facts are objective facts that outstrip our different perspectives and desires, then we do not have moral knowledge or justified beliefs.

I'll briefly explain why we might hold *disconnection*. If you're already convinced of *disconnection*, you can skip to the end of this section. (But, when you've read through the rest of this chapter, make sure to come back here to think about whether we should really accept *disconnection*, which is key to the explaining moral disagreement argument against objectivism.)

The idea of possible worlds models close and faraway possibilities and how close and faraway they are: what could have happened, or would have happened if something else happened. Suppose that I woke up at exactly 8am this morning. But that I could very easily have woken up at 7.52 or 8.08. In that case there are nearby possible worlds in which I woke up at 7.52. But in the actual world I woke up at 8. Now consider another principle:

> *Safety.* If S knows that (or is justified in believing that) *p*, then in nearly all nearby possible worlds in which S forms the belief that *p* in the same way as she forms her belief in the actual world, S only believes *p* when *p* is true.[9]

Our intuitions about cases support *safety*. Suppose that you're in the back of a car being driven around the countryside. You dose off. When you wake up you look out of the window and see what appears to be a barn. You believe that you've just seen a (real) barn. However, you're in fact driving around a bit of countryside in which elaborate barn facades have been constructed by film-makers wanting to shoot a film of this particular part of the countryside replete with barns. This piece of countryside replete with fake barns, *fake barn country*, proceeds for miles on end. But there is one genuine real barn in fake barn country and luckily enough you've just seen it. So your belief is true: you did just see a (real) barn. But it seems that you don't know that because your belief is just too luckily true to constitute knowledge. *Safety* explains this: had you woken up a minute earlier or later (as you could have easily done) and formed your belief about whether you're seeing a barn in the normal way, then you would've had a false belief: you'd have believed you were seeing a real barn but your belief would've been false.

Now if our moral beliefs are beliefs about an objective moral reality that outstrips our and our culture's attitudes, but our moral beliefs reflect something else that is entirely disconnected from this mind-independent moral reality, then even if moral beliefs happen to luckily line up with the lay of the land in moral reality, this will purely be a product of luck. Given the impact of culture, upbringing, and identification on our moral judgments, if we were in a different culture, had a different upbringing, or identified with different people, we'd form moral judgments in the same way but have different moral beliefs. So, whatever the moral truths are, in some nearby possible worlds in which we form moral beliefs in the same way we have false moral beliefs. So, it seems that there is a good case that

Disconnection. If our different moral beliefs are just the product of our different perspectives and desires but moral facts are objective facts that outstrip our different perspectives and desires, then we do not have moral knowledge or justified beliefs.

One response to this argument is to attack *safety*. Many philosophers have attacked *safety*. But most of these philosophers want to maintain that we lack knowledge in cases like the fake barn country case. So, most of these philosophers will still end up endorsing an epistemic principle that is quite close to *safety*. And these principles may well similarly imply *disconnection*.[10]

Alternatively, it might be argued that *safety* only shows that we do not have knowledge of moral claims that there is significant moral disagreement about. But we shouldn't believe that we have moral knowledge about issues that are controversial across cultures anyway; we should only believe that we have moral knowledge of that which is morally uncontroversial such as that we have moral reasons to keep promises, not harm others, and help others. This is a view that W. D. Ross (1930, esp. p. 30) held. According to Ross, we know what our basic moral reasons or *prima facie* duties are but we do not know how these reasons/duties stack up in any particular case. So, we know that we have moral reasons not to harm others and we know that we have moral reasons to help others, but we do not know whether the moral reasons not to harm trump the moral reasons to help such that, for instance, we shouldn't push the heavy man off of the bridge in the footbridge trolley case.

There are at least two problems for this kind of response. First, if we do not know any moral claims that are controversial, then we can't know that homosexuality is permissible, and that racial and gender inequality is wrong; for some people still reject these claims. But if objectivism entails that we do not and cannot know these things, this would seem to be a serious problem. Since, as we discussed earlier, that we know these things is one of the features of our practice that moral objectivism is motivated to preserve. Second, even if it is somewhat intuitive to think that we do not know whether euthanasia is permissible and abortion is wrong given the massive disagreements about these issues, pretty much any moral issue is controversial across and within cultures and we surely want to be able to say that at least some people have justified beliefs about the moral status of euthanasia and abortion such as those who have devoted their entire lives to thinking about these issues (see §6.2.8). So, it seems that there is at least a relatively good case for *disconnection*.

2.3. RESPONSES 1: PROBLEMS WITH OBJECTIVIST EXPLANATIONS

So far we've seen that an argument along the lines of Mackie's argument that non-objectivism provides a better explanation of moral disagreement than objectivism can be made. This argument is not as simple to make as Mackie and others thought it to be, and it in fact relies on some assumptions that can be challenged. But there is quite a good case for these assumptions. And in this case there is a good case that (i) the striking correlation between our moral judgments and our ways of life calls for explanation, (ii) such a correlation is predicted by non-objectivism but is not predicted by objectivism—unless objectivists want to hold that we are entirely disconnected from the objective moral facts. So, non-objectivism provides a good explanation of widespread moral disagreement, or the correlation between our differing moral views and our differing ways of life. But, so far, we have seen no similarly good objectivist explanation of the correlation between our differing moral views and our differing ways of life—for we have only seen an objectivist explanation that undermines most of our moral knowledge and justified moral beliefs.

Objectivists have made a variety of responses to the argument that we've been discussing. According to these responses, there are features of morality or our moral disagreements that enable objectivists to provide an explanation of why there is such widespread moral disagreement, and these explanations are at least as good as non-objectivists explanations of widespread moral disagreement. In the rest of this section I will discuss some objectivist responses that seem to somewhat miss the mark.

2.3.1. DIFFERING EMPIRICAL CIRCUMSTANCES AND NON-MORAL BELIEFS

Some objectivists respond to Mackie's argument by arguing that moral disagreements are the result of (i) differences in the circumstances in which moral judgments are made and (ii) differences in our non-moral beliefs about the consequences of particular policies or actions.

However, (ii) does not play a part in a good objectivist explanation of widespread moral disagreement. For, as we discussed in Chapter 1, there is widespread moral disagreement that does not boil down to disagreement about the consequences of particular policies or particular actions; there are widespread disagreements in moral principles or values.

David Brink (1989) made an influential response to the argument from explaining disagreement. He argued that many moral disagreements are the product of (i). Here's what he says in favour of this view:

> An economically underdeveloped country might think that in a society in its economic condition distributive inequalities provide incentives that benefit everyone and that this justifies such inequalities. A more economically advanced country might oppose distributive inequalities on the ground that in societies at its level of affluence distributive inequalities are divisive and so work to everyone's disadvantage. The economically underdeveloped society thinks it should promote certain distributive inequalities, whereas the economically more developed society

thinks it should oppose distributive inequalities. This might look like a moral disagreement but the fact is that the disagreement is only apparent.

(Brink, 1989, p. 200)[11]

Such apparent moral disagreements are not really moral disagreements. For people who make these different moral judgments are not making conflicting judgments. The people in the more economically advanced country are judging that inequalities in one circumstance are unjust and the people in less economically advanced country are judging that inequalities in another circumstance are just. And these judgments are completely compatible and so not in disagreement with one another. If many moral disagreements were like this, then this would undermine the claim that non-objectivism/relativism is the best explanation of widespread moral disagreement. For many seemingly moral disagreements would not genuinely be moral disagreements at all. And so there would not be widespread moral disagreement that needs to be explained.

However, as we discussed in Chapter 1, many moral disagreements are in fact genuine rather than merely apparent. People who disagree about the morality of eating animals, abortion, torture, and redistributive taxation, among many other issues, disagree about the morality of these things in the same circumstances as well as in different circumstances (remember Alice and Christina from Chapter 1 and the anthropological investigations we discussed in §1.2, for instance).

2.3.2. THE LACK OF MORAL PHILOSOPHICAL DISAGREEMENT

Derek Parfit (2011b, p. 554) argues that

a   There is widespread agreement among philosophers about which actions are right and wrong and what moral reasons there are; and
b   The fact that (a) holds shows (or contributes to showing) that objectivism explains the amount of disagreement that there is as well as non-objectivism/relativism.

There are issues with both of these claims. There are reasons to reject (a). As we discussed in Chapter 1, act-utilitarians disagree about trolley cases and related cases with deontologists, virtue ethicists, and others. They also disagree with deontologists about whether we have strong moral reasons to keep our promises and refrain from lying even if our doing so would not cause any benefit (see Ross, 1930; Dancy, 2000, p. 168). Particularists hold that the fact that doing something would cause another pain is not always a reason to refrain from doing it and that the fact that doing something is pleasurable doesn't always give us a moral reason to do it (Dancy, 2004). Other philosophers disagree with them about this. Some philosophers hold that we have reasons not to breach others' self-ownership and property rights for its own sake, many do not hold this view (contrast, for instance, Nozick, 1974 and Ross, 1930). Many philosophers are internalists about reasons who hold that we only have reasons to do things that there is a sound deliberative route from our current desires and other motivations to our doing (see Williams, 1981; Finlay & Schroeder, 2017). This view entails that if you don't care about keeping your promises or refraining from assaulting another, and there will be no costs to you of breaking your promise or assaulting another person, then you have no reason not to assault them and not to break your promises. Others believe that we have reasons not to assault others and to keep our promises even if we do not care about doing these things. Some Kantians hold strong views about lying and promise-breaking according to which we should never lie and we should never break promises even when doing so could save lives. This view is in conflict with the moral views of many of us. Relatedly, some Kantians hold extremely strong views about the treatment of animals such that we should never use animals as mere means to ours or others' ends (see Korsgaard, 2018). This view implies that pretty much all testing of products on animals is impermissible.

In political philosophy there are great debates about what justice requires. For instance, right libertarians believe that it is unjust to tax the rich to benefit the poor even if doing so will have very good consequences (see Nozick, 1974). Some egalitarians argue that justice requires that we do not give more resources to the rich even if the only alternative to doing this is to throw away these resources; others disagree that justice requires that we waste resources in this way.[12] Sufficientarians hold that justice only requires that we ensure that everyone has enough; egalitarians disagree.[13] And (some) luck egalitarians hold that equality only requires us to ensure that no one is worse off than others through no fault of their own; others disagree holding that equality requires that we also take care of those who are worse-off than others as a result of their own choices.[14]

Even if there were little moral philosophical disagreement about which actions are right and wrong and what moral reasons there are, relativism/non-objectivism could still provide the best explanation of why *non-philosophers* disagree. If this is right, then there are reasons to reject (b) as well as (a).

Perhaps Parfit's view would be that the absence of moral philosophical disagreement would show that if non-moral-philosophers thought about moral issues for as long as moral philosophers have, they would no longer disagree. However, it's not clear that moral philosophers are in an epistemically better position than non-moral-philosophers regarding the moral reasons that we have. Many argue that although there are experts about what the consequences of particular policies are there are no experts about the *pure moral facts*. That is, there are no experts about whether (putting what particular religions and moral theories imply aside) we have reasons to keep our promises for its own sake, about whether (assuming they are sentenient) animals have a moral status that makes it wrong to kill them for food or not, and about whether it is wrong to push the heavy man off of the bridge in the footbridge trolley case; there are no experts about which moral theory or religion is the correct one. Or if there are such experts, we have no good way of identifying them (see McGrath, 2011).

There are several reasons to be sceptical of the idea that there is identifiable expertise about pure moral facts. One reason is that we do not have an independent neutrally verifiable track record by which to compare someone's moral verdicts to the moral truth. We know that meteorologists are experts about the weather because we have an independent record that we can go to in order to check whether someone's predictions about the weather have been correct in the past or not. In contrast, there is no such independently mutually agreed verifiable record that we can go to in order to see whether someone has been right about morality in the past or not—for there is disagreement about what constitutes the correct answer about many moral issues (McGrath, 2008). A further reason to be sceptical of expertise about pure moral facts is that if there were such pure moral expertise, it would be reasonable to defer to others about pure moral facts. But many hold that such deference is odd, as we'll discuss in §6.3. If there's no pure moral expertise, this does not mean that moral philosophers have no expertise but only that their moral intuitions about trolleys, the moral status of animals, and promise-keeping, for instance, are no more reliable than those of non-moral-philosophers (Rini, 2015). And if we cannot identify who the pure moral experts are, this just means that we lack sufficient reason to believe that moral philosophers' intuitions about these matters are more reliable than others'.

2.3.3. BIASES

David Enoch and Derek Parfit argue that many moral disagreements may be the result of self-interested bias, status quo bias, or other biases. And because this explanation of many moral disagreements is entirely consistent with objectivism, objectivism can explain widespread moral disagreement just as well as non-objectivism/relativism.

According to Parfit (2011b, p. 553), 'if we ask whether people should be paid much higher salaries when their innate abilities make them more productive, our answer may depend on whether we ourselves have such abilities'. That is, our self-interest may bias our answer. Enoch elaborates at greater length:

> Peter Singer and Peter Unger believe that we should give almost all our money to famine relief, that unless we do so we are morally corrupt, that our behavior is (almost) as morally objectionable as that of murderers ... Perhaps they are wrong ...

But even assuming they are right, there is no mystery about the common—almost universal—belief that morality does not require all that Singer and Unger believe it does. Acknowledging that they are right would exert a high price: it would involve exposing 'our illusion of innocence,' leaving us either to give up almost all of our belongings or to the horrible acknowledgment that we are morally horrendous persons. Refusing to see the (purported) truth of Singer's and Unger's claims thus has tremendous psychological payoffs. Now, this is an extreme case, but it illustrates what is typical, I think, of many cases of moral debates—very much is at stake, and so false moral beliefs can rather easily be explained in terms of their psychological payoffs. And where mistakes can easily be explained, disagreement can easily be explained without resort to [non-objectivism/relativism]. Furthermore, given a standing interest in not revolutionizing one's way of life, in not coming to view oneself and one's loved ones as morally horrendous people, explanations in terms of the distorting effects of self-interest can explain the phenomenon Mackie was so impressed with—that our moral convictions seem to reflect our ways of life, and not the other way around.

(Enoch, 2009, p. 26)

According to this line of argument, there is only the amount of moral disagreement that there is because we are prone to certain biases. Call this objectivist explanation of widespread disagreement, the bias explanation.

Does the bias explanation of widespread disagreement provide as good an explanation of widespread moral disagreement as non-objectivism/relativism? One worry about the bias-based explanation of disagreement is that it can only explain why (certain) people hold certain moral views, namely:

i   non-consequentialist moral views that hold that our interests and the interests of our friends and family play a large role in determining what we may or morally ought to do;
ii economically right-wing political views held by the rich and economically left-wing political views held by the poor;
iii non-vegetarian/vegan views about the morality of eating animals and other similar status-quo based views such as that euthanasia is wrong.

So, it might seem that in order for the best explanation of widespread moral disagreement to be that moral disagreements are the result of biased reasoning, it needs to be the case that we can justifiably believe that views (i-iii) are false. But it's not clear that we can do this. It's not clear that we can be justified in believing that (i) is false. Many argue for (i). For instance, proponents of agent-centred prerogatives argue that although we generally ought to do what's best it is permissible for us to refrain from doing what's best in order to promote the well-being of ourselves or our family and friends instead. They have arguments for this view and believe that their beliefs in this view are not the result of biases.[15] There are many people who are not extremely rich who believe in economically right wing political views such as classical liberalism and libertarianism. And there are several arguments—such as those made by Gaus (2011) and Nozick (1974)—for such views. It's not clear that we can justifiably believe that those who hold these views only hold them due to biases.

A response to this worry can be made. It can be argued that there are biases or errors that might be responsible for people coming to hold the opposites of (i) and (iii) as well as (i) and (iii). For instance, if consequentialism is false, people might still believe it because they mistakenly think that moral reasoning is just like mathematical reasoning: we can just simply add up well-being to figure out what to do, and there's no alternative to this way of reasoning about morality. Similarly, meat eaters accuse vegetarians of anthropomorphising animals and might claim that those who believe in vegetarianism thereby only hold the views they hold due to biases. So, proponents of the bias explanation of disagreement might argue that we don't know who is biased (act-utilitarians or proponents of prerogatives, vegetarians or meat eaters) but we have good reasons to believe that everyone's moral judgments are biased. And these reasons furnish us with a good explanation of moral disagreement.

However, this response threatens to prove too much by showing that we have good reason to believe that no-one's moral beliefs constitute knowledge because everyone's moral judgments could very easily be caused by biases. This would not help objectivists (see §2.1 and §2.2.3). But without this response, the prospects of the bias explanation of disagreement are tied too directly to our being able to justifiably believe in consequentialism and vegetarianism. Is this a problem? It might seem to not be for consequentialists. However, this would mean that non-consequentialists have good reason to accept relativism/non-objectivism rather than objectivism on the basis of the explanatory argument from disagreement. Relatedly, many hold that, other things equal, theories about the nature of moral properties should be neutral regarding a large range of first-order views about moral properties. For instance, theories about what it is for act-utilitarianism, contractualism, or rule-consequentialism to be the correct moral theory should not entail the truth of one of these theories. Why? One idea is that what it is to be an account of the status of moral facts is to be an account of what widespread moral disagreements are about. But an account of the status of moral facts that takes a lot of sides on first-order moral questions will not be a good account of what widespread moral disagreements are about.[16]

Furthermore, it's not clear at all that recourse to biases can really explain all that much of the moral diversity that relativists believe should be explained and seek to explain. For instance, it's not clear how biases could explain the differences in moral views between ourselves and the Hopi or between Northerners and Southerners discussed in Chapter 1. (Why would biases explain why Southerners think violence is more justified than Northerners or that the Hopi think that it is okay to cause severe harm to birds in a way that we do not?) There are similar disagreements often discussed in this context that we didn't explicitly discuss in Chapter 1. Some, such as Doris and Plakias (2008a, pp. 322–325) argue, on the basis of empirical data, that there are disagreements in moral principles or values between non-Chinese Americans and Chinese people about whether the lives or well-being of a few should be sacrificed for the lives and well-being of a greater number (so about how governments should act in trolley-style cases). The Yanomamö are a group of approximately 35,000 indigenous people who live in small villages in the Amazon rainforest. According to anthropologists, they hold that it can be morally right for men to brutally assault their wives and to trade them as property. And that the disagreement that most in the West have with the Yanomamö about the wrongness of treating people in this way is a disagreement in moral principles or values. It's unclear how biases can explain these moral disagreements either.[17] In general it does not seem that by appealing to biases objectivists show that they can explain widespread moral disagreement as well as non-objectivists.

2.3.4. INDETERMINACY AND DEGREES OF WRONGNESS

Russ Shafer-Landau (1994) and Derek Parfit (2011b) argue that many moral disagreements are the result of (a) parties to these disagreements' failure to recognise that wrongness comes in degrees or (b) moral indeterminacy.

Let's take (a) first. Parfit says that some disagreements are caused by people

> mistakenly assuming ... that wrongness cannot be a matter of degree ... return next to the question of what we rich people ought to give to those who are very poor. If we assume that wrongness is all-or-nothing, we shall be most unlikely to agree on how much we ought to give. And it is hard to believe that there could be a definite answer here, so that what is wrong might be giving less than a tenth of our income, or less than a fifth, or less than half. For most of us, the truth is rather that we shall be acting less wrongly the more we give.

> (Parfit, 2011b, p. 555)

However, first, the idea that wrongness comes in degrees is very controversial. Many hold that wrongness is not gradable: actions are either wrong or not, it doesn't make sense to think of an action as more or less wrong. Of course, some actions that are wrong can cause more harm than others, and accordingly be morally or evaluatively worse. And we can have more reason to refrain from performing some actions that are wrong (e.g. killing millions) than refraining from performing others (e.g. stealing a chocolate bar from a supermarket). But these facts do not make it the case that some actions are *more wrong* than others; this is to misunderstand the status an action can have of being wrong. Of course, the view that wrongness comes in degrees is a view that consequentialists are attracted to. Since, according to consequentialism, wrongness is a function of the degree of negative consequences of an action. But non-consequentialists seem to have little reason to accept the view that actions can be more wrong than others.

Second, it's unclear how the idea that wrongness comes in degrees could explain any of the moral disagreements that non-objectivists hold need to be explained such as disagreements about redistributive justice, the morality of polygamy, scarification, and homosexuality, disagreements about the moral distinction between doing and allowing, and the disagreements between us and the Yanomamö and the Hopi and between Northerners and Southerners about the justifiability of violence.

Let's move on to the idea that moral indeterminacy can explain widespread moral disagreement. Some questions may be indeterminate in the sense that they have no answer. For certain numbers of hairs, it is not the case that someone who has that many hairs on their head is either bald or not bald: whether they are bald or not is rather indeterminate; this explains why there is no clear point at which (no number of hairs at which) someone who was hirsute becomes bald by losing a certain amount of hair. Similarly, it may be neither true nor false that there is no moral objection to abortion. Parfit says that

> if some normative questions are indeterminate, having no answer, this would provide another explanation of some normative disagreements. When people disagree about whether some act is wrong, they may mistakenly assume that this act must either be, or not be, wrong. If these people gave up this assumption, they might often cease to disagree.
>
> (Parfit, 2011b, p. 562)

However, we have good reason not to invoke moral indeterminacy in this way to explain moral disagreement because doing so involves attributing a mistake to both parties to the relevant moral disagreements: if we hold that abortion, for instance, is neither permissible nor wrong, then both pro-lifers and prochoicers are mistaken, and they are in fact doubly mistaken (see Enoch, 2009, p. 25, n. 39). Both parties think that abortion must be either (a) wrong or (b) permissible. And pro-lifers also think it is wrong, while pro-choicers think it is permissible. So, both parties to this disagreement are mistaken twice on this view. Pro-lifers are mistaken to think that abortion is (a); pro-choicers are mistaken to think that it is (b); and both are mistaken that abortion must be either (a) or (b). Now in order for this moral indeterminacy response to the argument from disagreement to be a good one, moral indeterminacy would have to explain a lot of moral disagreements. But if it did that, it would involve attributing a lot of errors to people on all sides of a lot of moral disagreements. And we should avoid doing this if possible. For we should charitably interpret people, which means interpreting as many of their claims as true as we can rather than interpreting them as making two errors for every disagreement in moral principles or values that they find themselves in (see Chapter 4). Furthermore, if moral indeterminacy played an important role in explaining disagreement, this would entail that there are few if any determinate moral truths; and it's hard to see how this would be a victory for objectivism about moral truth (Enoch, 2009, p. 25, n. 39). So, it seems that an appeal to moral indeterminacy and degrees of wrongness cannot form a significant part of a good objectivist explanation of widespread moral disagreement.

2.4. RESPONSES 2: THE BEST OBJECTIVIST EXPLANATION

A better response to the argument from explaining disagreement can be made. This response combines several explanations. First, Parfit (2011b, pp. 554–555) argues that many moral disagreements are the result of the moral issue at hand being a borderline case. The idea here is that foetuses, for instance, are borderline cases of human beings, they have some properties that human beings have but not others. And it's unclear what to say about the morality of treating beings in various ways when they are borderline cases of beings whom we believe have moral rights. (The same might be said of non-human animals.) In this case, we don't need non-objectivism/relativism to explain why some people hold that abortion is morally wrong and some hold that it is morally permissible; all we need is the insight that figuring out whether foetuses have the same status as children and adult human beings is difficult and our moral concepts are not sufficiently clear here for us to be easily able to tell what the moral status of a foetus is.

In addition to explaining why there is widespread disagreement about the morality of abortion and eating animals, this part of the explanation might also explain why there is so much moral disagreement about utilitarianism-related issues too such as whether we should kill one person to save five in the footbridge trolley case, and whether we should give 30% or more of our income to charity. For, we might think that there is little disagreement that we should sacrifice one person to save billions of lives and that those of us who are very well-off should give something to charity—the number of people who disagree with these claims might be similar to the number of people who disagree about whether dinosaurs once roamed the earth, whether the earth is very old, and whether anthropogenic climate change is happening. The issue is where we draw the borderline between it being permissible to sacrifice one person to save many more and it being wrong to do so (e.g. 5 people, 100 people, 1000 people, 1 million); where do we draw the borderline between the amount that it is our duty to give to charity and the amount that is praise-worthy for us to give but which we are not required to give (e.g. 5% of our income, 10%, 12%, 20%, etc.).

Second, Parfit (2011b, pp. 552–553) argues that many disagreements in moral principles or values are the result of the disagreeing parties having dif-fering religious beliefs or different beliefs about human nature. Some hold that abortion is wrong and eating animals is permissible because they believe that their religion implies these views; if they no longer held these religious views, they would no longer disagree with vegans and pro-choicers (respec-tively) about the morality of abortion and eating animals. Similarly, many of those who hold left-wing political views, particularly anarchists, hold that humans are naturally kind and charitable; some of those who hold more right-wing political views hold that humans are naturally selfish.[18] Many widespread moral disagreements can be explained as being a result of the fact that people hold different religious views and different views about human nature.

These two factors can be combined with a paired down subtle version of the bias explanation. We can hold that morality is very important to us for it affects how we are perceived by ourselves and others, as well as what we must do with our lives in order to live with ourselves (and to live in harmony with others). In this case, we're inevitably going to be driven to make mistakes about morality due to self-serving and other biases just as we make mistakes about whether our spouse is cheating on us or about whether our family and friends are people that we really like. We're not so prone to bias that it is highly likely that none of our moral judgments are justified. But the fact that biases do play into our moral judgments does explain some of our moral judgments and so some moral disagreements. And perhaps the view that many moral disagreements are disagreements about borderline cases, that many moral disagreement are due to people holding particular views about religion and human nature, and the fact that biases infect our moral thinking can be combined to completely explain why seeming irresolvable moral disagreement is so widespread.

This combination of factors does provide an explanation of widespread moral disagreement. And this explanation is not a bad one. However, it does have some limits which it seems to me make it a worse explanation of wide-spread moral disagreement than relativism.

First, let's think about the borderline cases part of this explanation. This part of the explanation might be able to account for why there is such wide-spread disagreement about the moral status of animals and foetuses, but can it explain why certain people put foetuses on one side of the borderline and others put them on the other side? Can it explain why those in conservative (sub-)cultures tend to put foetuses on the child and adult moral status side and those in more liberal (sub-)cultures tend to put foetuses on the other side of the borderline? As we discussed in §2.2, relativism/non-objectivism can explain this. But it is not clear that objectivism can.

You might think, 'why can't objectivists just say the obvious thing here: conservatives put foetuses on the child and adult side because they're in a culture that holds that view; liberals put foetuses on the opposite side because those in their culture and way of life put them on that side'. But, as I explained in §2.2.3, this is not a good option for objectivists because if they take this kind of explanation, then they undermine the possibility of an objectivist view that guarantees moral knowledge and justified moral beliefs.

Onto the second part of the explanation: many moral disagreements are the product of disagreements in religious views and views about human nature. There are several worries about this part of the explanation. First, holding that moral disagreements are the product of different religious views and views of human nature seems very close to holding that moral disagreements are the product of different cultures, perspectives, and ways of life. So, there is a worry that adopting this explanation of many moral disagreements undermines moral knowledge in the same way as an objectivist explanation of moral disagreement that holds that moral disagreements are due to parties to those disagreements' differing perspectives and ways of lives does.

Second, some philosophers are relativists/non-objectivists about religion and/or human nature.[19] One reason to adopt relativism about religion and human nature is the similar widespread disagreement about these issues. If disagreement about religion and human nature favours relativism/non-objectivism about truths about religion and human nature, then appealing to disagreement about religion and human nature to explain moral disagreement will not be an option for objectivists. To see this, see that it would not help to respond to the argument from explaining disagreement by arguing that moral disagreements are the product of disagreements in taste and aesthetics if we should be relativists about taste and aesthetics. For in this case, moral beliefs would not reflect objective facts (with more or less success) but rather be the product of non-objective or relativistic judgments and facts about our tastes and preferences. And, once again, the possibility of moral knowledge and justified moral beliefs would be undermined. Similarly, if we should be relativists about human nature and religion, then objectivists cannot appeal to disagreements about human nature and religion to explain widespread moral disagreement without undermining the possibility of knowledge of, and justified beliefs about, objective moral facts.

Third, there seem to be many moral disagreements that correlate with different perspectives and ways of life that cannot be explained by appeal to differing religious views and differing views about human nature. For instance, communities, such as the Nigerian Yoruba, who believe that it is permissible or required to scarify their children's faces do not believe that this is required by their religion. They rather scarify their children's faces 'for identification of a person's tribe, family or patrilineal heritage' and because they perceive the scarifications to be beautiful.[20] And it is not clear that most communities that practice female genital mutilation believe that it is required by their religion rather than by their traditions or conventions.[21] Many of the disagreements in moral principles or values that we discussed in Chapter 1 could be disagreements that are due to differences in religious views or views about human nature. It is not clear. But we have no evidence that gives us reason to believe that most of them are. For instance, as we discussed in Chapter 1, many of the disagreements between those in the Northern US and those in the Southern US about justified and excusable violence seem to be pure moral disagreements, that is, disagreement that are not the result of disagreements about religion or metaphysics. It might well be that at least some of those who believe that we should be loyal and obey authority for its own sake are in a pure moral disagreement with some of those who believe that we have no moral reasons to be loyal and obey authority for its own sake: it might well be that some of those who find themselves in this disagreement are not in this disagreement just because they hold different religious views or different views about human nature. More research is needed in order to determine this.

So, there are limits to the explanatory work that can be done by the borderline cases and human nature and religion-based explanations. If these two parts of the objectivist explanation of widespread disagreement cannot do so much of the explanatory work, then a lot of the burden to explain widespread disagreement falls back on biases. But as I explained in the last section, we should not want biases to play a great role in an explanation of widespread moral disagreement.

So, relativism/non-objectivism does seem to better explain widespread moral disagreement than objectivism. The real action is in how much better the relativist explanation of moral disagreement is. The relativist/non-objectivist explanation is very simple and straightforward. There are lots of issues with getting a powerful objectivist explanation of widespread moral disagreement. But an objectivist explanation of some amount of power can be given. Objectivists like David Enoch (2011, p. 34) think of the metaethical theory that we should accept as the one that accrues the most plausibility points from arguments in its favour without losing plausibility points that outweigh these due to problems that it faces and objections that are levelled at it. It seems that non-objectivism at least gains plausibility points from its neat explanation of widespread moral disagreement. And objectivism loses some plausibility points because it cannot explain widespread moral disagreement so well.

We should not accept or reject a metaethical theory on the basis of one argument or one set of reasons or plausibility points. Rather we have to look at all of the arguments in its favour and objections that it faces. This book cannot cover the entire terrain of metaethics and all the arguments in favour of and against objectivism and non-objectivism/relativism. However, although non-objectivism/relativism gains plausibility points by explaining widespread moral disagreements in the way that we have been discussing in this chapter, many argue that it loses a great deal of plausibility by being unable to make room for the view that we often are in genuine moral disagreements. In the next chapter we will discuss this argument from moral disagreement against non-objectivism.

SUMMARY

Objectivism is the view in metaethics that moral facts outstrip our and our culture's attitudes. Non-objectivism holds that moral facts do not so outstrip our and our cultures attitudes. In this chapter we explored the most famous argument from disagreement in metaethics. This argument, crystallised by J. L. Mackie, holds that non-objectivism better explains widespread moral disagreement than objectivism. This argument is not quite so straightforward to make as it might initially seem, but it can be made and does cut against objectivism. Objectivists have made a plethora of interesting responses to this argument. And objectivists can blunt the force of this argument. However, ultimately it does seem that non-objectivism can provide a (somewhat) better explanation of widespread moral disagreement than objectivism and this does count in favour of non-objectivism.

FURTHER READING

Shafer-Landau (2017, ch. 19–21) is a good place to start thinking about metaethics. Van Roojen (2015) is a more comprehensive good next step. Miller (2003) is a very sophisticated and thorough introduction to metaethics, it is a great place to go after getting a feel for the area after reading Shafer-Landau and van Roojen. Scanlon (2014) is the articulation and defence of realist objectivism that helped me most in getting interested in and understanding metaethics. For an introduction to constructivism see Bagnoli (2017) and Street (2010). If you are interested in thinking further about constructivism in metaethics, Korsgaard (1995) and the essays in Lenman and Shemmer (2012) are good places to start. For a view closest to what I've been calling constructivism in this chapter see Rawls (1980), Brink (1989, appendix 4), Smith (1994), and Jackson (1998). Harman and Thomson (1995) is a good place to start thinking about the debate between objectivists and relativists. Harman (1975) and Wong (1984) are classic defences of relativism; we will discuss more recent relativist views in the next chapter. Schroeder (2007) and Sobel (2016) are sophisticated contemporary defences of views along the lines of what, in this chapter, I called individualist relativism. An important part of this chapter discussed the relationship between objectivism and the view that we have a lot of moral knowledge and justified moral beliefs, for more on this topic see §11.4 and the further readings to chapter 11. The explaining disagreement argument that this chapter has focussed on holds that there is more moral disagreement than objectivism about morality would predict. Sauer (2019), interestingly, argues there is too much moral *agreement* for objectivism to be correct.

NOTES

1 The full story—along with multiple versions of this song—can be found in an episode of the podcast, Reply All (2020).
2 That is, we engaged in the best and widest form of Rawlsian reflective equilibrium reasoning; see Daniels (2003).
3 The view that I call constructivism in this chapter is really what is sometimes called Kantian constructivism; although it is also very close to views that are sometimes thought of as Humean forms of realism such as Smith (1994) and Jackson's (1998) realist views.
4 See, for instance, Enoch (2011).
5 Enoch (2009, p. 23) pushes on the need for proponents of the argument from explaining moral disagreement to answer this question.
6 See Shafer-Landau (2006) and McGrath (2010).
7 See Enoch (2011, p. 158) and Rowland (2019a, p. 58).
8 See Blackburn (1984, pp. 182–190) and Rowland (2019a, pp. 55–59) for further discussion of why the ability of theories to explain correlations are a big deal when assessing metaphysical views.
9 See, for instance, Pritchard (2005, p. 163), Sosa (1999, p. 142), and Hawthorne (2004, p. 56, n. 17).
10 For an introduction to the *safety* principle and problems for it see Rabinowitz (2011).
11 See also Parfit (2011b, p. 553).
12 See, for instance, Temkin (2003) and Crisp (2003).
13 For discussion see Shields (2018).
14 See, for instance, Anderson (1999).
15 See, for instance, Scheffler (1994).
16 See Dreier (2002) and Rowland (2019a, pp. 22–24).
17 See Chagnon (2000).
18 For discussion see, for instance, Wolff (1996, ch. 1); for a contemporary hopeful view see Bregman (2020).
19 See, for instance, McGraw (2008) and Ayer (2001).
20 See Lefeber and Voorhoeve (1998). Isn't this a non-moral difference? Well many of us don't believe that it is morally permissible to scarify children's faces for the sake of beauty. So, not entirely.
21 See Gruenbaum (2001).

3

MAKING ROOM FOR DISAGREEMENT

Sometimes it seems that we disagree but in fact we do not. Suppose that I say that the bank is open till 11 p.m., but you say it's only open till 5 p.m. We don't disagree if we have different things in mind: I'm talking about 'The Bank', the restaurant by the river, and you're talking about the bank in town. In this case we seem to be disagreeing but actually we're just using two words that sound the same but have different meanings. Sometimes we seem to disagree but in a sense we actually don't. Suppose that you say that Natalie Imbruglia is an amazing songwriter and I disagree. But you only think that she's an amazing songwriter because you think that she wrote 'Torn'. I explain that she didn't write it. You don't rate her other work. In this case there's a sense in which we never really disagreed about how good a songwriter Natalie Imbruglia is, we just had different understandings of what she wrote. Finally, sometimes we have different tastes, wants, or plans but it's not clear that this shows that we find ourselves in a disagreement rather than that we have a conflict of attitudes. Suppose I say 'I want to play *Fortnite* tonight.' And you say, 'No I don't want to do that.' We might seem to disagree. But this isn't clear. Perhaps I didn't realise that you had time to spend with me this evening. And even if I did, does the fact that I want to spend our evening one way and you want to spend it another way suffice to establish that we disagree? It might just seem that this means that we're inclined to or want to do different things. But differences in inclinations or wants might not be enough to create a disagreement: in general if I say that I want my team to win and you say that you want yours to win, we wouldn't say that we disagree, just that we want different things or have different allegiances.

DOI: 10.4324/9780429491375-4

Objectivism is a view about the nature of morality according to which there are objective facts about what we morally ought to do which outstrip our and our culture's attitudes about what we morally ought to do; non-objectivists hold that moral facts do not outstrip these attitudes, there are moral facts but only moral facts that are wholly dependent upon our or our culture's attitudes. Many worry that non-objectivism implies that we are never involved in genuine moral disagreements: if we accept a non-objectivist view, then although we may appear to be in moral disagreements, this is not the case. According to this worry, if we accept non-objectivism, all of our moral disagreements are instead misunderstandings or mere differences in preferences like those in the cases above. If this is right, then our seeming moral disagreements are not really moral disagreements and non-objectivism cannot make adequate room for moral disagreement. In this chapter we'll discuss whether non-objectivist views can make room for moral disagreement.

Before getting into this argument, however, you might think that non-objectivist views are wildly implausible for other reasons. The two toy non-objectivist views that we discussed in the previous chapter were: individualist relativism, according to which, for an action to be wrong is just for the individual who judges it to be wrong to disapprove of it; and cultural relativism, according to which, for an action to be wrong is for our culture to disapprove of it. In this chapter we will discuss more sophisticated non-objectivist views. However, none of these views hold that there are objective moral facts and truths that outstrip those to which individualist and cultural relativism are committed. But in this case, it might seem that these views are obvious non-starters. For it seems to many of us that it is very clear that not only is homosexuality morally permissible but it has always been morally permissible. But cultural and individualist relativism seem to imply that this is not the case. For certain (historical and contemporary) people and cultures disapprove(d) of homosexuality and thought it was morally wrong. So, aren't non-objectivist views wildly implausible?

Non-objectivists argue that non-objectivism does not imply that homosexuality has not always been morally permissible. One of the reasons for this is that non-objectivism is a view about moral facts, rather than moral thought and talk. It involves a kind of scepticism about objective moral facts existing in some kind of Platonic heaven. It asks how we could know about such facts or why they would matter. But it is perfectly consistent with such scepticism to hold the first-order moral view that homosexuality has always been morally permissible. Now suppose we take a view along the lines of individualist relativism. Some who hold views like this hold that it is only appropriate to hold that homosexuality was morally wrong in the past if you disapprove of homosexuality in the past. If you don't disapprove of homosexuality in the past, then it makes no sense for you to endorse the first-order moral judgment that homosexuality was wrong in the past. These non-objectivists hold that we don't need to be objectivists to hold onto our moral views. And, on this view, although there are no objective moral facts, truths, or properties, we can only appropriately assert the moral positions that accord with our own moral attitudes. Saying, for instance, that Anders Breivik's slaughter of 77 innocent people was permissible since he approved of his doing this is not, on this view, just to endorse non-objectivism about moral facts, but rather to endorse the first-order moral view that it was permissible for Breivik to do this; and to endorse such a moral view one has to not disapprove of his horrific actions.[1]

Perhaps this non-objectivist response doesn't work. But hopefully it is now clear how non-objectivism might not have quite the first-order moral subjectivist and relativist moral consequences that it may intuitively seem to have. Yet there are other significant challenges that non-objectivist views face. And one of the most significant involves whether they can adequately make room for the moral disagreements that we seem to have.

3.1. THE MAKING ROOM FOR DISAGREEMENT PROBLEM FOR NON-OBJECTIVISM

The two toy non-objectivist/relativist views that we discussed in Chapter 2 were individualist relativism, according to which, for an action to be wrong is just for the individual who judges it to be wrong to disapprove of it; and cultural relativism, according to which, for an action to be wrong is for our culture to disapprove of it. According to these views there are no moral facts beyond facts about what's wrong relative to the views of us and our culture (respectively). According to individualist relativism, if utilitarianism matches up with all the actions that I (morally) approve and disapprove of, then utilitarianism is correct (for me). And according to cultural relativism, if utilitarianism matches up with all the actions that our culture (morally) approves of and disapproves of, then utilitarianism is correct (for us).

Now suppose that we use these views to give accounts of moral thought, that is, to give accounts of what it is to think that and judge that an action is right or wrong. A natural view that fits with our toy cultural relativist view is that when we say that an action is wrong we report our belief that our culture disapproves of it. And a similar natural view that fits with individualist relativism is that when we say that an action is wrong we report our disapproval of that action.

However, these views face a disagreement problem. Take individualist relativism first. Suppose that I say 'I have a headache'. And my colleague says 'I don't'. We are not disagreeing. We both report our headaches but my having a headache is consistent with my colleague's not having a headache. Now suppose that I express my judgment that Australia's policy of detaining asylum seekers offshore in awful conditions is wrong and unjust. But my colleague expresses her judgment that this policy is perfectly right and just.

My colleague and I disagree. But this individualist relativist view struggles to yield this result. For if by asserting our moral judgments, my colleague and I just report our disapprovals, then it seems that there can be no disagreement here. For the state of affairs in which I disapprove of Australia's policy is entirely consistent with the state of affairs in which my colleague does not, just as the state of affairs in which my colleague does not have a headache is entirely consistent with the state of affairs in which I do. Or put another way, although the two statements in the left-hand column of Table 3.1 below intuitively involve a disagreement, the statements in the middle and right-hand column of Table 3.1 do not seem to involve a disagreement.

Table 3.1 When we disagree and when we don't.

Disagreement	No disagreement	No disagreement
A: Australia's policy is just	A: I approve of Australia's policy	A: I have a headache
B: Australia's policy is unjust	B: I disapprove of Australia's policy	B: I do not have a headache

This means that we should reject the view that our moral claims *report* our disapprovals or approvals of various actions, policies or other things. For this view doesn't make room for moral disagreements: when we assert a moral judgment and we find that we have a different moral judgment from another, such as in the Australian policy case, we seem to find ourselves in a disagreement with them, we seem to be saying something incompatible with what they are saying. But if moral judgments just report our disapprovals, this isn't the case. So, this view doesn't make room for the moral disagreements that we have.

There is no similar problem for objectivist views. But in order to see this, we need to first understand the difference between cognitivism and non-cognitivism. Objectivists are cognitivists, and this is what allows them to evade this problem. Individualist relativists hold that moral judgments consist in non-cognitive states rather than cognitive states. Cognitive states are belief and belief-like states. They are states that aim to match reality in a certain way. When all is going well my beliefs match external reality. For instance, if there is a cup of coffee on the table in front of me, I believe that there is a cup of coffee in front of me: I represent the table as having a cup of coffee on it. But, at least when my brain is functioning well, if someone takes the cup of coffee away, my belief will go away too: I will no longer represent the table as having a cup of coffee on it. Non-cognitive states are desire-like states, they do not aim to match the way the world is but rather aim to change the world. For instance, if there is no cup of coffee in front of me, this doesn't mean that I have no desire for one. In fact when there's no cup of coffee in front of me, I normally want one. Desires don't aim to match the way the world is, instead they motivate us to change it. So, in this case, if there's no cup of coffee in front of me, but I desire one, I will be motivated to get one: my desire will dispose me to go to make a coffee. Disapprovals, approvals, plans, acceptances of norms. These are all non-cognitive rather than cognitive states. For instance, if I plan to do something this means I am disposed to do it; if I disapprove of something, this motivates me not to do it.

According to cognitivists, the relationship between your judgment that stealing is wrong and the fact that it is wrong to steal is analogous to the relationship between your judgment that it's raining outside and the fact that it is raining outside. In both cases your judgment represents something a particular way: the action of stealing as having the property of being wrong; there being rain outside. Non-cognitivists disagree. They do not believe that moral judgments are belief-like, that they primarily represent the way the world is. Instead they hold that moral judgments are more like desire-like states. Suppose that you plan to never go to France again; you absolutely hated it when you visited before. Non-cognitivists hold that the judgment that an action is wrong is more like the plan to never go to France than the judgment that it is raining outside. This is because moral judgments primarily motivate us rather than representing the world in a particular way. When we judge that an action is wrong this disposes us not to perform it and when we judge that something is just good or valuable, this disposes us to pursue it. Of course, we often do end up doing things that we judge to be wrong and failing to do things that we judge to be right. But this is because other motivating considerations get in the way: if we judge that it's wrong to steal, we might still steal because the benefits of stealing are so great. But still our judging that stealing is wrong to some extent motivates us to refrain from stealing. Cognitivism struggles to explain how moral judgments are necessarily related to motivation in this way. For beliefs on their own do not motivate us to action: beliefs represent the world, that's it. In contrast, non-cognitive states are purely motivational, all they do is motivate us to do particular things.

Objectivists are (generally) cognitivists, they hold that our moral judgments are representation of something as having a moral property: when I say that stealing is wrong I believe that stealing has the feature or property of being wrong; and when you say that it is right, you believe that stealing has the property of being right. But although it is consistent that I believe that stealing is wrong and that you believe that stealing is not wrong, stealing's having the property of being wrong is not consistent with stealing having the property of being right. So in this disagreement we have representations of the world that are inconsistent: I represent the world as being one way (stealing as having a particular property), you represent the world a different way (stealing as not having this property); just as when I judge that it's raining outside and you judge that it is not we have inconsistent representations of the weather outside. In contrast, if, as per individualist relativism, moral judgments consistent in approvals/disapprovals, then when people have different moral judgments and seem to be in a moral disagreement, they will not be holding inconsistent representations: for my disapproval of X is consistent with your not disproving of X. So, one reason to endorse non-cognitivism is that it explains the relationship between motivation and moral judgment neatly. But one reason to accept (objectivist) cognitivism is that it more clearly makes room for moral disagreement than non-cognitivism.

However, the cultural relativist view that we discussed at the start of this chapter is a cognitivist relativist view. It holds that when we assert our judgment that an action is wrong we report our belief that our culture disapproves of it. This view also seems to face something like the making room for disagreement problem. Suppose that I meet someone at a conference who comes from a very conservative country where homosexuality is prohibited and punishable by imprisonment. We spend the day together, they are very nice, funny, smart, and seem quite liberal. But after we have dinner I ask them about their country's imprisonment of couples for involvement in same-sex sexual relationships. They tell me that it's very sad that people feel the need to debase themselves in this way. Shocked, I tell them that it's a gratuitous wrong to put people in prison for loving someone else. They tell me that, no, it's right and good that the state imprisons them, it stops them engaging in such immorality, what's wrong is people thinking that it's fine to act in such morally awful ways. We are engaged in a genuine moral disagreement. But cultural relativism implies that we are not engaged in a genuine moral disagreement. For according to cultural relativism, my claim that it is wrong to imprison people for having sex with someone of the same gender just means that my culture disapproves of such imprisonment. And my conference buddy's claim that it is right to imprison people for having sex with someone of the same gender just means that their culture approves of such imprisonment. Given that we are from different cultures, these two claims are consistent and compatible just as my claim 'I have a headache' and my colleague's claim, 'I don't have a headache' are compatible. Given that the reason why my colleague and I don't disagree is because our claims are consistent, similarly, my conference buddy and I don't disagree if cultural relativism holds because our claims are consistent. Or put another way: in response to my colleague saying 'I have a headache', it would be odd to respond by saying, 'No, I don't have a headache'. But if my colleague says that an action is wrong, it is not odd to respond by saying, 'no, that's not wrong'. So, cultural relativism cannot make room for many seemingly genuine moral disagreements either.[2]

So, far we've been discussing toy non-objectivist views to make the making room for disagreement problem as clear as can be. In the rest of the chapter we'll switch to looking at contemporary non-objectivist views and how they try to overcome the making room for disagreement problem. First, in §3.2, we'll discuss contemporary non-cognitivist responses to the making room for disagreement problem before discussing contemporary relativist responses to the making room for disagreement problem in §3.3.

3.2. THE EXPRESSIVIST RESPONSE

Contemporary non-cognitivists have developed plausible general views about the meaning of sentences which help them to overcome the making room for disagreement problem. Some of the first non-cognitivists were A. J. Ayer and Charles Stevenson in the early 20th century. Their non-cognitivist views were associated with the Wittgensteinian idea that meaning is use. Contemporary non-cognitivists hold a similar view. For instance, Gibbard (2003, p. 7) holds that the meanings of sentences are determined by the states of mind that sentences can be used to express; we'll call this an *expressivist* account of meaning. To start to understand this view, let's first see that we should distinguish between reporting a mental state and asserting a sentence that expresses a mental state. When we say 'it's sunny outside' we are normally in the state of believing that it's sunny outside. So, we can say that the claim 'it's sunny outside' expresses our belief that it is sunny outside. (Note that this is a technical use of the term 'expresses'; by 'X expresses Y' contemporary non-cognitivists just mean that X stands in the relationship to Y that is the same relationship that my claim 'it's sunny outside' bears to my belief that it's sunny outside; see Schroeder, 2010, ch. 4.) But although my claim 'it's sunny outside' expresses my belief that it's sunny outside, it does not *report* this belief. For if I were reporting this belief I would not say 'it's sunny outside'; I would rather say, something like 'I believe that it is sunny outside'.

Now let's look at a particular non-moral disagreement and what this *expressivist* account of the meaning of sentences implies for it. Suppose that Ann and Beth both see a bird on a gate but disagree about which bird this is:

Ann (1):   Look, there's a sparrowhawk on the gate.
Beth (2):   No, that's not a sparrowhawk, that's just a cuckoo.

This is a disagreement. (Sparrowhawks and cuckoos look very alike!) But Ann's claim, 'there's a sparrowhawk on the gate', expresses her belief that there's a sparrowhawk on the gate and Beth's claim that the bird on the gate is a cuckoo expresses her belief that there's a cuckoo on the gate. According to this *expressivist* account of the meaning of terms and sentences that we've been discussing, because (1) is used to express the belief that there is a sparrowhawk on the gate, (1) means

Ann (3):   *I believe that there's a sparrowhawk on the gate*
           And because (2) is used to express the belief that there is a cuckoo on the gate rather
           than a sparrowhawk, (2) means
Beth (4):   I believe that there's a cuckoo on the gate rather than a sparrowhawk.

Now there is no inconsistency between (3) and (4): it's perfectly possible for Ann to believe that there's a sparrowhawk on the gate and for Beth to simultaneously believe that there's a cuckoo on the gate. Yet Ann and Beth are in a disagreement just in virtue of their asserting (1) and (2). And the meaning of (1) and (2) is (3) and (4). But proponents of the expressivist account of meaning hold that there is a disagreement between (1) and (2) because it is inconsistent to have the belief specified by (3) and the belief specified by (4). To see this see that to have the belief specified by (3) is to represent the sparrowhawk as on the gate; to have the belief specified by (4) is to represent the sparrowhawk as not on the gate.

Non-cognitivists hold different views about what moral judgments consist in, to make the expressivist response to the making room for disagreement problem strongest and clearest, I'll take Allan Gibbard's view that moral judgments are a particular type of plan. On this view, the judgment that (A) consists in the state that (B):

(A)   Stealing is wrong;
(B)   I plan not to steal (and plan not to do so even for contingencies where I would like to steal or benefit a lot from stealing).

In this case, according to this expressivist account of meaning, when I assert (A), the meaning of (A) is (B) because to think that (A) is to be in the mental state specified by (B).

Let's put this all together and see where we are left regarding the making room for disagreement problem. Suppose that Alex and Blake disagree about whether stealing is wrong:

Alex (i):   Stealing is wrong.
Blake (ii):   No, stealing is morally fine.
      These assertions mean:
Alex (iii):   I plan not to steal (and plan not to do so even for contingencies where I would like to steal or benefit a lot from stealing).
Blake (iv):   I do not plan not to steal even in contingencies where I would like to steal or benefit a lot from stealing.

That is, (i) means (iii) and (ii) means (iv). How does the disagreement between Alex and Blake about the morality of stealing—in (i) and (ii)—amount to a disagreement? Remember that Ann's claim (1) that there is a sparrowhawk on the gate is in a disagreement with Beth's claim (2), that there is not, because it is inconsistent to have both the belief specified in (3) and the belief specified in (4) for the content of the beliefs in (3) and (4) represent inconsistent things: the sparrowhawk being on the gate and not being on the gate respectively. And the proposition that there is a sparrowhawk on the gate is inconsistent with the proposition that there is not a sparrowhawk on the gate: we cannot simultaneously have two beliefs that represent the world in two inconsistent ways: it is impossible to both represent the world as being a certain way and represent as not being that way at the same time. For instance, it is impossible to represent a post box as red all over while simultaneously representing it as not red all over but instead blue all over.

Now, similarly, Alex's claim that (i)—'stealing is wrong'—is in disagreement with Blake's claim that (ii)—'no, stealing is morally fine'—because the content of the non-cognitive states that the meaning of (i) and (ii) consist in conflict: the plan not to steal is inconsistent with the plan to steal. To see this, suppose that someone tells you that they both plan to steal and do not plan to steal. It seems that there is an inconsistency in what they plan to do. So, expressivists argue that this account of the meaning of sentences, inclusive of moral sentences, allows us to make room for moral disagreement. For it yields the conclusion that in cases like Alex and Blake's disagreement about the morality of stealing there is genuine moral disagreement.

Non-cognitivist theories that involve different views of the mental state that moral judgments consist in can also make room for moral disagreement in the way we've been discussing. For instance, suppose that instead of consisting in plans, we hold that moral judgments consist in disapprovals/approvals. In this case, I disagree with my friend when I claim that stealing is wrong and she claims that it is not because to judge that stealing is wrong is to disapprove of stealing and to judge that stealing is not wrong is not to disapprove of stealing. And it is inconsistent to both disapprove and not disapprove of stealing. Of course, it is consistent to disapprove of stealing in some respects (or some instances) while not disapproving of stealing in other respects (or other instances). But still it is not possible to both *all things considered* disapprove of stealing and not disapprove of stealing at all at the same time.

The combination of non-cognitivism and an expressivist account of meaning seems to make room for disagreement and overcome the problem that we encountered in the previous section. The problems for this response to the making room for disagreement problem are problems with the expressivist account of meaning generally. These problems go far beyond the scope of this book. But I will briefly discuss one issue that we might have about expressivist non-cognitivism's way of making room for moral disagreement. This problem arises because a perhaps more traditional account of the meaning of sentences may seem to provide an account of what disagreements are that may be more intuitive than the account given by an expressivist account of meaning. This may cast doubt on the idea that non-cognitivist expressivism really adequately makes room for moral disagreement.

Expressivists' account of meaning is controversial, it attributes the meaning of sentences to the mental states that they are used to express. But we might want to accept an alternative theory of meaning. For instance, expressivists hold that the meaning of 'there is a sparrowhawk on the gate' consists in the belief that there is a sparrowhawk on the gate. But we might alternatively want to hold that the meaning of this claim consists in the proposition that there is a sparrowhawk on the gate rather than in the belief that there is a sparrowhawk on the gate. Such a, perhaps more traditional, view makes sense of the disagreement between Ann and Beth very straightforwardly: they disagree because the meaning of the claims that they make consist in propositions about the world that are inconsistent: that there is a sparrowhawk on the gate; that there is a Cuckoo instead. But expressivists reject this account of meaning.

Couldn't non-cognitivists hold the more traditional view of the meaning of claims like 'there is a sparrowhawk on the gate' while holding the view that moral claims have a different kind of meaning, where their meaning consists in the mental states that they are used to express? There are two problems with holding this asymmetrical view about meaning in morality and elsewhere. First, such an asymmetrical view would seem to treat moral discourse as very different from non-moral discourse about objective matters. But, like objectivists, contemporary non-cognitivists, such as Gibbard and Simon Blackburn, want to preserve all of the objective-seeming features of our moral practice and our thought and talk: the ways in which talk about morality seems to be talk about things that there are correct objective answers to in the same way that talk about mathematics and physics seems to be.[3] For they think that our moral thought and talk is in good order and serves a useful purpose. In this case, they want to be able to treat moral discourse as very similar to non-moral discourse about objective facts. If we adopt this asymmetrical view, we do not do this.

Second, this more traditional account of meaning provides a very straightforward way of explaining why Ann and Beth are in a disagreement: the meanings of their assertions consist in propositions about the way the world is and the propositions that the meaning of their assertions consist in are inconsistent; one proposition is that there is a sparrowhawk on the gate, the other is that there is not. But, then, we might think that to disagree with another is to say something that is inconsistent with what they say rather than to express a mental state that one could not have consistent with having the mental state they expressed. And this view might seem very attractive. Suppose that we're watching City play United. I say, 'C'mon City' and you say 'C'mon United'. This does not really seem like a disagreement. We have different desires; we support different teams. This seems different to the disagreement that Beth and Ann are in: they are disagreeing about the way the world is and this manifests in their asserting inconsistent propositions. Whereas, 'C'mon City' and 'C'mon United' do not assert inconsistent propositions. But even expressivist non-cognitivism seems to equate all disagreements to clashes like the one between my friend and I about which team we want to win: it is inconsistent to both (all things considered) want City to win and (all things considered) want United to win. But some disagreements seem to come to more than that. Some disagreements seem to involve an additional form of inconsistency like that in the sparrowhawk/cuckoo case. And moral disagreements, at least on the surface, seem to present that additional layer of inconsistency. Suppose that I say 'fox-hunting is an awful wrong' and you say, 'no, it's right, hunting helps out farmers by stopping foxes ravaging their crops'. We seem to be in a disagreement of the inconsistency kind: this disagreement is different from the mere clash of attitudes we would be in if, seeing some fox-hunters trot by you cheered them and I said 'boo to fox-hunting'.[4]

So, we might have doubts about the expressivist response to the making room with disagreement problem. But whether these doubts give us any reason to reject this response seems to depend on the technical question of which general account of meaning we should hold (see also §4.2.1 below).

3.3. CONTEMPORARY RELATIVISM AND THE MAKING ROOM FOR DISAGREEMENT PROBLEM

Contemporary relativists are generally cognitivists about moral judgments. So, they disagree with non-cognitivists about what kind of mental states moral judgments are but they also disagree with objectivist cognitivists because they hold that there is no single set of objective moral truths. Rather there are just a variety of moral standards and frameworks. And all moral truths—as well as all of our moral judgments—are relative to particular standards or frameworks.

3.3.1. FRAMEWORK RELATIVISM

According to what I'll call framework relativism, there is no such thing as an action being simply morally wrong or being simply good. Rather there are only actions that are wrong-relative to particular moral standards or frameworks and good for particular people and from particular perspectives. For instance, relative to the moral standards operative in certain countries it is wrong for someone born a Muslim to convert to Christianity (apostasy is wrong); relative to other countries this is entirely morally permissible. So, on this view all claims or truths about wrongness that are not explicitly relativised to standards are elliptical, they are not fully spelled out, when fully spelled out they will be so relativised: e.g. the true claim 'apostasy is permissible' is elliptical, short for, a not fully spelled out version of the claim that 'apostasy is permissible *relative to atheist Western liberal moral standards*'—or another such true standard-relative claim. Similarly, pushing the heavy man off the footbridge in the trolley case is wrong relative to a Kantian moral framework and right relative to a utilitarian moral framework. But, according to framework-relativism, there is no such thing as it being right or wrong-*sans*-framework to push the heavy man off the footbridge. Harman (1996, p. 3) compares this kind of moral relativism to relativism about motion. The view that motion is always relative is widely accepted. Suppose I'm standing still in my living room. Relative to the living room floor I am not in motion, I am moving at 0 metres per second. But relative to the Sun I am currently in motion, I am moving at a speed of something like 30,000 metres per second. I am also in motion—and in motion at a greater speed—relative to other things: we're currently moving at something like 50,000 metres per second away from the centre of the universe. So, relative to the centre of the universe I am travelling at 50,000 metres per second when I'm stood still in my living room.[5] Truths about whether something is in motion are always relative to particular spatiotemporal frameworks: something is only ever in motion relative to a particular thing or framework: there is nothing such as being in motion without being in motion relative to some other thing. Similarly, according to relativists like Harman, all moral truths are relative to particular frameworks.

But doesn't it seem to some that there are objective moral facts? According to Harman, the reason why it seems to some that there are non-relative facts about moral right and wrong is the same reason why it seems to some people that there are objective non-relative facts about motion or mass:

> In the case of motion or mass, one particular system of coordinates is so salient that it seems to have a special status. Facts about motion or mass in relation to the salient system of coordinates are treated as nonrelational facts.
> In a similar way, the system of moral coordinates that is determined by a person's own values can be so salient that it can seem to that person to have a special status.
>
> (Harman, 1996, p. 13)

Framework relativism needs to be combined with a view about the meaning of particular moral claims that individuals make. When A claims that an action or practice is wrong what does this mean? It could mean that:

a   This action or practice is wrong-relative to A's moral standards;
b   This action or practice is wrong relative to the standards of the country that A is in or is talking about; or that
c   This action or practice is wrong relative to the contextually salient standards.

Whichever view we select, some form of the making room for disagreement problem akin to the making room for disagreement problem for cultural relativism that we discussed in §3.1 will arise. This is clearest with (a). If I claim that no-platforming is permissible and my friend claims that it is not, it seems that we disagree. But if 'wrong' and 'permissible' in our claims should be understood as relativised to the different moral standards that we hold, then our claims are compatible. For my claim that no-platforming is permissible just amounts to the claim that by my moral standards no-platforming is permissible and my friend's claim just amounts to the claim that by her different moral standards no-platforming is wrong. So, if we select (a), then our relativist view will entail that certain seeming disagreements are not genuine disagreements. Selecting answer (b) will also create problems with disagreement. Suppose that I'm in Brunei where I know that homosexuality is generally judged to be wrong (and punishable by death). I go on a tour and my Bruneian tour guide tells me 'homosexuality is wrong', which they sincerely believe. I respond, by claiming that 'homosexuality is very clearly morally permissible'. Intuitively we disagree. If we select (b), then what I say is false and I am saying something that I know to be false. This seems implausible.[6] If we select (c), it seems that—in order to make progress beyond the results that (a) and (b) yield—we must claim that either my Bruneian tour guide or I do not understand what the contextually salient moral standard is. This does not seem to be a particularly plausible or attractive view. For it is clear from the context that the moral standard that I have in mind is not that held by the majority of Bruneian's. However, it is equally clear that my tour guide does not have my moral standards in mind.[7]

3.3.2. THE CONCEPTUAL NEGOTIATION RESPONSE

There are at least three contemporary relativist responses to the making room for disagreement problem. The first involves conceptual negotiation. We can ask questions about how we should use various words and concepts. For example, some working in the philosophy of race and gender have recently started adopting ameliorative accounts of race and gender. These accounts do not aim to provide accounts of our concepts of race and gender; they do not aim to give a unified descriptive conceptual analysis of how we use these concepts. Rather these accounts propose particular race and gender concepts and argue that we should adopt and use them for particular purposes rather than our current race and gender concepts—we might think of these accounts as proposing reforming definitions. Sally Haslanger (2000, esp. pp. 36–39) proposes the following concepts of woman and man:

> S is a woman iff$_{df}$ S is systematically subordinated along some dimension (economic, political, legal, social, etc.), and S is 'marked' as a target for this treatment by observed or imagined bodily features presumed to be evidence of a female's biological role in reproduction.
>
> S is a man iff$_{df}$ S is systematically privileged along some dimension (economic, political, legal, social, etc.), and S is 'marked' as a target for this treatment by observed or imagined bodily features presumed to be evidence of a male's biological role in reproduction.

These accounts are probably implausible as descriptive accounts of everyone's current concepts of a woman and a man. For a lot of people (still) think of women as people who were born with particular bodily features and men as people who were born with different bodily features; these people's concepts of women and men involve nothing to do with systematic subordination. But Haslanger proposes these concepts not as descriptive analyses of our current gender concepts but rather as proposals for the concepts that we should adopt because they would be useful for revealing and fighting against injustice.

According to the conceptual negotiation approach, many instances of moral disagreement are moral disagreements not because the parties to these disagreements make inconsistent claims but rather because speakers use their words in different ways to advocate for different concepts or different ways of using particular concepts and terms (Plunkett & Sundell, 2013, p. 3). Plunkett and Sundell argue for the conceptual negotiation approach. They make this view seem plausible via several examples. First, they show that it is quite plausible to think that we sometimes disagree even though the claims that we make are logically consistent. For instance, suppose that Alana says that 'there is one proton in the nucleus of a helium atom' and Bryony disagrees saying, 'no, there are two protons in the nucleus of a helium atom'. These two claims are logically compatible. But there is still disagreement between the speakers. This is because Alana believes that there is exactly one proton in the nucleus and Bryony believes that there is exactly one proton in the nucleus. And not only do Alana and Bryony believe these incompatible claims, they communicate them via the compatible claims that they utter (ibid., p. 12).

Second, Plunkett and Sundell show that sometimes our evaluative disagreements are intuitively quite plausibly understood as conceptual negotiations. They consider a disagreement about whether the racehorse Secretariat was an athlete, modelled on an actual disagreement on sports radio. Alda says that 'Secretariat was an Athlete'; Belle says, 'No, Secretariat was not an Athlete'. If Alda systematically applies the term, 'athlete', in such a way as to include non-human animals, and Belle systematically applies 'athlete' to exclude non-human animals, then it is plausible that they mean different things by 'athlete'. But even if this were the case—and even if they both knew that they meant different things by 'athlete'—it would still seem plausible that Alda and Belle disagree here. Plunkett and Sundell (2013, pp. 16–17) plausibly claim that the way to explain this disagreement is to hold that Alda and Belle disagree about how 'athlete' should be used in this context, that is, whether it should be used to include racehorses or not.

They then claim that this approach can be extended to moral terms. One plausible example that they give concerns debates about torture. Suppose that we are in the context of a policy debate about torture. McCain says, 'waterboarding is torture', and Cheney says, 'waterboarding is not torture'. Suppose that McCain understands torture in line with the UN definition as involving any infliction of severe mental or physical suffering in order to obtain information or to punish, and Cheney understands torture according to the US justice department definition: only acts inflicting pain rising to the level of death, organ failure, or permanent impairment of body function are acts of torture. Plunkett and Sundell say that, in light of these facts,

> [e]ven if we suppose that the speakers mean different things by the word 'torture', it is clear that we have not exhausted the normative and evaluative work to be done here. After all, in the context of discussions about the moral or legal issues surrounding the treatment of prisoners, there is a substantive question about which definition is better. By employing the word 'torture' in a way that excludes waterboarding [Cheney] communicates (though not via literal expression) the view that such a usage is appropriate to those moral or legal discussions. In other words, [he] communicates the proposition that waterboarding itself is, in the relevant sense, unproblematic—a proposition that is, we submit, well worth arguing about.
>
> (Plunkett & Sundell, 2013, p. 19)

The conceptual negotiation approach is interesting and somewhat plausible. But there are two challenges it faces. The first is that it struggles to do a good job of making room for disagreements in moral principles or values among normative ethical theorists: Kantians and utilitarians, for instance, hold different moral standards and are not just advocating for different ways of using 'wrong'. Rather they seem to disagree and think of themselves as disagreeing about *which actions are wrong* as well as disagreeing about how we should use the term 'wrong' in the future - and part of the reason why they disagree about how we should use 'wrong' in the future is that they disagree about which actions are wrong.

Second, the examples that make the conceptual negotiation approach seem plausible share several features. Thick moral and evaluative concepts are concepts such as 'kind', 'cruel', 'tactful', 'selfish', 'boorish', 'shrewd', 'imprudent', 'open-minded', and 'gracious' (see Väyrynen, 2019). Sometimes these terms are understood as combining, or at least implying, both evaluative and non-evaluative content: to say that someone is cruel is to say something negative about them, to say that they are bad in a way, but also to say something descriptive too, that is, to specify some features of their conduct that makes them bad: to say that they have a bad feature because they are disposed to try to hurt or wound people deliberately. Thin moral concepts, such as good and wrong, do not involve or imply any such descriptive content: to say that something is good is not to describe it in any way.[8] The examples that make the conceptual negotiation approach seem plausible all involve concepts that are often thought of as thick concepts: 'athlete' and 'torture' are examples of thick concepts; to say that someone is an athlete is to evaluate them positively and say something descriptive about them, to say that someone is being tortured is to say that something bad is happening to them but also to describe what that bad thing is.[9] Although the conceptual negotiation approach is plausible with thick concepts it may be less plausible with thin concepts: is there an example like the secretariat and torture examples that you can think of where people are plausibly advocating for different uses of the word right or wrong rather than just holding that different actions are right and wrong? If there is, are all disagreements about right and wrong plausibly like this example?[10]

3.4.3. THE QUASI-EXPRESSIVIST RESPONSE

A second relativist response to the making room for disagreement problem is a quasi-non-cognitivist expressivist approach. According to this view, some cases in which A asserts that 'it is wrong for C to act', B asserts that 'it is permissible for C to act' and A and B seem to thereby be in disagreement, are disagreements in virtue of the fact that A and B express different conflicting attitudes to C's acting by asserting 'it is wrong for C to act' and 'it is permissible for C to act'. Namely, A expresses a negative attitude, such as disapproval of C's acting with her statement and B expresses no such disapproval, or that she does not feel such disapproval, with her statement (see Finlay, 2017, p. 191). For instance, suppose that Vicky the moral vegan and Megan the meat-eater hold different moral standards: vegan and meat-eating standards. In this case, relativism holds that when Vicky says, 'factory farming is wrong' and Megan says, 'factory farming is permissible' they mean different things: Vicky's claim means that factory farming is wrong according to her vegan moral standards; and Megan's claims means that factory farming is permissible relative to her meat-eating moral standards. According to the quasi-expressivist view, Vicky and Megan still disagree when Vicky asserts that factory farming is wrong and Megan says that it is permissible. This is because in saying that factory farming is wrong Vicky expresses her approval of moral standards forbidding this practice; in saying that factory farming is permissible, Megan expresses approval of moral standards that do not forbid factory farming (Harman, 1996, p. 35).[11]

Relativists normally hold this view of what makes certain moral disagreements moral disagreements rather than all moral disagreements. That is, they add an expressivist explanation of what makes seeming disagreements like Megan and Vicky's genuine disagreements onto their cognitivist relativist account of the meaning of moral terms rather than giving up their view and adopting non-cognitivist expressivism (Harman, 1996; Wong, 2011; Finlay, 2014, 2017). But Jonas Olson (2014, pp. 126–135) argues that this kind of add-on does not work. He argues that we often find ourselves in moral disagreements where we know that we and those with whom we disagree have conflicting moral standards. Kantians and utilitarians find themselves in these situations, so do libertarians and socialists, conservatives and feminists, and vegetarians and meat eaters. But in these circumstances the disagreements that we find ourselves in seem to be of just the same kind as the disagreement that I might have with someone about whether redistributive taxation will have bad consequences or about who the next president will be: if I say that redistributive taxation will not cause bad economic consequences and you claim that it will, we disagree because we make inconsistent claims; and it seems that our disagreements in moral principles or values (with e.g. utilitarians/Kantians) are disagreements in just the same way. The quasi-expressivist approach is to that extent counter-intuitive: it cannot preserve the idea that disagreements in moral principles or values are always disagreements in just the same way that many other moral and non-moral disagreements are disagreements.

3.3.4. TRUTH RELATIVISM

In response to the making room for disagreement problem—as well as for other reasons—some relativists adopt a form of relativism according to which the *meanings of moral claims are not relativised* to standards. Rather these claims are only *true relative* to standards or perspectives. The claim, 'it's wrong to push the heavy man off of the bridge in the footbridge trolley case' when uttered by a Kantian is not a claim about this action being wrong-relative to a Kantian moral framework—it is a claim that it is wrong-*sans*-framework. But the truth of such claims is only framework-relative: this claim is true, and is only true, relative to a Kantian framework, or perspective; it is false relative to a utilitarian framework. By adopting a view according to which moral truth is only truth relative to a moral framework or perspective, rather than a view on which the meaning of all moral claims is relative to particular standards, truth relativism may seem to avoid the making room for disagreement problem. For according to moral truth relativism, if I'm a Kantian and I claim that it's wrong to push the heavy man, and you tell me that in fact it's right to push the heavy man, we are talking about the same thing: I'm affirming the same proposition that you're denying, that it's wrong to push the heavy man. The relativity here is instead in what makes the propositions true. And, given my moral framework, what I say is true (due to the framework or moral perspective that I hold) while what you say is true (due to your moral framework or perspective).[12]

Truth-relativism may only evade the making room for disagreement problem by creating a similar problem elsewhere however. For Kantians and utilitarians, libertarians and sociologists, and meat eaters and vegans, think that their claims cannot both be true and that is why they are disagreeing; truth-relativism entails that both their claims are true. It might also seem that truth-relativism does not even quite solve the disagreement problem. In explaining moral truth-relativism, Jamie Dreier (2009, pp. 86–90) compares it to the view that the truth about who is the President is relative to a particular perspective or time: the claim, 'Trump is the president' is true now but was not true in 2010. So, we can say that 'Trump is the president' is true relative to 2020 but not true relative to 2010. But if we model moral truth-relativism on the truth relativity of 'Trump is the president', then it seems that this view will not give us as much disagreement as we want. For someone who says, in 2010, that Trump is not president and someone who says, in 2020, that he is do not seem to us to be disagreeing. So, if the moral disagreement between different moral frameworks or perspectives (e.g. between proponents of Kantian and utilitarian perspectives) is just like the disagreement between these people making claims about who is president, there seems to be no real moral disagreement between people with different moral frameworks or perspectives.[13]

3.4. ERROR THEORY?

In this chapter we've seen how non-objectivist views try to make space for the many genuine moral disagreements that they initially seem to preclude. In the next chapter we'll discuss how non-objectivist views have been argued to in fact make room for more disagreements than (certain) objectivist views. But before doing this it might be useful to note where one could take the combination of the arguments in this chapter and the last to lead. Remember that in Chapter 2 we discussed J. L. Mackie's argument that objectivism explains widespread moral disagreement worse than non-objectivism. Well, Mackie was a non-objectivist, but he wasn't a non-cognitivist, and nor was he a relativist of the form that we discussed in §3.3. Non-cognitivists and contemporary relativists tend to believe that non-cognitivism and relativism fit well with how we understand morality. But Mackie thought that this was not the case. Mackie thought that we do think and talk as if there is an objective morality but that this is a mistake, just as people used to think and talk as if there were witches, but that was a mistake. He was what is called a moral error theorist. According to Mackie, our moral judgments are beliefs about an objective moral reality, but there is no such objective moral reality. There is only a more culturally and individually relative moral reality. If you think that objectivist views are severely undermined because they cannot explain widespread moral disagreement (Chapter 2) but that relativist and non-cognitivist views don't provide an account of our moral thought and talk that could possibly be a good account of *our* moral thought and talk because they cannot make room for all the moral disagreements that we think that we find ourselves in (this chapter), then you might similarly be attracted to the moral error theory. You might hold that our moral thought and talk is mistaken and misguided: there is no objective moral reality but the best explanation of our moral thought and talk is that we think that there is one.

Alternatively, you might conclude, as we discussed at the end of the last chapter, that the vices of objectivism aren't as serious as the vices of non-objectivism or that sophisticated non-objectivist views can adequately make space for moral disagreement. In the next chapter we'll discuss positive arguments from disagreement for particular contemporary non-objectivists views.

SUMMARY

In this chapter we saw that non-objectivist views face a challenge with making room for moral disagreement. We started off by seeing how the toy non-objectivist views that we introduced in the previous chapter face this problem. Then we discussed contemporary non-cognitivist non-objectivist views. We saw that contemporary non-cognitivists have a plausible and interesting response that seems to show that their view can make room for enough moral disagreement. Contemporary relativists have a variety of ways of responding to the disagreement problem. These responses at least mitigate the problem. But these responses may not seem to make room for all moral disagreements such as the disagreements in moral principles or values between Kantians and utilitarians and libertarians and socialists that we discussed in Chapter 1.

FURTHER READING

Schroeder (2010) is a fantastic introduction to non-cognitivism, as well as to the problems that non-cognitivism and what I've called individualist relativism face with disagreement and how non-cognitivist expressivism seems to overcome these problems. Dreier (2009) is a similarly fantastic introduction to non-cognitivism and relativism's problems with disagreement. Enoch (2011, ch. 2) provides a contemporary slightly different articulation of the making room for disagreement problem. If you're attracted to the idea that non-cognitivists cannot really make room for moral disagreement due to the problem that I briefly discussed at the end of §3.2, a natural next place to go—after Schroeder (2010)—would be Blackburn (1999). Blackburn (1993, 1998) and Gibbard (1990, 2003) are the most well-known and well developed expressivist views. Blackburn and Gibbard also develop 'quasi-realist' expressivist non-cognitivist views, that claim to be able to say everything that robust realists say but without the existence of objective non-natural moral facts. On whether non-cognitivist views have subjectivist and relativist consequences see Blackburn (1998), Schroeder (2014), Köhler (2014), and Olson (2010). For an introduction to relativism see Harman (1996); see also Wong (1984). For a complex relativist view and how it deals with problems of disagreement see Finlay (2014) and Finlay (2008). Finlay (2017) also provides a very useful overview and discussion of contemporary relativists' responses to relativism's problem with disagreement. For an alternative relativist view see Silk (2016, 2017). For an introduction to the moral error theory see Olson (2014); this also involves an argument against contemporary relativism. Joyce (2002), Olson (2014), Streumer (2017), and Kalf (2018) provide defences of the error theory. For one much discussed problem for the error theory see Rowland (2013).

NOTES

1 See, for instance, Blackburn (1998), Schroeder (2014), and Köhler (2014). For a conflicting view see Olson (2010).
2 My discussion in §3.1–2 is indebted to, and draws heavily on, Schroeder (2010: ch. 4).
3 See the further readings and Blackburn (1999) for a clear picture of how this works.
4 This is Joyce's (2006, p. 58) example.
5 These examples are from Brightstorm (2010).
6 This view also seems to be in conflict with the principle of charity that we will discuss in Chapter 4.
7 This view similarly would seem to uncharitably interpret us. But there may be good technical reasons for holding this view.
8 For discussion see Elstein and Hurka (2009), Roberts (2011), and Väyrynen (2013).
9 On 'athlete', see Eklund (2011, p. 37).
10 Cf. Plunkett and Sundell (2013, pp. 28–31).
11 See also Wong (2011) and Finlay (2014, 2017).
12 See Dreier (2009, pp. 86–90), Kölbel (2004), and MacFarlane (2007, pp. 21–22).
13 See Dreier (2009, p. 99). There is more to be said regarding whether non-cognitivists and relativists really fail to make sufficient room for disagreement. For instance, in note 3 of Chapter 4, I discuss how it might be argued—on the basis of Janice Dowell's (2016) argument in a different context—that in fact neither view really needs to make room for disagreement in the way that I've explained that it can seem that they need to.

4

INTERPRETING MORAL DISAGREEMENTS

This first part of the book is about the descriptive implications of moral disagreement. When we're trying to describe the social world, to describe what people do or say, it's generally a good idea to charitably interpret their assertions and actions. To see this, take a couple of examples. First, take the work of the ancient philosopher Thales. We only have fragments of what Thales wrote. But we know that he was immensely influential in the ancient world. One of the fragments of Thales' writing that we have is his claim that all is water. We could interpret his claim as showing that he thought that solid objects like tables and chairs are somehow really composed of water. This interpretation of his view would be uncharitable. We can see this because if we understand his claim this way we have to see Thales as holding a ridiculous view about the nature of things. This uncharitable interpretation of his views fits poorly with his great influence and esteem in the ancient world. A more charitable interpretation of Thales' claim that all is water would understand this claim as meaning something along the following lines: water is the most fundamental of all the elements and everything else in the world depends on or originates from water. Interpreting Thales' claim in this way does not make him seem as silly or his claim as very obviously false, and it fits better with his influence in the ancient world (Andale, 2019).

We should charitably interpret practices too. Satanism is growing in the contemporary United States. Satanists gather in churches dressed in black hoods saluting 'Hail Satan'. Some of these contemporary Satanists gather in ceremonies where naked men in chains put dead pigs' heads on spikes. And some of these contemporary Satanists are involved in a campaign that aims

DOI: 10.4324/9780429491375-5

to erect a statue of a goat, Baphomet, on public governmental land. We could uncharitably interpret this practice as being one in which people who hate the good and love the bad gather together to plot the downfall of all that's good in our civilisation in order to serve their hideous desires and those of their Satanic lord. But this wouldn't account for what contemporary Satanists actually say. Most claim that they do not believe in an actual Satanic lord. Rather they use the Satan as a symbol of liberty and heroic rebellion. They do not seek to plot the downfall of what's good in civilisation but rather preach diversity and tolerance while also having a penchant for a certain kind of dark aesthetic. And their attempts to have Baphomet erected on public, politically important land is part of a campaign to try to stop the encroachment on religious pluralism in the US; they will stop their campaign if Christian statues and artefacts are removed from their positions outside state buildings (see Lane, 2019; Gander, 2017).

So, when we are describing human assertions and practices there is a good case that we should interpret these assertions and practices in a charitable manner. As we'll see in this chapter, some have argued that once we understand the importance of charitable interpretation, moral disagreement favours non-objectivist metaethical views because they are the only views that allow us to charitably interpret many moral disagreements.

4.1. THE INTERPRETATION ARGUMENT FOR NON-COGNITIVISM

As we discussed in the last chapter, according to non-cognitivism, our moral judgments consist in non-cognitive desire-like states such as disapprovals/ approvals or plans, rather than beliefs, and the meaning of moral sentences is explained in terms of such non-cognitive states. For instance, according to one kind of non-cognitivist view, to judge that an action is wrong is to disapprove of it and the meaning of 'stealing is wrong' should be understood in terms of what it is to think that stealing is wrong, which is to disapprove of stealing. One of the most well-known arguments that non-cognitivists make for their view is that it offers a better interpretation of moral disagreements than alternative objectivist views. The core of this argument is that a charitable interpretation of the way in which we disagree about moral issues requires that we interpret moral terms not as terms we use to try to refer to the objective and external moral properties that objectivists believe exist but rather as terms that we use to express our non-cognitive attitudes. The first claim in the interpretation argument is the following:

1   For any class of judgments J (such as judgments about colours, cars, horses, philosophical judgments, moral judgments), we should interpret agents making Js mostly making true or correct judgments when they make Js.

Don Loeb (1998, pp. 294–295) discusses an example that simultaneously explains (1) and renders it plausible:

> Imagine a conversation in which Kevin and Konstantin are discussing their common interest in horses. They talk about how useful horses are for getting around town, how expensive they are to take care of, how much each cherishes his own, how they rub them down each day, and how beautiful they are to look at – especially the wild mustangs both have recently seen out in the country. Still, we would give up the claim that they are both referring to horses if it became clear that their other beliefs diverge in certain ways – if, for example, Konstantin says that his horse has a red steering wheel and bucket seat ... Konstantin's belief that 'horses have bucket seats' gives us excellent evidence that he is not really referring to horses.
>
> (Loeb, 1998, pp. 294–295)

Davidson's principle of charity is very close to (1). According to the principle of charity, theories of how to interpret speaker's sentences must render speakers' sentences mostly true. The principle of charity is a principle about how we should interpret sentences rather than about judgments but speakers' judgments correlate with their sentences: if I judge that stealing is wrong, I will assent to the sentence 'stealing is wrong'.[1]

Tersman (2006, pp. 88–90) sees two types of reasons to accept (1). First, it fits with and explains the intuitively correct verdicts in cases like Loeb's as well as others. For instance, suppose that whenever we see something and say that it's red our friend says that it's blue: we say that Ferraris, British post boxes, and Manchester United shirts are red, but our friend always says that they aren't red, they're blue. In this case we should not interpret our friend's sentences that involve 'red' and 'blue' as meaning and referring to the same things as we mean and refer to when we use 'is red' and 'is blue' and make judgments about things being red and blue. Similarly, suppose that we find ourselves disagreeing with someone about the shape of the earth: they believe that it's flat, we don't. But we then come to believe that they also disagree with us about other features of the earth too: for instance, they believe that it's uninhabited and hasn't been around for a very long time. In this case, we should question whether they really have the same thing in mind as we do when they talk about the earth. (1) fits with and explains our intuitions about the red/blue and earth cases.

Second, (1) fits with the idea that language and the meaning of our sentences are essentially social phenomena. It makes it impossible for the meaning of someone's claims and sentences to be something that is private, inaccessible to others, and only accessible to them. It does this by ensuring that what someone means by a term is essentially available to others interpreting them: what someone means by a term is a function of how reasonable interpreters can understand their claims and sentences as being mostly true. So, if we want to preserve the idea that language is essentially social, then we need to accept something like

1   For any class of judgments J (such as judgments about colours, cars, horses, philosophical judgments, moral judgments), we should interpret agents making Js as mostly making true or correct judgments when they make Js.

But, according to the interpretation argument:

2   Given (1), if we are cognitivists about moral judgments, we must interpret many seeming moral disagreements as not really genuine moral disagreements at all; and
3   It is implausible to interpret many seeming moral disagreements as not really genuine moral disagreements.

R. M. Hare, Simon Blackburn, Charles Stevenson, and Folke Tersman each discuss an example that they argue is an instance of (2). That is, which they argue is an instance of a seeming moral disagreement which cognitivists must hold to not be a genuine moral disagreement given (1). Hare (1952, pp. 146–149) discusses a missionary who comes across a group of cannibals. The missionary finds that the cannibals use 'good' in the same way that he does, that is, as the 'most general adjective of commendation'. But he finds that they apply 'good' to different things than those that he applies it to. Namely, the cannibals apply 'good' to people who are 'bold and burley and collect more scalps than average' while the missionary applies 'good' to people who are 'meek and gentle and do not collect large quantities of scalps'. According to cognitivism about moral judgments, moral judgments, and the sentences that express these judgments, aim to describe or represent the world (§3.1). Now, assuming (1), if we hold that moral judgments aim to describe and represent the world, in order to interpret the missionaries and cannibals' judgments as mostly correct, we must hold that they mean and refer to different things with their judgments of goodness.

Similarly, Blackburn (1984, p. 168) considers a priest and a utilitarian who disagree about whether contraception should be abolished. The utilitarian rejects this claim in virtue of the fact that he believes that permitting contraception promotes more happiness while the priest assents to it because he believes that contraception is against God's wishes. So, similarly, it seems that if we are to interpret the priest and utilitarians' differing moral judgments as beliefs about the world that are mostly correct, then we must hold that they mean different things by 'contraception should be abolished': the utilitarian means 'abolishing contraception promotes the most happiness', which they believe to be false, and the priest means, 'contraception is forbidden by God'.

Stevenson (1963, p. 49) and Tersman (2006, pp. 86–87) discuss cases in which two people discuss whether particular policies and laws are unjust: suppose that Alice and Christina share all the same non-moral empirical beliefs about the effects of a taxation policy but disagree over whether the policy is just (§1.1). Christina thinks that the policy is unjust because it breaches the self-ownership rights of those earning a lot and Alice thinks that the policy is just because it will make things much better for the least well-off. So, they systematically and frequently disagree about sentences like, 'this policy is just'. If we accept cognitivism and hold that Alice and Christina are trying to describe the world with their judgments and claims, we must hold that they mean different things, and refer to different properties, by 'is (if we are to charitably interpret them).

So, there is a good case that

2   Given (1), if we are cognitivists about moral judgments, we must interpret many seeming moral disagreements as not really genuine moral disagreements at all.

The strength of this case for (2) does, to some extent, depend on the extent of actual disagreement that there is. For if there were only a few such disagreements where cognitivists must interpret the disagreement as one in which the parties to it are talking past one another and not genuinely disagreeing, then cognitivism would not be severely undermined. If it only entailed that some possible people would not genuinely disagree or that only the missionary and the cannibals (an example close to the real example of the Yanomamö discussed in §2.3.3) do not disagree, then this might not undermine cognitivism. But cognitivism would be far more severely undermined if it entailed that many everyday seeming moral disagreements, and most moral philosophical (seeming) disagreements, are not genuine moral disagreements.

However, according to Hare, Blackburn, Stevenson, and Tersman, it is implausible to hold that the aforementioned seeming disagreements between the missionaries and cannibals, priests and utilitarians, and libertarians and socialists are not genuine disagreements. One argument for this claim is that these (seeming) disagreements are paradigmatic moral disagreements. They share all the standard features of moral disagreements: parties to the disagreement will assent to conflicting propositions, they are motivated to do and support different conflicting things, they will feel opposed in their disagreements. If we hold that the parties to these seeming disagreements are not genuinely disagreeing, then we hold that they are talking past one another when they're talking about actions, practices, and policies being right, wrong, or just. In this case, 'good' or 'just' when uttered by one of the parties to these disagreements will have as much in common with 'good' or 'just' when uttered by one of the other parties to these disagreements as 'bank' in 'financial bank' has in common with 'bank' in 'riverbank', that is, nothing at all beyond sounding the same when pronounced. But 'good' when uttered by the missionaries seems to have more in common with 'good' when uttered by the cannibals than 'bank' in 'financial bank' has in common with 'bank' in 'riverbank'. And, similarly, 'just' when uttered or written by egalitarians like Rawls seems to have more in common with 'just' when uttered or written by libertarians like Nozick than 'bank' in 'financial bank' has in common with 'bank' in 'riverbank'. So, it seems that there is a good case for

3   It is implausible to interpret many seeming moral disagreements as not really genuine moral disagreements.

So, it seems that there is a good case for the three premises of the interpretation argument. If this argument is sound, these facts about the seeming genuineness of several moral disagreements seem to favour non-cognitivism.

How exactly, you might wonder, do non-cognitivists understand these disagreements as genuine disagreements? Well according to non-cognitivist expressivists, moral judgments express our non-cognitive attitudes (our approval or disapproval of redistributive taxation for instance). And we disagree with one another when we have a clash of such non-cognitive attitudes to the same proposition. So, the utilitarian and the priest are in a genuine moral disagreement because they have different incompatible non-cognitive attitudes towards whether contraception should be abolished; and the missionaries and cannibals disagree about what's good just because they approve of different things (for more discussion see §3.2).

What does (1) entail for expressivists, though? How can they hold that the missionaries and cannibals and utilitarians and priests are mostly making true or correct judgments when they make their seemingly conflicting judgments? Non-cognitivists expressivists can hold that moral sentences express non-cognitive judgments such that it's appropriate and correct to utter a sentence (e.g. stealing is wrong) that expresses a mental state (e.g. disapproval of stealing) only when you have that non-cognitive judgment (e.g. when you disapprove of stealing). There is no external moral standard that dictates the aptness of your uttering a moral sentence, whereas when your judgment is cognitive there is: it's appropriate for you to assert p (e.g. Trump is president) only if p (e.g. only if Trump is in fact president).[2]

So, non-cognitivists hold that they can charitably interpret the disagreements that we've been discussing in a way that cognitivists cannot. The general idea is that the missionary and cannibals, priest and utilitarian, egalitarians and libertarians, are all making correct judgments in a sense because they are all making judgments that accord with their attitudes. We should accept such an account because otherwise we will not charitably interpret people like these in such disagreements. And the only view that allows us to accept a view like this is non-cognitivist expressivism which aligns the meaning of moral claims with the non-cognitive mental states that they are used to express; if we align the meaning of moral claims with cognitive mental states instead, then we will have to say that these disagreements are not genuine disagreements because in order to charitably interpret the people involved in these seeming disagreements we will have to hold that they are talking about different things. Otherwise, we will have to hold that one of the parties to these disagreements is making an incorrect judgment because they are expressing their beliefs that aim to represent the world with their judgment—rather than expressing their non-cognitive judgments that do not so attempt to represent the world—and in this case one of the parties to these disagreements must be making many mistakes. And such a conclusion would conflict with the charitable interpretation of the parties to these disagreements.

You might wonder how this argument interacts with relativist views such as framework relativism (§3.3). It is not aimed at such views—for it is aimed at objectivist cognitivist views—but as far as I can tell it will militate against cognitivist relativism. It will provide a kind of dilemma for views like framework relativism of the following form: either the meaning of the utilitarian and priest's, cannibal and missionary's, and egalitarians' and libertarians' claims are relative to different frameworks or they are not. If they are relative to different frameworks, then they are not in genuine moral disagreements and this is implausible. If they are not relative to different frameworks, then relativism must uncharitably interpret these claims. And, according to proponents of the interpretation argument, either option is implausible. Relativists might respond by invoking one of the three strategies that we discussed in §3.3. However, as we discussed, there are problems with these three strategies.

The interpretation argument is mainly aimed at objectivist cognitivists, that is, those who hold that there are moral facts that outstrip the desires, frameworks, and other standards of individuals' and their cultures, such as the constructivists and robust realists that we discussed in Chapter 2. As we'll discuss in the next section, objectivist cognitivists have developed interesting and plausible responses to this argument.

4.2. RESPONSES TO THE INTERPRETATION ARGUMENT

The best response to the interpretation argument is to argue that we should reject (1): that we should reject Davidson's principle of charity and similar principles. If we pursue this strategy, we must offer a different way of determining when people's moral judgments are correct or true amenable to realist cognitivism.

4.2.1. A CAUSAL THEORY OF REFERENCE, AND MORAL TWIN EARTH

Some cognitivist objectivist (realists) such as Richard Boyd (1988) and David Brink (1989) have argued that we should accept a causal theory of meaning and reference for moral terms. If we accept a causal theory of reference for a term T, then the meaning and referent of sentences involving T is determined by whatever causally regulates our use of T. This means that our judgments, beliefs, and assertions using T can be widely mistaken because whether our judgments involving T are correct is a matter of the nature of what T refers to rather than a matter of how we use T. For instance, Aristotle and contemporary chemists both refer to water with their terms for water even though Aristotle had many different beliefs about the nature of water that conflict with those of contemporary chemists. This is because 20th-century chemists' and Aristotle's terms for water were both causally regulated by the same natural property: by using their terms for water Aristotle and 20th-century chemists were both trying to refer to that substance that they bathed in, drank, that falls from the sky, and that gathers in lakes. And because they both observed, felt, and otherwise perceived water (by drinking it, bathing in it, seeing it fall from the sky and gather in lakes), their use of the term 'water' refers to that substance they perceived and otherwise felt and were trying to refer to with their terms for water (Loeb, 1998, pp. 293–294). So, the causal theory differs from Davidson's principle of charity. It does not hold that we need to interpret people so that most of their judgments are true. And according to the causal theory, the fact that two people apply a term differently doesn't establish that their use of this term is regulated by different properties. If we have good reason to accept this view of meaning and reference, as Boyd and Brink argue, then we must reject (1).

However, there is a disagreement-based problem for proponents of the causal theory of reference for moral terms: moral twin earth. Suppose that Kantian properties direct and regulate our practice of calling actions 'wrong'. So, we say that lying and promise breaking are always wrong and that it is always wrong to use someone as a mere means to our ends. But suppose that there is a twin earth, an earth that is identical to our earth except for one feature, namely that twin earthers' use of 'wrong' is directed and regulated by act-utilitarian properties; they say that we're morally required to give most of our income away and that we always ought to do what will bring about the greatest happiness. Now if we accept the causal theory of reference, we and twin earthers' would not be disagreeing if we claimed that pushing a heavy man in front of a runaway trolley in order to save the lives of several people is wrong and twin earthers' claimed that pushing a heavy man in front of a runaway trolley in order to save the lives of several people is right. But it seems implausible to hold that we and twin earthers do not genuinely disagree about whether pushing the heavy man in front of the trolley is wrong (Horgan & Timmons, 1991).

In response to this argument, Janice Dowell (2016, pp. 13–16) argues that we have no reason to trust the reliability of ordinary speakers' judgments about whether hypothetical linguistic communities' terms share a meaning and reference. She argues that theories of meaning and reference (semantic theories) are more like empirical theories in biology than philosophical theories. This is because semantic theories—like biological theories—aim to fit with and explain empirical data about what competent speakers of a language are able to do with their language, namely 'communicate, coordinate, and collect information'. Non-experts' judgments about whether two token biological processes are of the same type are not reliable because the notion of a biological process is a theoretical notion; we determine what a biological process is by determining the account of a biological process that has the most explanatory power rather than by trying to figure out which account fits best with any common-sense views about what biological processes are. So, the question of whether two biological processes are the same is a theoretical one requiring expert theoretical knowledge. Similarly, whether we should accept that two communities' claims are in disagreement with one another depends on the view of meaning and reference we should hold. And the view of meaning and reference that we should accept depends on which view is most explanatorily useful. So, the question of whether two communities' claims are in disagreement with one another is a theoretical question. But in this case, in order to have reliable intuitions and judgments about whether two communities are genuinely disagreeing we need to have a high level of theoretical knowledge of which semantic theory is the most explanatorily useful. So, our ordinary judgments about whether we are genuinely disagreeing with moral twin-earthers are not necessarily reliable.

Dowell (2016, pp. 25–26) claims that this argument shows that we should be agnostic about whether ordinary people's judgments about whether we are disagreeing with twin earthers' are reliable or not until we know which semantic theory holds and whether it vindicates the pre-philosophical judgments of ordinary speakers. But such agnosticism does not help proponents of the moral twin earth argument for this argument works only if we should trust our pre-philosophical judgment that twin earthers are in fact disagreeing with us.[3]

One worry about Dowell's response to the twin earth argument is that many proponents of the twin earth argument, such as Horgan and Timmons, appear to be experts about semantic theories. So, even if we should not trust most people's intuitions about twin earth this wouldn't clearly undermine the twin earth argument.

4.2.2. CONCEPTUAL ROLE SEMANTICS

Another way of avoiding the twin earth problem is to adopt a different but non-causal theory of meaning and reference for moral terms. One such alternative theory is Ralph Wedgwood's (2001) conceptual role semantics for moral terms. According to Wedgwood's theory, the meaning of a term is given by the 'rules of rationality' that govern its use. And for moral and eva-luative terms the relevant rules are 'rules of practical reasoning'. For instance:

> A sentence S in some language other than English, which involves X-ing and Y-ing, means the same as the sentence 'X-ing is (all things considered) a better thing for A to do than Y-ing' iff accepting S commits one to have a preference for X-ing rather than Y-ing. This is because accepting the sentence 'X-ing is (all things con-sidered) a better thing for A to do than Y-ing' commits one to having a preference for X-ing rather than Y-ing.

And, similarly, *mutatis mutandis* for other moral and evaluative terms and sentences.

Accepting a view like Wedgwood's allows cognitivist realists to evade the problems with moral twin earth as well as the problems with the disagree-ments discussed in §4.1. Take, for instance, Hare's missionaries and cannibals. They count as disagreeing about what is good because the cannibals have a word that functions just like 'good' in that they use it as a general adjective of commendation. So, plausibly, when they call something 'good' in their lan-guage this rationally commits them to having a preference for it or otherwise commending it; just as when we call something good this rationally commits us to preferring it or otherwise commending it.

We and twin-earthers count as disagreeing on Wedgwood's proposal because the sentences accepted by twin earthers and ourselves involving the predicate 'is wrong' have the same conceptual role. Exactly what this is will depend on the particular conceptual role semantics that we accept for 'is wrong'. But suppose that it is, crudely, that judging that an action is wrong commits you to being averse to or blaming people who perform actions of that type. In this case, a sentence shares the same meaning as our sentence 'assault is wrong' iff some-one's uttering it rationally commits them to being averse to or blaming some-one who assaults another. And by claiming that a kind of action (e.g. stealing) is wrong both we and twin earthers are plausibly committed to being averse to or blaming those who steal (assuming that this is the right conceptual role that 'is wrong' plays in our society). For when we judge that it's wrong to sacrifice the one to save the many in the footbridge trolley case we are committed to being averse to people who perform actions like this one. And if twin earthers really disagree with us and judge that it's wrong to do anything but sacrifice the one to save the many, they will be committed to being averse to people who don't do things like sacrifice the one.

Tersman (2006, pp. 96–98) argues that at least realist objectivist cognitivists cannot evade the interpretation argument by accepting Wedgwood's con-ceptual role semantics. First, he argues that Wedgwood's conceptual role semantics seems more congenial with non-cognitivism than with cognitivism. Wedgwood claims that his semantics can be reconciled with realist objectivist cognitivism. Thoroughly evaluating whether Tersman's response is a fair response to Wedgwood's view would take us too far afield. But we can at least see why Tersman is worried here. For Wedgwood might be seen as sneaking the non-cognitive element of moral disagreements into the method of determining their meaning: the strong relationship between moral judgments and non-cognitive attitudes (blame, aversions, preferences) is part of what makes non-cognitivism an attractive view about moral judgment (§3.1). Giving an account of the meaning of moral terms that allies moral terms' meaning so strongly with these attitudes, as Wedgwood's does, might seem like a suspicious move to make if we want to preserve objectivist cognitivism in light of the interpretation argument.

According to realism, moral properties are not determined or constituted by our actual or hypothetical attitudes; moral facts are as mind-independent as facts about physics are for instance (§2.1). Wedgwood argues that his conceptual role semantics is consistent with realist objectivist cognitivism. But Tersman argues that we should think of realism as a 'continuity thesis' according to which moral facts, moral judgments, and the meaning of moral terms are not different in kind from judgments about, facts about, and the meaning of terms in physics. But if we adopt Wedgwood's proposal, then the continuity thesis is lost for we determine the meaning of moral terms via the rules of practical reasoning while even if we adopt a conceptual role semantics for non-moral non-evaluative terms and sentences, such as sentences about physics, we will not determine the meaning of sentences about physics via the rules of practical reasoning. For assenting to the claim 'that is a proton', for instance, does not commit you to having any kind of practical attitude such as a preference towards it. So, Wedgwood's proposal abandons the continuity thesis.

However, not all realists hold the continuity thesis. Most clearly, many robust realists, such as David Enoch, Michael Huemer, Derek Parfit, T. M. Scanlon, and Russ Shafer-Landau, hold that moral facts are very different from natural facts, like facts about physics, and are not reducible to natural facts in the realm of cause and effect.[4] So, in this case, such realists give up nothing by taking up Wedgwood's conceptual role semantics. But there are costs to holding that there are completely person- and reasoning-independent moral facts that are very different from natural facts.[5] And, Tersman seems to be right that naturalist realists who embrace the continuity thesis cannot take up Wedgwood's theory without giving up something important (see also Loeb, 1998).

4.3. INTERPRETING OUR INTUITIONS ABOUT DISAGREEMENTS

In Chapter 3 we discussed framework-relativism, according to which there is no such thing as an action being simply morally wrong or being simply good *sans* framework. Rather there are only actions that are wrong-relative to particular moral standards or frameworks and good for particular people and from particular perspectives such as wrong-relative to utilitarian standards or wrong-relative to Western moral standards.

Some have argued that framework relativism provides the best interpretation of some of our judgments about moral disagreement and have used experimental survey evidence to support this claim. Justin Khoo and Joshua Knobe (2018) argue that across a set of experimental studies people's judgments about whether parties disagree about a moral claim come apart from their judgments about whether these parties hold inconsistent beliefs or assert inconsistent claims. And the best explanation of this data is that a form of relativism holds.[6] In Khoo and Knobe's first study (ibid., p. 116–118), 248 participants were split into three possible conditions: same-culture, other-culture, or extra-terrestrial. Those in the same-culture condition received the following introduction to the characters that would be involved in their vignette:

> Sam is having a discussion with one of his classmates. Eventually, the conversation turns to a recent event. A person named Dylan bought an expensive new knife and tested its sharpness by randomly stabbing a passerby on the street.
> Sam says, about this case, 'Dylan didn't do anything morally wrong.'
> As it happens, Jim is listening in on Sam's conversation, and believes that Dylan did do something morally wrong. Jim jumps into Sam's conversation and says, 'No, Dylan did do something morally wrong.'

The other-culture and extra-terrestrial conditions were exactly the same except that Sam and his classmate were replaced by two individuals from an Amazonian tribe in the other-culture condition and two aliens from another planet in the extra-terrestrial condition. Within each condition participants were assigned to either the incorrectness or rejection condition. Those in the incorrectness condition were asked a question of the form:

> Given that Jim and Sam have different judgments about this case, we would like to know whether you think at least one of their judgments must be incorrect, or whether you think both of them could actually be correct.
> Please tell us to what extent you agree or disagree with the following statement:
> *Since Jim and Sam have different judgments about this case, at least one of their judgments must be incorrect.*

Those in the rejection condition were asked a question of the form:

> Given that Jim and Sam have different judgments about this case, we would like to know what you think about Jim's response to Sam's claim.

> Please tell us to what extent you agree or disagree with the following statement: *Since Jim and Sam have different judgments about this case, it was appropriate for Jim to reject Sam's claim by saying 'No'.*

Across all three conditions, there was strong agreement that rejection was appropriate. But people had different intuitions about incorrectness: they agreed less strongly that one of Jim and Sam's judgments must be incorrect.

Khoo and Knobe (2018, pp. 118–119) ran a second similar experiment involving 521 participants. The setup was very similar, the most important difference was that instead of a rejection condition participants were asked to evaluate a statement of the form, 'in making the claims that they do, Jim and Sam disagree'. They found a statistically significant difference between judgments of disagreement and judgments of incorrectness: people agreed more with the claim that the parties were disagreeing across conditions than that one of the parties was making an incorrect judgment; and this difference in judgments was magnified across conditions: in the same-culture condition there was a significant difference between judgments of disagreement and incorrectness but there was a (statistically significantly) larger difference between judgments of disagreement and incorrectness in the extra-terrestrial condition. Khoo and Knobe (ibid., p. 121) also ran a third experiment to see whether the statistically significant difference between judgments of incorrectness and judgments of appropriate rejection and disagreement regarding moral questions were mirrored regarding non-moral disagreements. They found that it was not.

Khoo and Knobe conclude that their data favours the view that people understand certain cases of moral disagreement as cases in which people disagree but do not hold views that are incompatible. Relativism predicts this, since according to relativism, A's claim that 'φ-ing is wrong' means that φ-ing is wrong relative to her standards, and B's claim that 'φ-ing is right' means that φ-ing is right relative to her standards, so when A and B make these claims to one another and hold different standards they make compatible claims, but A and B are still in a moral disagreement.[7]

This does seem to be the best interpretation of this data. But it should be noted that though the differences that Khoo and Knobe find are statistically significant they are not massive. They asked participants to evaluate statements on a scale from 1 ('Completely disagree') to 7 ('Completely agree'). In the first experiment the mean response in the same-culture condition was just above 5.5 to the rejection question and just above 5 to the incorrectness question; in the other-culture condition the mean response to the rejection question was 5 and the mean response to the incorrectness question was just under 4.5. And it is these exact differences in degrees that they use to support their claim that people understand certain cases of moral disagreement as cases in which people disagree but do not hold views that are incompatible, and that this fact favours relativism, which predicts this, unlike alternatives to relativism. So, although Khoo and Knobe recorded differences in degree of agreement with statements, often they did not in fact find differences in all-or-nothing agreement/disagreement responses. That is, Khoo and Knobe did not find any significant difference in participants' agreement/disagreement that the relevant two moral claims were inconsistent between the case in which the parties to this disagreement were in the same culture and the case in which they were not; all they found was a slight differences in the *extent to which* participants agreed/disagreed with these statements in these different conditions. We might wonder whether this data is really enough to show that we should accept a relativist account of the meaning of moral terms or even to give us good reason to accept it.

In this first part of the book we've discussed four kinds of arguments from moral disagreement for and against particular positions in metaethics. Where does our discussion leave us? Well, I hope to have shown that all views apart from the moral error theory do in fact face genuine and important challenges regarding moral disagreement. The arguments that we've discussed so far may show that all things considered moral disagreement may present more of a challenge for realism and other objectivist views than for non-cognitivist expressivism (and perhaps relativism). But it's not clear that these problems are severe enough on their own show that we should reject objectivist views. We'll come back to these issues, once we've seen further metaethical problems that moral disagreement leads to in Chapter 11. But in order to understand these problems we first need to discuss how moral disagreement impacts on what we can know and reasonably believe, and on what we ought to do.

Aren't these issues moot if relativism, non-cognitivist expressivism, or the error theory are true? I don't think so. Non-cognitivist expressivists hold that their view does not have first-order normative ethical consequences—as we discussed in Chapter 3 (this is especially true for quasi-realist non-cognitivists who hold that if we accept their view, we can say everything that objectivists say about morality, and its objectivity). But non-cognitivist expressivists hold that we still have strong reasons to accept non-cognitivist expressivism regardless and to care about how we understand the nature of our moral practice. (These strong reasons are that non-cognitivism explains the relationship between moral judgment and motivation (Chapter 3), enables us to make sense of our moral judgments and the place of morality in the natural world without positing a mysterious realm of Platonic facts, as well as enabling us to charitably interpret many moral disagreements). Some proponents of the moral error theory also claim that their view doesn't have practical implications (see Streumer, 2013). But even if there were practical implications of the moral error theory or relativism, we all need to reasonably and rationally decide what to do, and to figure out what laws to live by in light of disagreement about their justice. And even if non-cognitivism, relativism, or the error theory have normative implications for what we morally ought to do, there may be other first-order normative implications of moral disagreement that do not derive from metaethics. So, whatever the metaethical implications of moral disagreement, we can still gain by thinking about the practical implications of moral disagreements.

SUMMARY

Some relativists argue that relativism provides a better explanation of empirical data concerning people's judgments about moral disagreements that non-relativist views. This data is extremely interesting. But it is not clear that in order to explain this data we need to adopt relativism. Non-cognitivists argue that non-cognitivism provides the most charitable interpretation of many moral disagreements, and that cognitivist objectivism is incompatible with charitably interpreting many genuine moral disagreements. Cognitivist objectivists have responded to this problem by articulating new somewhat complicated cognitivist-friendly theories of the meaning of moral terms. These theories create other (disagreement-based) problems for cognitivist objectivism but these problems may not be insurmountable and may only affect certain forms of cognitivist objectivism.

FURTHER READING

Tersman (2006) is the only book-length discussion of moral disagreement and metaethics. The book focuses on moral disagreement as an argument for a non-objectivist non-cognitivist view and on developing the interpretation argument for that view discussed in this chapter. See the further reading section in Chapter 3 for further readings on non-cognitivism In §4.2.1 we discussed the moral twin earth problem. For other responses to this problem, not discussed above, see Dunaway (forthcoming), Dunaway and McPherson (2016), Väyrynen (2018), Merli (2002), and Sayre-McCord (1997). In that section we also discussed causal theories of reference for moral terms. For an introduction to reference and the causal theory of reference more generally see Michaelson and Reimer (2019). For an overview of experimental work regarding whether people are objectivists or relativists about morality see Pölzler and Wright (2019).

NOTES

1 See Tersman (2006, pp. 88–89) and Davidson (2001, pp. 168, 200).
2 There will be other ways of making a similar manoeuvre, but this seems to be the most straightforward. On this view there is an external standard for beliefs due to what it is to be a belief and in virtue of this, what it is to believe that p, namely, to represent p as being objectively the case; when one believes that p one has a mental state that is answerable to the way the world is. Remember that to say that it is appropriate to assert that an act is wrong just when one disapproves or plans not to perform that action (whatever the relevant mental state is according

to your preferred version of non-cognitivism) does not mean that we must hold that serial killers are correct to assert that serial killing is right; for more on this strategy see the introduction of Chapter 3.

3 Dowell's argument might also seem to enable a response to the making room for disagreement problem for non-cognitivism and relativism too. For expressivists and relativists might plausibly argue on similar grounds that whether A and B are disagreeing is a theoretical question that depends on the theory of meaning that we should accept. In this case, this question should be settled by the views and intuitions of those with knowledge of our best theories of meaning rather than by our everyday intuitions—which are not informed by theories of meaning—about whether two people are in a genuine disagreement.

4 See Shafer-Landau (2003), Huemer (2007), Enoch (2011), Parfit (2011b), and Scanlon (2014).

5 This view faces particular problems with evolutionary debunking, supervenience, and the seemingly odd nature of such *sui generis* facts; see Blackburn (1984, pp. 182–90), Street (2006), Olson (2014), and Streumer (2017).

6 Wong (2011, p. 426) argues that framework relativism provides a good explanation of Goodwin and Darley's (2008) experimental data. However, this data would only at most seem to show—the unsurprising conclusion—that many undergraduates are relativists. This data also seems best explained by cultural relativism rather than framework relativism; it does not seem to be straightforwardly explained by the latter at all. And there are serious problems with cultural relativism as we discussed in the last chapter.

7 A and B make compatible claims, but according to relativism we can be in a moral disagreement even when we make compatible claims so long as our moral verdicts about what to do in a particular circumstance are different.

PART II

EPISTEMOLOGY AND NORMATIVE ETHICS
NORMATIVE PERSONAL CONSEQUENCES OF MORAL DISAGREEMENT

5

THE EPISTEMIC SIGNIFICANCE OF PEER DISAGREEMENT

The first part of the book discussed how facts about moral disagreement impact on how we should describe the world. This second part of the book's focus is normative rather than descriptive: it focusses on what moral disagreement implies for what we ought to believe and do.

Many moral philosophers, such as Henry Sidgwick and Derek Parfit, have been concerned with moral disagreement's implications for the moral claims that we can believe and know. Both Sidgwick and Parfit were concerned with the moral disagreements that we find ourselves in with our epistemic equals. Sidgwick (1981: 341–342) says that

> if I find any of my judgments ... in direct conflict with a judgment of some other mind, there must be error somewhere: and if I have no more reason to suspect error in the other mind than in my own, reflective comparison between the two judgments necessarily reduces me to a state of neutrality.

Parfit was worried that the moral disagreements that he found himself in with other moral philosophers he respected a lot should lead him to drop some of his moral beliefs. Parfit had great respect for Bernard Williams. But Williams thought that if we don't want to give to the Against Malaria Foundation, and we couldn't come to a position where we decide to give to them from our current motivations, we have no reason to help them. Though he respected Williams greatly, Parfit thought he was dead wrong about this: Parfit thought we have external reasons, that is, reasons to help people just because of the

DOI: 10.4324/9780429491375-7

value of doing so even if our doing so doesn't connect up with any of our desires or other motivations. Influenced by Sidgwickian ideas, Parfit (2011b, p. 17, p. 426) worried how he could rationally maintain his belief in external reasons in light of his disagreement about their existence with Williams whom he believed to be at least as competent as he was regarding the issue of whether there are external reasons.

Finding yourself in a disagreement about a moral issue with another whom you believe to be your epistemic equal on that issue is one of the most clear and important ways in which moral disagreement can impact on what we ought to believe. It may be the only way that *disagreement itself* impacts on what we ought to believe about what's right and wrong, which is why we focus on it in this part of the book.[1] In the next chapter we will discuss particular moral disagreements and how moral disagreements with our epistemic equals can affect what we can justifiably believe and know about morality. But before this we need to know what it is to find yourself in a disagreement with an epistemic equal. As well as how we should respond, and what we can reasonably believe, when we find ourselves in disagreements with our epistemic equals.

5.1. PEER DISAGREEMENT

Finding yourself in a disagreement with someone whom you know to be your epistemic inferior on that topic seems to have no epistemological implications. Suppose I'm talking with some friends about the new football (soccer) season. I say that United have a great shot at the title this year: I believe they'll win. My friend Jerry says: 'that's absurd, they haven't won a title in years'. If I know that Jerry doesn't follow football, doesn't know how close United came last year, and how smart their transfers have been recently, the fact that he disagrees with me about United's prospects has no epistemic upshot at all: I shouldn't lower my confidence that United will win just because he disagrees with me. This is because I know that Jerry is my epistemic inferior regarding United's chances this season.

Our epistemic peers about a matter are our epistemic equals on this matter. Those with whom we took high school math classes and who were about as good as we were at mental math in these classes are our epistemic peers when it comes to mental math questions. We might see those with whom we went to, or are at, grad school with in philosophy as our epistemic peers about any randomly chosen question about contemporary philosophy or the history of philosophy. And most people that we talk to in person are our epistemic peers about whether the sun is shining where we are when we talk to them.

Disagreements with our epistemic peers sometimes seem to require us to reduce our confidence in our beliefs. For instance, suppose that you and I believe that we're epistemic peers about early noughties pop. We're at a trivia night. The host asks whether Britney Spears was born before Christina Aguilera. I express the belief that she was. You assert that she wasn't. Neither of us are massive Britney or Christina fans. When we discover that we disagree about who was born first it seems that we should reduce our confidence in our beliefs about this and suspend belief about who was born first.[2]

Almost everyone agrees that finding yourself in a disagreement with someone you believe to be your epistemic peer about whether some proposition p (e.g. it is raining) is true should sometimes lead you to revise your view about whether p. But there are different views about whether you should typically do this. In this chapter, we'll first explore two different views about how we should respond to disagreements with our epistemic peers. According to conciliatory views, we should typically revise our judgment about whether p when we find ourselves in a peer disagreement about whether p. According to steadfast views, we typically should not revise our judgments in light of finding ourselves in a peer disagreement.

In order to get an accurate account of conciliatory and steadfast views on the table we need to distinguish different accounts of exactly what it takes for another to be our epistemic peer on some matter. According to the epistemic virtues view, A is our epistemic peer about p if and only if A has been exposed to the same evidence and arguments regarding whether p as we have, has the same relevant background knowledge as we have, and possesses general epistemic virtues (e.g. intelligence, freedom from bias, reasoning skill) to the same degree that we do.[3] According to the *likelihood* view, A is our epistemic peer about whether p if and only if A is as likely as we are to be right about whether p.[4] (Being as likely as we are to be right about whether p will often involve having at least similar evidence to ours about whether p.) There are cases in which these two views come apart. Suppose that Alex is a professional mathematician who is generally more epistemically virtuous than I am. And suppose that Alex and I are both asked to figure out 4×12. The likelihood that we will provide the right answer is the same, so according to the likelihood view, we are epistemic peers on this issue. But according to the epistemic virtues view, Alex is my epistemic superior regarding 4×12 (see Frances, 2014, p. 45). Yet, it does not seem right that Alex is my epistemic superior in this case. For although Alex is my epistemic superior regarding mathematics—and regarding other matters that engage the capacities that make her more epistemically virtuous than I am—she seems to be my epistemic equal about the answer to 4×12 (see Rowland, 2017a, p. 2).

However, in order to figure out whether another is as likely to be right about a particular proposition p as we are we need to ascertain whether they have similar evidence and background knowledge to ours regarding p and whether they have similar reasoning skill to ours regarding p. And sometimes the only evidence that we have regarding another's reasoning ability regarding a particular proposition is their reasoning ability regarding other (relevantly similar) propositions. So, even if we should accept the likelihood view, we might often talk as if we accept the epistemic virtues view because often when thinking about whether another is as likely to be right about a particular proposition p as we are we will think about the evidence they possess, their reasoning skill, or other epistemic virtues that they have.

Issues about the significance of peer disagreement are often complicated by issues about the significance of epistemic superior disagreement. For instance, we might know that some who are our epistemic superiors about whether p (such as some relevant scientific or economic experts regarding whether p) agree with us about whether p but that many of our epistemic peers disagree with us (see Frances & Matheson, 2018, §4). I'm going to mostly put circumstances like these aside because we are interested in how we should respond to peer disagreement due to its implications for moral epistemology. And there are reasons to be sceptical of the view that we can identify people whom we should believe to be experts on issues of moral principle or moral values, or on pure moral issues (we'll come back to this issue in §6.3).[5] So, for the rest of this chapter I will focus on cases in which we have no epistemic superiors, or we don't currently have access to who they are or what they think.

5.2. CONCILIATIONISM

Views about the epistemological significance of peer disagreement are views about the implications of finding yourself in a peer disagreement about whether p. The most interesting and important debates about the epistemic significance of peer disagreement are about the significance of being in a situation where you *should* judge that someone is your *approximate* epistemic peer about whether p (rather than circumstances in which someone objectively *is* your *exact* epistemic peer). Where for A to judge another to be her approximate epistemic peer about whether p is for A to either (a) judge them to be her peer about whether p or (b) judge that they are either her peer or just her superior or just her inferior about whether p, she doesn't know which. To make things easier to read, for the rest of this book I'll refer to this kind of situation as one in which A judges that she is in a peer disagreement about whether p. That is, I'll just use the following shorthand for the rest of this book:

> To find yourself in a peer disagreement about whether p = to find yourself in a disagreement with another *whom you should believe to be* your *approximate* epistemic peer about whether p.[6]

According to conciliatory views, in these circumstances we typically ought to lower our confidence regarding whether p or suspend judgment about whether p.

If we believe that p, peer disagreement about whether p defeats our justification for believing that p—and ensures that we cannot know that p—unless we have a defeater-defeater; e.g. we come to know that someone who seemed to be our peer is not in fact our peer because they have been lying about their credentials or are drunk or otherwise inebriated. According to conciliationism, in our Britney and Christina case, we should suspend belief about whether Christina was born first. The reason why we should suspend belief in this kind of case according to conciliationists is that the fact that our epistemic peers disagree with us is evidence that we have made an error, we have misremembered or misjudged who was born first.

The most plausible version of conciliationism is a view about what we should do when a significant number of our approximate peers disagree with us. Take a variant of the trivia example. Suppose you're at the trivia night with 99 other friends. The host asks people to shout out their answer to the question. You and 98 of your friends shout out 'Britney' but you hear one dissenting 'Christina'. You should stick to your guns and believe that Britney was born first even though one of your epistemic peers disagrees with you. The fact that 50% of your peers on an issue rather than 1% of your peers on an issue disagree with you seems to matter for how you should respond to the disagreement. We will get back to issues about exactly how and why the number of peers matters in a second, but it will help to first have the whole picture of what conciliationism is in view.

We can see the version of conciliationism that we're going to be interested in as the principle that:

> Conciliationism. If we should believe that there is a substantial division of opinion among our (approximate) epistemic peers regarding whether p, then, other things equal, we should suspend belief about whether p or significantly lower our confidence about whether p.

Why should we accept conciliationism? One argument is that it fits with and explains our intuitions about cases. One case has famously been used to motivate the view. Suppose that

> Restaurant. You're at dinner with a large number of your friends whom you consider to be just as good as you at mental mathematics. At the end of dinner you all decide to split the bill. You and one of your friends mentally calculate how much everyone owes. You calculate that everyone owes $35. But your friend says that you each owe $40.

It seems that in this case you should suspend belief about whether everyone owes $35 or $40 for dinner (Christensen, 2007, pp. 193–194; 2009, p. 757). Conciliationism entails this and explains why we should suspend belief in this case. *Conciliationism* fits with and explains our intuitions about other cases too. Suppose that

> *Horse race.* You're watching a horse race. You're sitting next to a stranger who seems perfectly sober, fit, and healthy. The race is a tight one and the winner hasn't been announced yet. You believe that Prince of Penzance won. But the stranger says that Excess Knowledge won.

It seems that in this case you should at least reduce your confidence that the Prince of Penzance won (Elga, 2007, p. 486). And conciliationism explains this, as well as our intuitions about other cases like the Britney/Christina case from the previous section.

A second argument for conciliationism is that alternative views have implausible consequences. If we hold that we should not lower our confidence in our belief that p after realising that a significant number of our epistemic peers disagree with us about whether p, it seems that we are (at least implicitly) committed to the view that we should attribute more epistemic significance to a belief because it is one of our own. But the bare fact that a belief is our own rather than someone else's does not make it more likely to be true; and so seems to be an epistemically irrelevant feature of a belief. (Two further arguments for conciliationism are discussed in the context of more specific arguments in §5.4 and §6.2.7.)

In the rest of this section I'll further clarify and precisify conciliationism before discussing the view with which it competes in the next section. I promised to discuss issues about the number of peers. There are some important questions about how and why the numbers of disagreeing peers matters. First, why do the numbers matter? The more of your peers disagree with you, the stronger the reason you have to believe a contrary proposition, to believe that you have made an error in your reasoning or assessment of the evidence, and the higher the likelihood that you are mistaken. But is this always the case? In a sense, yes. If you believe that A and B are both your epistemic peers about whether p but then you come to know that B, instead of trying to figure out whether p, simply says and thinks whatever A thinks—B parrots A's views—then the fact that B disagrees with you in addition to A, is no reason to review your belief about whether p in addition to the fact that A disagrees with you about whether p. However, in this case it might seem that we should not take B to be our epistemic peer regarding whether p, since if she is literally just deferring to A's view whatever it is, merely parroting their view, then she is not assessing or evaluating it in any way (see also §6.2.3). Jennifer Lackey (2013) argues that in all other cases the number of peers does make a difference to what we have reason to believe.

If different epistemic peers have used different sources to come to the same belief that p, then we have more reason to believe that p because they have come to believe that p via different means. But even if two peers have used the same sources to come to the same belief that p, if they have autonomously and rationally engaged with the sources—which involve e.g. monitoring these sources for errors—the fact that two peers believe that p rather than one still provides additional epistemically significant testimony that we would not have if only one believed that p, and more greatly increases the likelihood that we are mistaken if we believe that p. Furthermore, the fact that such an additional (non-parroting) peer disagrees with you about whether p may provide additional information about the reliability and trustworthiness of the sources that they used to come to their belief that p. To ignore such additional beliefs that are formed and retained using an individual's epistemic agency is to ignore the epistemic agency used in the formation and retention of these beliefs (Lackey, 2013, p. 261).[7] In this case, because we in general don't know that any peer who holds that p is just parroting this belief, we must take the presence of an additional peer who holds p's belief to be epistemically significant.

Okay, so there is a good case that the number of peers in disagreement with us matters. But how extensive does the disagreement need to be in order to make a difference to what we should or can reasonably believe: how large a proportion of our peers need to disagree with us about p in order for this disagreement to show that we should lower our confidence in our belief or suspend belief about whether p? This is a tricky question. It is plausible that it is scalar. If only 1 of your peers disagree with you about whether p, but 99 agree with you, then you do have a reason to believe that you reasoned in error due to the peer disagreement you encounter. But this reason is outweighed by the reasons to believe that this 1 peer reasoned incorrectly in virtue of the fact that 100 of their peers disagree with them. Similarly, when 2 peers disagree with you but 98 agree with you, you have a slightly stronger reason to think that you made an error, but this reason is still massively outweighed by the reason to think that they made an error (a reason that is slightly weaker than the reason when there is 1/100 rather than 2/99 split). Take a substantial division of opinion among peers about whether p to be (approximately) between a 40/60 and a 60/40 split about whether p. In this case, even if the topic is quite specific (e.g. some specialist topic in applied ethics such as the ethics of surrogacy contracts), there can be a significant division of opinion regarding that topic among those who understand it. Conciliationism holds that when there is such a significant division of opinion about p, one should generally suspend belief about whether p.

Conciliationism involves an 'other things equal' clause: when other things are not equal we need not suspend belief in light of significant peer disagreement. When can other things be unequal? Proponents of conciliationism normally adopt a view about when we can justifiably downgrade someone's status as our epistemic peer about a proposition. Conciliationists normally hold that we may sometimes respond to a disagreement with an epistemic peer about whether p by downgrading their status as a peer about whether p but we may not downgrade someone on the basis of a consideration that is part of our peer disagreement with them about whether p. For instance, you cannot justifiably respond to the peer disagreement in *restaurant* by coming to believe that your friend must not be as good as you are about mental math because she came to the conclusion that you each owe $40 but in fact you each owe $35.

So, we should understand conciliatory views as involving a view along the following lines:

> *Independence.* We can justifiably downgrade another's status as our (approximate) epistemic peer regarding whether p post-disagreement with them about whether p only if we have a reason to downgrade their status that is independent of the disagreement that we are in with them regarding whether p.[8]

Some proponents of conciliationism argue that we must accept *Independence* because if we do not, then non-experts about whether p would (implausibly) be able to legitimately dismiss the disagreement with them about whether p of a large number of experts about whether p on the basis that they are not their epistemic peers regarding whether p since they disagree with them about whether p (see Christensen, 2011, p. 2).

An example of such an independent consideration on the basis of which we may be able to reasonably downgrade another's status is the following: that we reasonably believe that it is more likely that they are drunk or joking than that they in fact hold the view that they have asserted (Lackey, 2010, pp. 307–308; Christensen, 2011, p. 10). In general, if post-disagreement you have good reason to believe that the person with whom you disagree is cognitively malfunctioning in a certain way, then you can be justified in downgrading their status from that of your epistemic peer on the relevant proposition. And if you can be so justified in downgrading their status as that of your epistemic peer, then you should not revise your belief that is contrary to theirs due to peer disagreement with them. For instance, suppose that you are having dinner with Jack and Jill at their house. Jack and Jill haven't spoken through dinner and you've only spoken to Jack. Halfway through dinner you turn to Jill and ask her how she is. But Jack asks you who you are talking to; he says Jill isn't there. In this case, it seems that it is more likely that one of you is drunk, joking, temporarily blind, or otherwise cognitively malfunctioning than that you are both in fact peers who disagree about whether Jill is at dinner with you both. Suppose, that you know that you're not drunk, you haven't had any other weird substance that might make your perceptual faculties malfunction, and that you're perfectly well otherwise. But you don't know that the same is true of Jack, and you don't know whether he's really joking or not. In this case, it seems that you can downgrade Jack from the status of your epistemic peer about whether Jill is there for the moment, since it is more likely that he is not than that you and he are peers about whether Jill is at dinner with you and disagree (Lackey, 2008, pp. 307–308; Christensen, 2011, p. 10). (Another reason one might have to downgrade another's status as your peer might be that you knew before the disagreement that your epistemic superiors were on your side rather than theirs.)

One final clarification. I'll mainly focus on conciliationism as a view about our all-or-nothing beliefs. In *restaurant* it seems that we should adjust our all-or-nothing belief about how much everyone owes (that is, we should adjust whether we believe or do not believe that everyone owes \$35).[9] But it's also worth noting that if we should endorse conciliationism as a view about our all-or-nothing beliefs, we should also embrace conciliationism as a view about our degree of confidence, credences or degrees of belief. (This will be somewhat important later and in Chapter 7). A standard view is that in addition to all-or-nothing beliefs we also have credences or degrees of belief. To have a credence of 1 in a proposition, p, is to be certain that p is true. To have a credence of 0 that p is to be certain that p is false. And to have a credence of 0.5 that p is to think that p is as likely to be true as it is to be false. How do credences/degrees of belief relate to all-or-nothing beliefs? Dealing with this issue thoroughly is beyond the scope of this book. But according to a common view, there is a threshold of less than 1 and more than 0.5 such that when one's credence in p passes this threshold, one has a belief that p: others hold that one believes that p when one has a credence in p of 1; and others hold that there are no all-or-nothing beliefs, only credences.[10]

Sometimes peer disagreement can require changes in our degree of confidence or degree of belief without requiring a change in our all-or-nothing belief. For instance, suppose that my friend Laura is my epistemic peer about whether we have free will but her degree of belief that we do not have free will is barely sufficient to constitute an all-or-nothing belief that we do not have free will and I have a degree of confidence that we have free will that is extremely high. In this case, if I take Laura's belief and my own about free will equally seriously, and so split the difference between our views, it seems that I will still have an all-or-nothing belief that we have free will; I will just have less confidence in this belief (Christensen, 2007, p. 214). So, a conciliatory view about the consequences of peer disagreement for the epistemic status of both our degrees of belief and our all-or-nothing beliefs seems plausible.

5.3. STEADFAST VIEWS

Conciliatory views are at odds with steadfast views. Steadfast views hold that we can generally stick to our guns when we find ourselves in disagreements about whether p with those whom we should judge to be our epistemic peers about whether p.

There are several arguments for adopting a steadfast view. I'll discuss two which argue that conciliationism underestimates the epistemic significance of (i) the rationality and reasoning that goes on in coming to hold particular beliefs and (ii) the epistemic significance of our own intuitions.

Suppose that you and your friend wake up in a dark room, not knowing what time it is. There is a row of watches on a table in the room. You pick up a watch. According to this watch it is 6 p.m. Your friend picks up a watch. According to that watch it is 7 p.m. In this case you should suspend belief about whether it is 6 p.m. or not. For you have no reason to believe that one watch is more reliable than the other. But intuitively our relationship to beliefs that we have formed through reasoning is different from our relationship to these watches' readouts of the time. Take the Parfit and Williams example from the start of the chapter. Parfit had engaged in a long chain of reasoning to come to his belief in external reasons. If he suspended belief in them in light of his peer disagreement with Williams, he would be treating his belief in external reasons as if it were equivalent to one of the watches' readouts. But to treat our beliefs that are the product of detailed reasoning in this way is to not give these beliefs their due; to treat them in this way is to not give enough weight to the reasoning that we did that made it reasonable for us to have the belief prior to the disagreement (see Enoch, 2010).

However, it's not clear that conciliationism does require us to treat the beliefs that we have formed on the basis of reasoning just like the read-outs of the watches. For, as we discussed in the previous section, conciliationists hold that we may downgrade another's status as our epistemic peer about some matter in certain conditions. Namely, when:

i   We can reasonably believe that it is less likely that we are both epistemic peers regarding whether p and have contradictory beliefs about whether p than that although we seemed to be epistemic peers regarding p we are not; and

ii   We can reasonably believe that the person with whom we disagree is more likely to be the one of us who is the epistemic inferior regarding p.

And if we can reasonably believe that our reasoning about some matter is sufficiently good that another could not have reasoned about the matter equally well and come to a different conclusion, then we satisfy conditions (i) and (ii) regarding this matter and our disagreement.[11]

Ralph Wedgwood (2010, pp. 239–240) makes another argument for accepting a steadfast view. He argues that we are justified in sticking to our guns and not revising our belief that p in light of a disagreement with our epistemic peers about whether p when our disagreement is the result of our having different moral or philosophical intuitions. Wedgwood says that we can come to have moral and philosophical beliefs directly on the basis of one of our own intuitions but we cannot come to have moral and philosophical beliefs directly on the basis of the intuitions of others. And that this asymmetry is epistemically significant. In virtue of this fact, Wedgwood says that our current intuitions have an epistemic significance that could not be matched by others' intuitions or beliefs.

Wedgwood's claim is not just that we cannot typically form moral judgments directly on the basis of others' moral intuitions but that the state of having an intuition that p is epistemically significant in a way that coming to believe that another has an intuition that p is not. To see how this view works it is easiest to start out with how an analogous view about perception works. According to some, we gain justification that there is a red table in front of us purely through being in the state of having a perceptual experience of the red table. Perceptual experiences on this picture provide basic non-derivative justification. That is, we gain justification just by having the experience: our justification for believing that the table is red derives just from the fact that we see it as red, rather than deriving from the fact that we know that our seeing a table as red is a reliable indicator that it is red. On a contrasting view, perception does not provide basic non-derivative justification. Rather we each have an *a priori* entitlement to believe that our perceptual faculties are reliable absent evidence to the contrary – and our perceptions only provide justification because we enjoy this more fundamental entitlement to believe in the reliability of perception. Wedgwood's view is an analogue of the former view: intuitions are mental states of a special epistemic significance because once we have an intuition that p we thereby gain fundamental non-derivative justification for believing that p; we don't need any further prior entitlement to believe that our intuitions are reliable. This view attributes epistemic importance to your being in the state of having an intuition. And the justification that we get from that is different from any justification that we could get from someone else having that intuition or another's being such that they used to or will have an intuition.[12]

However, there are some problems for Wedgwood's view. Suppose that you read Nozick's (1974, pp. 33–35) raygun thought experiment for the first time. In this case you're supposed to imagine that you've been thrown down a deep well by Zelda. You can't get out of the well. Zelda has taken another innocent person, Hilda, hostage. Zelda is about to throw Hilda down the well. If Hilda lands on you, your body will cushion her fall and she will live. But you will die, crushed by Hilda's body. However, you have a raygun. If you shoot Hilda with the raygun as she falls, her body will disintegrate, you will not be crushed by her body, but she will die. Is it permissible for you to shoot Hilda with the raygun or would it be wrong for you to do so? You carefully consider the case. And it strikes you that it is permissible to shoot Hilda. You go out for an hour for lunch with a friend, you talk about music, eat some great food, completely forget about philosophy and the raygun case. After lunch, you get back to work, re-read the raygun case, and you now have the intuition that it would be wrong for you to shoot Hilda with the raygun. But you remember that just half an hour ago you had the opposite intuition. So, you don't know what to think. It seems that in this case you wouldn't be justified in siding with your present clear anti-raygun intuitions, given that you had the opposite clear pro-raygun intuition half an hour ago. Suspending judgment about whether it's permissible to fire the raygun seems to be the right response in this case.[13] But Wedgwood's view seems to entail that this is not the case: it seems to entail that you may permissibly believe that it is wrong to fire the raygun based on your current intuition.

It might be tempting to respond that we should think that intuitions that are stable over time are the relevant special kind of mental state that Wedgwood has in mind. But it's hard to understand how stable intuitions could provide non-derivative justification for belief, since the stability of a state is not a feature of that state that is accessible from the inside.[14] If we think that our stable intuitions that p justify our beliefs that p, then it seems that this is because we have reason to believe that stable intuitions that p are reliable guides to whether p. But in this case, our intuition that p does not non-derivatively justify our belief that p; rather our intuition that p justifies our belief that p because our intuition that p is reliable regarding whether p. But the intuitions of our epistemic peers regarding p could also be—and may well seem to be, given that they are the intuitions of our epistemic peers regarding p—just as reliable.[15]

5.4. CONCILIATIONISM AND SELF-DEFEAT

So, there are problems with alternatives to conciliationism and arguments for them, and we have some good reason to accept concilationism. Perhaps the most persistent and intuitive objection to conciliationism is that it is self-defeating. This is of particular interest for us, since arguments about the implications of disagreement in political philosophy and metaethics are also argued to be self-defeating (see §9.5 and Sampson, 2019).

The simplest version of the self-defeat objection is the following:

1   There is disagreement among epistemologists about whether con-ciliationism is true.
2   Given (1), conciliationists should believe that there is peer disagreement about whether conciliationism is true.
3   According to conciliationism, we should suspend belief about p if there is peer disagreement about whether p. So,
4   Conciliationism entails that we should suspend belief about conciliationism.

One response to the self-defeat argument is to deny that (4) is problematic for conciliationism. For the fact that we cannot justifiably believe conciliationism (or cannot do so right now) does not show that conciliationism is false. Some radical sceptics believe that we cannot be justified in holding any beliefs at all. But the fact that such radical sceptics cannot justifiably believe their radical scepticism does not show that their radical sceptical view is false but only that they cannot justifiably believe it (see Matheson, 2015b, pp. 148–149).[16] One problem with adopting this response, however, is that conciliationism seems to provide useful advice for how to revise our beliefs. If conciliationism might be true though it cannot be reasonably believed, then it seems that we cannot reasonably utilise it to guide our belief formation and revision.

Adam Elga (2010, pp. 180–181) articulates an influential response to the self-defeat problem. Imagine that *Consumer Reports* is a magazine that rates appliances and gives advice on which appliances to buy. Suppose that *Consumer Reports* rates the Hotrod 2000 toaster as the best toaster and prints the advice: if you're going to buy one toaster buy the Hotrod 2000. But its competitor *Smart Shopper* rates the Classic Toastie Toaster as the best toaster. *Consumer Reports*, however, also publishes ratings for consumer ratings magazines and rates *Smart Shopper* as the best ratings magazine and says: if you're going to buy a particular kind of appliance, buy the one that smart shopper rates best. *Consumer Reports* gives conflicting advice: it cannot coherently both recommend that its readers follow the advice of *Smart Shopper* and buy the Hotrod 2000; for it is not possible to do both of these things at the same time.

Elga argues that this example shows that any fundamental policy, rule, or method must be dogmatic regarding its own correctness because otherwise it may give incoherent advice, as *Consumer Reports* does. This is why *Consumer Reports* should not rate other appliance advice magazines. Furthermore, according to Elga, if *Consumer Reports* did rate other appliance advice magazines it should always rate itself number 1. Elga (2010, p. 185) imagines that a picky reader writes in a letter to complain that *Consumer Reports* has for its twenty-eighth year in a row rated itself as the number 1 consumer ratings magazine: the reader complains that although the magazine is rigorous and even-handed when rating toasters and cars, it has an ad-hoc exception to its standards regarding consumer ratings magazines, and the magazine ought to apply its standards across the board. Elga says that this complaint has no force. And the editors of *Consumer Reports* should reply that it is not arbitrary for them to always rate themselves number 1, rather they are forced to rate themselves number 1 in order to be able to give consistent advice about toasters and cars. In this case, Elga argues it is not ad-hoc to revise conciliationism so that it does not apply to itself. Elga argues that just as *Consumer Reports* need not apply its own standards to its ratings of itself, so conciliationism need not require that we suspend judgment about the truth of conciliationism when we are confronted with peer disagreement about the truth of conciliationism.

Jonathan Matheson (2015b, pp. 151–152) argues that Elga's rationale for the restriction is flawed. Take *Consumer Reports*'s conflicting advice about the toaster. Matheson says that it is natural to take *Consumer Reports*'s recommendations about ratings magazine as meta-advice that should guide you first: if you want to follow their all-things-considered advice you should go to *Consumer Reports* see who they think the best ratings magazine is, then forget *Consumer Reports*'s advice about particular products and follow the advice of *Smart Shopper* which it rates as the top ratings magazine; *Consumer Reports*'s advice about particular products can then be seen as their best pass, but not by their own lights worth taking as seriously as *Smart Shopper*'s advice: if you're stuck without access to *Smart Shopper*, then get the hot rod toaster 2000, otherwise buy whatever *Smart Shopper* tells you to buy. If Matheson is right about this, then Elga doesn't establish that any fundamental policy, rule, or method must be dogmatic regarding its own correctness because otherwise it may give incoherent advice. In which case, his restriction of conciliationism so that it doesn't apply to itself lacks an independent rationale and appears to be ad-hoc.

A further problem with Elga's response to the self-defeat objection is that there's a nagging sense that the kind of epistemic humility that conciliationism counsels should guide us whatever we're disagreeing about including when we're disagreeing about the epistemology of peer disagreement. And in this case, we should not restrict the dictates of conciliationism so that it only applies to peer disagreements about topics other than the epistemic significance of peer disagreement. We are drawn to conciliationism because peer disagreement exhibits a kind of sceptical pressure on our beliefs. If Elga's restricted conciliationism were correct, then there would have to be an explanation of why this sceptical pressure is not exerted when we are in peer disagreements about conciliationism. But Elga does not provide such an explanation: if Elga is right, then fundamental policies or methods must make exemptions for themselves. But this does not show that the sceptical pressure that disagreement seems to exert on our beliefs, and that conciliationism's requirements aptly captures, is not also exerted on our beliefs about the epistemology of disagreement when we are in a peer disagreement about conciliationism (see Pittard, 2015, p. 448).

John Pittard (2015, pp. 449–450) provides a different justification for restricting conciliationism so that it doesn't apply to itself. Pittard argues that the key commitment of conciliationism, and the force of the considerations that seem to favour conciliatory views, consist in the view that we should defer (epistemically) to epistemically well-credentialed thinkers in a way that is proportionate to their epistemic credentials. According to Pittard, this commitment is more basic to conciliationists than any particular conciliationist principle. But such a commitment to deferring appropriately to the well-credentialed does not entail that we should reduce our credence in conciliationism when we find ourselves in a peer disagreement about it. In normal cases, when we find that we disagree about whether p, the only way to satisfy a commitment to appropriate deference is to reduce our confidence in p. But the same is not true when we find ourselves in a peer disagreement regarding conciliationism.

Suppose that I have a credence of 1 in conciliationism but I realise, for the first time, that an epistemic peer, Amy, disagrees with me about conciliationism. According to Pittard, my decreasing my credence in conciliationism exhibits no greater deference than remaining steadfast in my conciliationism. Suppose that I decrease my credence in conciliationism to 0.5. According to Pittard, if I do this, my credence is deferential because it gives weight to Amy's view, but my reasoning that gets me to lowering my credence in conciliationism is not deferential to Amy's view; for my reasoning depends entirely on conciliationism rather than to any extent on Amy's steadfast view. Similarly, if I stick to my guns and do not modify my credence in conciliationism, then my reasoning can be deferential for it can be based on the reasoning of Amy's steadfast view even though my credence in conciliationism is not deferential for it does not take into account Amy's different view. Given that whatever I do either my reasoning or credence will fail to be deferential, I can satisfy the idea that conciliationism is based on and be appropriately deferential to well-credentialed others by sticking to my guns and not lowering my credence in conciliationism. Even though when I find myself in a peer disagreement about a topic other than conciliationism I cannot so satisfy the appropriate deference requirement by being steadfast in my confidence about this topic.

One problem for Pittard's view is that it seems to implausibly entail that a conciliationist is not required by conciliationism to reduce their confidence in conciliationism even if all of the experts in the epistemology of disagreement (or everyone in the world) comes to hold a steadfast view regarding peer disagreement. It is not entirely clear that this objection does present a problem for Pittard's response to the self-defeat objection, however. For Pittard (2015, p. 460) claims that epistemic modesty is just impossible in this situation. For reducing one's confidence in conciliationism in this circumstance would be a product of conciliationism and so would necessarily involve a lack of epistemic modesty regarding conciliationism; this would not obviously involve greater epistemic modesty than sticking to your guns as those with whom one disagrees believe one should. So, he concludes, in this circumstance '[e]pistemic modesty would simply not be an option. And where modesty is impossible, immodesty is not objectionable' (ibid.). Whether this is a reasonable response is up for debate.[17]

SUMMARY

Sometimes we disagree with our epistemic equals about particular topics. When there is a significant number of these epistemic peers with whom we

disagree, conciliationism about peer disagreement tells us to suspend judgment or significantly lower our confidence in the proposition that we find
ourselves in a disagreement about the truth of. The steadfast view says that
we are generally not required to do this. Conciliationism is plausible and there
are problems with accepting the alternative steadfast view. Conciliationism
faces a problem with self-defeat because many conciliationists' epistemic peers
do not accept conciliationism. However, there is at least one plausible way for
conciliationism to avoid this problem with self-defeat.

FURTHER READING

Christensen (2009), Matheson (2015a), and Frances and Matheson's (2018)
introductory articles on the epistemology of disagreement are a good place to
start. Frances (2014) and Matheson (2015b) have written extremely useful
introductory textbooks on this topic. Christensen (2007) and Elga (2007) are
classic defences of conciliationism. Kelly (2005), Enoch (2010), Lackey
(2010), and Wedgwood (2010) are important defences of alternative views.
Van Inwagen (2010) makes another important argument for a steadfast view,
which I did not have space to discuss; see Matheson (2015b, p. 42) for a
response. Christensen (2013) and Decker (2014) are important resources on
conciliationism and self-defeat. The essays in Feldman and Warfield (2010)
and Christensen and Lackey (2013) are good next steps for thinking about the
broader issues and discussion about the epistemology of disagreement. De
Cruz (2018) is a (short) book length treatment of the epistemology of religious disagreement. Frances (2010), Carter (2018), and Barnett (2019b)
discuss the epistemological implications of philosophical disagreement.

NOTES

1 The cases and considerations discussed in §5.1 and §6.1 give us some reason to believe that
disagreements with non-peers about whether p do not themselves undermine the justification
of our belief about whether p; I make an argument for this conclusion in §11.4 too; see also
Vavova (2014). One might think that Condorcet's jury theorem is relevant to moral disagreement. For the jury theorem seems to show that if voters are only a little better than random,
and choices are between two alternatives, then the majority are nearly infallible about which of
the two alternatives are better. However, although Condorcet's jury theorem may well be relevant regarding the epistemology of certain disagreements it is not obviously relevant for the
epistemology of disagreements in moral principles or values for we do not know whether
people are better than random regarding questions of moral principles or values; see, for
instance, McGrath (2008). Condorcet's jury theorem is sometimes discussed regarding epis-
temic/instrumental justifications of democracy. I do not discuss it in this connection (in Chapter 10) because recent proponents of such justifications, such as Estlund (2009, ch. 12), argue
that it does not provide a compelling epistemic/instrumental justification.

2 This is a variant of Carter's (2018, p. 1358) example.

3 See Kelly (2005, p. 168, n. 2) and Christensen (2009, pp. 756–757).

4 See, for instance, Elga (2007, p. 493). For discussion of both views see Killoren (2009, pp. 15–20).

5 See McGrath (2008, 2010) and §2.3.2.

6 See Christensen (2009, p. 756), Matheson (2015a, §2.2), van Wietmarschen (2013, p. 395), and Setiya (2012, pp. 16–17).

7 Even if there are some cases in which the number of non-parroting peers with whom we disagree does not matter, in many cases they do; cf. Barnett (2019a).

8 And other disagreements with them that are such that we should take them to be our peers regarding whether *p*. See, for instance, Frances and Matheson (2018, §5.1) and Vavova (2014, pp. 308–309).

9 See Christensen (2007, pp. 213–214).

10 For discussion see Clarke (2013, pp. 1–18) and Staffel (2017, pp. 39–48).

11 Although, it seems that, regarding controversial moral issues, we will very infrequently be in a position such that we can reasonably downgrade someone's epistemic status in this way, since, as we discussed in §2.3.2, and will discuss more in the next chapter, we know that people who have reasoned extremely well about moral matters frequently disagree about them.

12 See Wedgwood (2010, p. 240); this is Mogensen's (2017, pp. 290–291) reconstruction of Wedgwood's argument. On the analogous view about perception view see Pryor (2000).

13 See Mogensen (2017, p. 292) and McGrath (2014, pp. 207–211).

14 It might be claimed that the instability of the intuition defeats the justification for it in this case. However, in this case, it's not clear that you have good reason to believe that the intuition is unstable; for instance, it might well be that the second intuition will be extremely stable but the first one was not.

15 An alternative response to the argument that I've been making on behalf of the proponent of a Wedgwood-style view would be that in the raygun case I described we gain evidence of the unreliability of our intuitions about this case; for discussion of this response see Mogensen (2017, p. 293).

16 For a discussion of such scepticism see Streumer (2013) and Cuneo (2007).

17 There may be alternative ways to respond. For instance, appropriate deference to experts in this case might involve both deferring to their steadfast view and then sticking to it.

6

APPLIED EPISTEMOLOGY OF MORAL DISAGREEMENT

In the previous chapter we found that there was a good case that

> *Conciliationism.* If we should believe that there is a substantial division of opinion among our (approximate) epistemic peers regarding whether *p*, then, other things equal (e.g. unless we have disagreement-independent reason to believe their views to be mistaken or to downgrade their status as our peer), we should suspend belief about whether *p* or significantly lower our confidence about whether *p*.

The first two sections of this chapter are about the implications of conciliationism for particular moral disagreements, and for the justification of particular moral beliefs that we, and others, have. The focus of this chapter is on applied moral epistemology: what we ought to believe and can be justified in believing regarding particular ethical issues and in particular circumstances; and how moral disagreement impacts on what we can so justifiably believe. The purpose of this discussion is not to come to definitive conclusions about how disagreement affects what we can justifiably believe about particular applied ethical issues. But rather to give you (the reader) ideas about how to think about applying principles like conciliationism to your own and others' beliefs about particular ethical issues.

In §6.1 we start off by trying to figure out when, if ever, we are in a position in which we should judge another to be our (approximate) epistemic peer about an issue of moral principle or value. We'll discuss a variety of principles involving necessary and/or sufficient conditions for judging someone to be your

DOI: 10.4324/9780429491375-8

epistemic peer about an issue of moral principle or value. These principles do not compete with the different abstract accounts of the circumstances for when someone is one's peer (in terms of epistemic virtues and reliability) discussed in §5.1. Rather the principles we discuss in §6.1 are aimed to help us identify who our peers are on some issue—when someone has the relevant set of epistemic virtues or is approximately as reliable as we are. Accordingly, these principles are principles for when we should judge that another is our (approximate) epistemic peer rather than for when they are our peer. In §6.2 we'll discuss the implications of conciliationism for our beliefs about particular moral issues such as abortion and the moral status of animals. Finally, in §6.3 we'll discuss a general challenge to the view that finding oneself in a disagreement of moral principles or values can ever affect what we should believe.

6.1. WHICH MORAL DISAGREEMENTS ARE PEER DISAGREEMENTS?

Some moral disagreements are nested in disagreements about a variety of related moral and non-moral issues. For instance, pro-choicers don't just disagree with pro-lifers about the morality of abortion; pro-choicers also disagree with pro-lifers about whether human beings have souls and whether we ought to do whatever the Bible says we should do (see Elga, 2007, p. 493).

We might think that conciliationism has no implications for our nested disagreements and that almost all moral disagreements are nested disagreements. As we discussed in §5.1, according to conciliationists, we can justifiably downgrade another's epistemic status regarding whether p only if we have a rationale for doing so that is independent of our disagreement with them regarding whether p. This idea suggests that

> Independence for peerhood judgments. We should believe that another is our epistemic peer about whether p if and only if setting aside our disagreement with them regarding whether p we should believe that they are our epistemic peer about whether p.

So, if I want to know whether I have reason to believe that Jo is my epistemic peer about how much we each owe for dinner, I must ask whether I would judge Jo to be my epistemic peer about whether p if I didn't know her view about whether p. And I must ask whether considering only the reasons independent of our different interpretations of the relevant evidence (and similar relevant factors) in this particular case, should I believe Jo to be my epistemic peer regarding p. (Such independent reasons might include whether Jo has gotten mental math questions right in the past.)

Adam Elga (2007, pp. 492–494) claims that once we accept *independence for peerhood judgments* it follows that conciliationism has no implications for nested disagreements. According to Elga, if A finds herself in a nested disagreement with *B* about whether *p*, *A* should not judge that *B* is her epistemic peer about whether *p*, because setting aside their disagreement about whether *p*, *A* should not judge that *B* is her epistemic peer about whether *p*. For instance, setting aside their reasoning about the morality of abortion, pro-choicers should not judge that pro-lifers are their epistemic peers about the morality of abortion because pro-choicers disagree with pro-lifers about other related issues such as about whether human beings have souls and whether we should do whatever the Bible says that we should do. So, if very often moral disagreements are nested in this way, then conciliationism will very often have no implications for the epistemic status of our moral beliefs.

However, we often find ourselves in non-nested moral disagreements with others whom we think are trustworthy and morally insightful people. For instance, we frequently find ourselves in disagreements about the moral status of animals with those with whom we agree about pretty much all other moral issues. And this great amount of agreement about other moral issues seems sufficient to make it the case that we can and should judge those with whom we disagree about many moral issues to be our epistemic peers about the moral status of animals.[1] So, *independence for peerhood judgments* seems plausible. But it does not establish that conciliationism has few implications for the justification of our moral beliefs. In the rest of this section we'll discuss some other principles we might use to determine who our peers are that might have further implications.

We might think that

> *Non-moral agreement is sufficient for peerhood.* If we should believe that A agrees with us about non-normative, non-moral topics, and is just as generally intelligent and socially developed as we are, then we should believe that A is our epistemic peer about moral issues.

Kieran Setiya (2012, pp. 19–20) seems to hold this view. He asks us to imagine that we are confronted with members of a large community of moral monsters who share all of our non-moral beliefs and are clearly just as intelligent and socially developed as we are but who have uniformly horrific moral beliefs; suppose that they believe that we should brutally kill the innocent for the pleasure of the many. He argues that conciliationism entails that in this case we should suspend judgment about whether it is wrong to brutally kill the innocent for the pleasure of the many because of our disagreement with the moral monsters. And because of this Setiya claims that conciliationism is implausible (as a view that applies to the epistemic status of our moral beliefs). For 'we should not defer to moral monsters but condemn them, however numerous they are'.

Setiya's argument is only sound if we presuppose *non-moral agreement is sufficient for peerhood*. But this claim is implausible. We have no reason to believe that Setiya's moral monsters, or anyone who is such that we only know that they agree with us about non-moral matters and are generally intelligent and socially developed, are our epistemic peers about moral issues. In order to have reason to believe that someone is our epistemic peer about some matter we have to have reason to believe that they are as likely to be right about this matter as we are. But the fact that someone shares all the same non-moral beliefs as us is no reason to believe that they are as likely to be right about moral matters as we are; just as the fact that A is as likely to be right about any mental mathematical calculation as we are is no reason to believe that A is as likely to be right about any matter of physics or philosophy as we are. Furthermore, one can be good at non-moral reasoning without being good at moral reasoning: robots and sociopaths are very good at reasoning about non-moral matters but not at moral reasoning. And conciliationism only holds that we should revise our beliefs about an issue in light of disagreement with others whom we should believe to be our epistemic peers about that issue rather than that we should revise our beliefs about an issue in light of disagreement with others whom we do not know are not our epistemic peers about that issue.[2]

More plausible than *non-moral agreement is sufficient for peerhood* is Fritz's (2018a, p. 114) idea that

> *Background agreement is sufficient for peerhood.* If we should believe that another shares a background of general agreement with us about many propositions in domain D, then we should believe that they are our epistemic peer about (all) propositions in domain D.

Background agreement is sufficient for peerhood does not entail that we should believe that Setiya's moral monsters are our epistemic peers because we do not share a general background of moral agreement with them. But it would entail that we should believe that pretty much everyone whom we might meet in our society is our epistemic peer about moral issues because we share a background of general agreement about morality with them: nearly everyone we might meet agrees that (i) pain is bad, (ii) we should generally keep our agreements, (iii) we should generally not torture others, (iv) we ought not kick puppies, and that (v) it's wrong to refrain from saving millions of lives when one knows one can do so at no cost (Fritz, 2018a, p. 114). But the combination of this principle and conciliationism would entail that we must suspend belief about whether gender and racial equality is right or required, about whether slavery is wrong, about whether horrific and torturous public executions are wrong and about whether homosexuality is permissible. For many of those in the past (and present) who have believed that slavery is permissible, that public executions were permissible and right, that gender and racial equality is wrong, and that homosexuality is impermissible agree with us about (i–v).

We should reject *background agreement is sufficient for peerhood*. Just knowing that someone shares a background of agreement with you in some domain is not sufficient to establish that you should believe them to be your epistemic peer about a particular proposition in that domain. For example, I agree with professional logicians about the general principles of logic that are taught in a first year logic course. So there is a background of agreement between them and me. But they should not judge me to be their epistemic peer about any matter in logic. I could read the *Stanford Encyclopedia* article on set theory and thereby agree with most philosophers working on set theory about which axioms hold. But set theorists should not then believe that I'm their epistemic peer about set theory. I share a background of general agreement about how British politics works with Professors who have written multiple books and articles about British politics. But I'm not their epistemic peer about British politics; they know a lot more about it than I do. And they should believe this. So, we should reject *background agreement is sufficient for peerhood*.

However, there is a similar principle to *background agreement is sufficient for peerhood* that is more plausible. Consider

> *Great background agreement is sufficient for peerhood.* If we should believe that another agrees with us about *pretty much all propositions in domain D*, then, other things equal, we should believe that they are our epistemic peer about (all) propositions in domain D.[3]

If someone shares a great background of moral agreement with us, then this is good reason to believe that, to the extent that we are reliable regarding moral issues, they are too. *Great background agreement is sufficient for peerhood* does not have the problematic implications that *background agreement is sufficient for peerhood* has: it doesn't entail that professors of British politics should believe that I'm their peer about British politics, for I don't agree with them about pretty much all propositions about British politics (I don't have sufficient knowledge for that). And *great background agreement is sufficient for peerhood* will not entail that we should judge that those who disagree with us about the morality of horrific torturous public executions are our epistemic peers about the morality of such executions. For they do not agree with us about pretty much all moral propositions.

Great background agreement is sufficient for peerhood only provides a sufficient condition for being justified in believing that another is our epistemic peer about a proposition in a domain; there may be other ways in which we can be justified in believing that another is our peer about some issue. For instance, we may have good reason to believe that another is our peer about a logical proposition because we have reason to believe that their reasoning about logic is very good even though we have no knowledge of how many matters of logic we agree with them about. However, it might be that for moral issues there are no other sufficient conditions and that great background agreement is both necessary and sufficient for peerhood.[4] The view that such great background agreement is both necessary and sufficient for peerhood would explain why it seems that we should judge that Setiya's moral monsters are not our epistemic peers about morality.

6.2. IMPLICATIONS OF CONCILIATIONISM FOR PARTICULAR MORAL ISSUES

What does conciliationism imply for the justification of our particular moral beliefs?

6.2.1. SCEPTICISM

Some suggest that it implies a general scepticism about moral knowledge and justified moral beliefs. This can't quite be right. As we discussed in §5.2, conciliationism only kicks in when there is a substantial division of opinion among our epistemic peers about a particular proposition. There are many moral propositions that there is no such substantial division of opinion about. Consider the following propositions:

Enjoyment is better than suffering.
If A is better than B and B is better than C, then A is better than C.
It is unjust to punish a person for a crime that they did not commit.

These claims are moral claims. And almost everyone who considers them accepts them (see Huemer, 2007, p. 102). Furthermore, I recruited 196 participants from Amazon's Mechanical Turk platform and asked them whether they agreed that (a) it is [at least] sometimes wrong to kill others; (b) we should [at least] sometimes help people; and (c) we should [at least] sometimes keep our agreements. 99% agreed with (a); 97% agreed with (b); and 99% agreed with (c). There is not a substantial division of opinion about these claims. I expect that if I had asked my participants whether it's wrong to refrain from saving millions of lives when one knows one can do so at no cost by pressing a red button that is within reach, over 90% would have agreed too. So, conciliationism does not entail that we have no justified moral beliefs or no moral knowledge.

Even if it does not entail wholesale moral scepticism, conciliationism may entail that many of our moral beliefs do not amount to knowledge and are not justified. Sarah McGrath (2008) argues that conciliationism implies that our controversial moral beliefs are not justified and implies epistemological scepticism about controversial moral issues. *Great background agreement is sufficient for peerhood* explains how this could be the case without conciliationism entailing a broader scepticism. Remember that according to

> *Great background agreement is sufficient for peerhood.* If we should believe that another agrees with us about *pretty much all propositions in domain D,* then, other things equal, we should believe that they are our epistemic peer about (all) propositions in domain D.

And according to

> *Conciliationism.* If we should believe that there is a substantial division of opinion among our (approximate) epistemic peers regarding whether *p,* then, other things equal (e.g. unless we have disagreement-independent reason to believe their views to be mistaken or to downgrade their status as our peer), we should suspend belief about whether *p* or significantly lower our confidence about whether *p.*

The combination of *great background agreement is sufficient for peerhood* and conciliationism seems to provide a *prima facie* case that we should suspend belief about, or reduce our confidence about, most of the moral issues that are currently controversial in our society and in the applied ethics literature: the morality of euthanasia, eating animals, strongly redistributive taxation, immigration controls, torturing in a ticking-bomb case, etc. Since for all of these issues there seem to be many people who agree with us about pretty much all moral propositions but who disagree with us about one of these particular moral issues. (Around half of the people in the US believe that such torture is permissible and that abortion is wrong for instance; see §1.2.) And for any controversial moral issue that we have a view about, we may seem to find ourselves in disagreement with a very large number of people who agree with us about pretty much all other moral issues. For instance, many libertarians agree with egalitarians about which actions are right and wrong. They just disagree with egalitarians about what it is permissible for a state to tax us for. We can disagree about whether there are some (hypothetical) cases in which it is permissible to torture someone while agreeing about pretty much all other moral issues. Similarly, vegetarians and non-vegetarians often agree with one another about pretty much all moral matters except about whether it's morally permissible to eat meat.

6.2.2. ABORTION

However, it is not obvious that conciliationism entails that we should suspend belief about the permissibility of certain actions because there is disagreement about whether they are permissible. Suppose that like me you are non-religious and on the left politically. In this case, it's not obvious that among those who agree with you about pretty much all moral propositions there is a substantial division of opinion about the morality of abortion. Most of those who have the same moral perspective as you only state that they vigorously affirm women's rights to choose to have an abortion; most either hold that it is permissible to have an abortion or do not state a view about whether it is permissible or not, only claiming that coercing women to refrain from having an abortion is wrong. The same may well be true for those who hold the opposite views, who are religious and on the right politically; they may not find themselves in disagreements about the morality of abortion with others with whom they share a great background of general agreement about moral issues. And so *great background agreement is sufficient for peerhood* and conciliation-ism do not seem to entail that those on either side of the disagreement about abortion must suspend belief about its permissibility.

There is a general implication here: when a moral topic is particularly polarised in the sense that those on each side share little background moral agreement, then *great background agreement is sufficient for peerhood* and conciliationism do not entail that those who disagree should lower confidence in their view. This might seem quite depressing. But there's a way in which this conclusion diagnoses what is so lamentable about polarised moral dis-agreements: parties to them no longer have reason to believe that those with whom they disagree are in the ball park of being their epistemic equals about the topic about which they disagree. This means that parties to such dis-agreements cannot afford one another an important kind of epistemic or cognitive respect about the issues that they disagree about.

6.2.3. GENDER AND MARRIAGE EQUALITY

Ben Sherman discusses the implications of conciliationism for the epistemic status of beliefs about the rightness of marriage and gender equality. Sherman (2014, esp. pp. 11–14) argues that

We should not take others to be our epistemic peers regarding whether p if

a   We have reason to believe that their beliefs regarding whether p

   i   Are dogmatic or are the result of other dogmatic beliefs;
   ii   Are status-quo beliefs; and
   iii Are the result of, or are informed by, other cognitive biases, such as 'implicit prejudices, misunderstandings of statistics, predictive errors and uncharitable interpretations of positions; and

b   We do not have such reason to believe that our beliefs regarding whether p instantiate (i–iii).

Sherman (2014, pp. 9–15) argues that those who believe that gender and marriage equality are wrong have beliefs about these issues that satisfy (i–iii), that is, their beliefs are dogmatic, status quo beliefs that are the result of biases and/or prejudices. But most of us who believe that gender and marriage equality are right have beliefs about these issues which do not satisfy (i-iii). So, we should believe that most of those who believe that gender and marriage equality are wrong *are not* our epistemic peers about these issues. But we should also believe that most of those who believe that gender and marriage equality are right *are* our epistemic peers about these issues. And in this case, peer disagreement does not undermine the epistemic status of our beliefs that gender and marriage equality are right because most of our epistemic peers about these issues agree with us.

There are issues with some of Sherman's claims. One worry is about (ii), the claim that the fact that A's belief that p accords with the status quo gives us reason to downgrade the epistemic status of A (and her belief) regarding whether p. (ii) does not initially seem to point to a plausible epistemic vice of a belief. According to a certain kind of Nietzschean immoralist, we should only pursue our own flourishing and we should only treat others as instruments to this pursuit. This kind of view entails (and is designed to entail) that many actions that we think are morally wrong are in fact required. Egoism entails that when it would be slightly inconvenient for us to press a button that would save thousands of lives, and we don't care about saving these lives, we ought not do so. And egoism entails that we are not required to save a drowning child from a pond if we'd prefer not getting our clothes and shoes wet to saving their life. So, egoism and Nietzschean immoralism both have implications that are radically at odds with the moral status quo. In this case, if a belief's having feature (ii) is an epistemic vice of a belief, then Nietzschean immoralists and egoists can claim an epistemic advantage for their moral beliefs over beliefs in all alternative ethical theories on the basis that they, unlike their opponents, hold radically contra-status-quo views.[5] But this doesn't seem to be a particularly plausible or attractive view.[6]

However, Nietzschean immoralism and egoism are extremely unpopular ethical theories. If a view is both popular or gaining in popularity and an anti-status quo view, then perhaps those who hold the anti-status-quo view—let's call them the revisionaries—can claim an epistemic advantage over those who hold the anti-status quo view—let's call them the traditionalists; especially in the context of the significance of peer disagreement, where (gaining) such popularity matters (see §5.1).[7]

A different worry is that (i) seems to be true of the beliefs about gender and marriage equality of at least many of us who believe that gender and marriage equality are right: many of us are very dogmatic about the immorality of gender inequality. For it seems that to be dogmatic about such claims is to believe them to be undeniably true and to be entirely resistant to changing belief in these claims. But if this is what it is to be dogmatic in our beliefs, then many of us are definitely dogmatic in our beliefs about the immorality of gender inequality and marriage inequality: we think it's undeniably true that these things are immoral and we are entirely resistant to changing our beliefs about this.

However, Sherman may have a different understanding of what it is to be dogmatic in mind. Namely that for A's belief to be dogmatic is for it to be the result of following religious or moral rules given to A by others and never questioned by A. It might be that if A's belief that p is dogmatic in this sense, then we should not take A to be our epistemic peer regarding p. For in this case A's belief that p is not really a product of A's reasoning about whether p but is rather the product of others (B's) reasoning about whether p. So, perhaps we should take these others (B) to be our epistemic peers regarding whether p but we should not take A to be our peer regarding whether p; for to do so would be to engage in a kind of double-counting of our epistemic peers regarding whether p. Since A's belief on this topic is not of any epistemic importance beyond B's belief; p is not more likely to be true given that A and B believe that p than given that B believes that p (see §5.1).

Now it might be the case that at least many of us who believe that gender and marriage equality are right are not dogmatic in our beliefs in this second sense. It simply seems very clear to many of us who believe this that we should have such equality, that any departure from equality would need to meet a high bar of justification, and that there is no such justification that can be made. If we hold these beliefs on this kind of basis, we do not hold them dogmatically (in the second sense of 'dogmatic').

Should we hold that we may downgrade another's status as our peer about whether p if their belief about whether p is dogmatic in this second sense of dogmatic? This seems plausible. For suppose that Amie forms all her beliefs about economics solely on the basis of what Brie believes about economics without questioning her views at all. In this case it seems that we should not take both Amie and Brie to be our epistemic peers about economics but only Brie.[8] So, Sherman does seem to be right: conciliationism does not entail that we should suspend judgment that gender and marriage equality are right because of disagreement about this.

6.2.4. EATING MEAT AND THE MORAL STATUS OF ANIMALS

There is disagreement about the morality of eating meat among those who agree about pretty much all other moral matters. Many intelligent, informed, and open-minded people believe that it is morally permissible to eat meat in all (or most) circumstances. But many also believe that it is morally wrong to eat meat (at least when one is affluent and can easily do otherwise). So, it seems that conciliationism entails that we should suspend belief about the morality of eating meat.

Can meat-eaters who think that it is morally fine to eat meat resist? Some claim that those who believe that eating meat is typically wrong hold this belief as the result of a cognitive shortcoming or bias. For instance, some hold that vegans hold this belief because they (illegitimately) anthropomorphise cuddly and cute animals. However, it's not clear that this is a plausible view. For many moral vegans who believe that non-human animals have a moral status believe this because they hold the plausible view that all beings that are sentient or can feel pleasure or pain have a moral status such that they should not be eaten. If we do not hold this view, it's unclear why babies, people in comas, and extremely cognitively deficient people have a moral status such that they should not be eaten.[9]

Alternatively, meat eaters could claim that there is not a significant division of opinion about the morality of eating meat since over 90% of people act as if it is morally fine (§1.2). However, this data about how people act may not show too much about their moral judgments: around 50% of people cheat on their spouses, but over 90% of people believe that infidelity is wrong; similarly, many of us believe that we should give more to charity than we do (Trustify, 2018; Haltzman, 2013). Furthermore, most of those working on the morality of eating meat, and over a quarter of philosophers, believe that eating meat is typically wrong (Leiter, 2012). Meat eaters might respond by arguing that those who work on farms are in the best epistemic position to ascertain the morality of eating meat. However, their epistemic position while much better in some ways, may be compromised by tradition and self-interest, so it's not clear that it's better or much better than that of those who study animals (or their moral status) in other ways. In this case, it's not clear that this strategy will work to show that there is not a significant number of others whom meat eaters should believe to be their epistemic peers about the morality of eating meat who believe that eating meat is wrong. This said, some of those who believe that it is typically permissible to eat meat may hold very traditional moral views. And because of this it is probably true that most of those who share a great amount of background moral agreement with them agree with them about the moral permissibility of eating meat. In this case, those with very conservative or traditional moral views can reasonably believe that eating meat is permissible even though there is disagreement about this.

Can moral vegans justifiably hold onto their belief in light of disagreement about it? Moral vegans might be able to justifiably hold onto their beliefs in light of Sherman's criteria for downgrading someone's status as an epistemic peer about whether p, which we can boil down to: we have disagreement-independent reason to believe that their belief about whether p is dogmatic, or based on its status quo or traditional status rather than being a result of their own reasoning and questioning, and propelled by cognitive biases, and ours is not. But many meat eaters don't obviously just believe that eating animals is morally fine because this is what everyone else around them believes. Rather it seems to them clear that beings with the features that animals have do not have the kind of moral status that precludes us from eating them. So, in order for moral vegans to justifiably hold onto their beliefs we must be able to justifiably downgrade another's epistemic status as our peer about an issue when not all of Sherman's criteria are met. We might be able to do this. We might hold that

> *Tradition & bias.* We can justifiably downgrade someone's status as our epistemic peer about whether *p* if
> (a) their view about whether *p* is the status quo or traditional view (and our view is a non-traditional view that is gaining popularity);
> (b) we have some reason to believe that their view regarding whether *p* is driven or sustained by cognitive biases; and
> (c) our view regarding whether *p* is not a traditional or status quo-based view and we have good reason to believe that our view regarding whether *p* is not driven or sustained by cognitive biases.

Should we accept *tradition & bias*? One argument would be that if someone's belief about *p* has the features specified in (a-b) and ours does not (as per (c)), then this establishes that they are importantly less reliable (or epistemically virtuous) than we are regarding *p*. So, when we would otherwise judge that another is our epistemic equal about whether *p*, and ours and their relevant beliefs satisfy the other features of *tradition & bias*, we may reasonably downgrade their status as our epistemic peer about whether *p*.[10]

Does *tradition & bias* allow moral vegetarians to downgrade the epistemic status of the meat eaters with whom they disagree? It may do. It could be argued that the practice of factory farming and eating meat is maintained largely because it is traditional and the status quo. Opponents of factory farming have long argued that it is only maintained on the basis of a kind of cognitive bias, namely speciesism; that is, the bias of seeing other species as less important than humans just because they are not humans. And it can seem that the only justification for treating non-human animals as different from any possible human is on the basis of speciesism. (The important question here, of course, is whether speciesism is the result of a genuine cognitive bias.)[11]

It might seem that many meat eaters believe that tradition itself provides us with reasons to do things (see §1.2). It will then seem strange and question-begging to use *tradition & bias* as a basis to downgrade their epistemic status about the morality of eating animals. However, it may be that those who believe that tradition itself provides a morally significant reason to do things disagree with moral vegetarians on such a sufficiently large number of topics that moral vegans do not have sufficient reason to believe that they are their epistemic peers on moral topics. (For, traditionalists are often socially conservative, and many vegans are very socially liberal, and the socially conservative disagree with the socially liberal on a vast number of moral issues)

Regardless, it seems that most of those who share a great background of moral views with moral vegetarians and vegans cannot justifiably believe that eating meat is permissible if *great background agreement is sufficient for peerhood* and conciliationism hold. In this case, if you agree about almost all other moral issues with your friends, except for about whether eating meat is permissible, then you should suspend belief about this, unless you can reasonably believe that the vast majority of those who share a great background of moral agreement with you share your view.

6.2.5. DISTRIBUTIVE JUSTICE

Libertarians and classical liberals like Robert Nozick (1974) and Gerald Gaus (2011) argue that a state that taxes the better-off for the purpose of improving the lot of the less or least well-off is unjust and/or illegitimate. Gaus and Nozick have spent large portions of their lives making—and have many extremely adept former students making—sophisticated arguments for their positions. And their positions are incompatible with my own view, which is that such taxation is legitimate and just. I don't believe that I have a reason to believe that Gaus and Nozick are not at least my epistemic peers (if not superiors) about distributive justice that is independent of our disagreement about distributive justice. There is considerable overlap between my first-order moral and philosophical views and their own—apart from in the area regarding libertarianism/classical liberalism. I respect their arguments, and methods, and I believe that they are thoughtful and considerate about redistributive justice and other moral matters. If I learnt about their lives, methods, and work before learning of their particular views about distributive justice, it seems that I would definitely hold that they are at least my epistemic peers—if not my superiors—about distributive justice. So, assuming that there are enough of those who disagree with me about distributive justice who have the features like those that I've been attributing to Nozick and Gaus, it seems that I should suspend belief about whether libertarianism and classical liberalism are right—or at least reduce my confidence that they are incorrect in light of this disagreement. Others might be in a similar position.

According to luck egalitarianism, justice requires that we ensure that no one is worse-off than others through no fault of their own. Luck egalitarianism is an attractive view which many of the most creative, adept, and generally great political philosophers of the 20th and 21st century, including G. A. Cohen (1989) and Ronald Dworkin (2002), have argued for or endorsed at various times. It seems to me that it's false. For I don't share luck egalitarians' intuitions that it is permissible by the lights of equality to allow some to be worse-off than others just because they are worse-off as a result of their choices rather than as a result of brute luck (see, for instance, Anderson, 1999). But I agree with luck egalitarians about most moral matters, judge

most well-known luck egalitarians to be extremely insightful and sophisticated moral thinkers, and because of this it seems to me that they are my
epistemic peers (if not superiors) regarding distributive justice (and other
matters). In this case, it seems that I—and others like me—cannot justifiably
believe that luck egalitarianism is false or mistaken (assuming conciliationism
and *great background agreement is sufficient for peerhood*).

6.2.6. ACT-UTILITARIANISM

According to act-utilitarianism, we ought to do whatever will produce the
most impartial happiness; and it's wrong for us not to do so. Act-utilitarianism generates counter-intuitive verdicts in a large number of cases. When you
can do a little more good by giving your money to a child other than your
own it entails that you ought to give the money to the other child rather than
your own and that it's wrong not to. When you can savagely kill one person to
save five more without any additional cost it entails that you ought to kill the
one and that it's wrong not to. When you can do great good for two far away
people by selling your house and all of your possessions it entails that you're
morally required to do so. When you can make the lives of many millions of
people very slightly better by killing one person (e.g. when doing so is the
only way of ensuring that the world cup continues to be broadcast around the
world), it entails that you're required to do this and that it's wrong not to.[12]
Many of us disagree with act-utilitarians' verdicts about these cases. Should
we suspend judgment about what it is permissible to do in these cases because
act-utilitarians disagree with us?

It might be argued that there is just not enough act-utilitarians around to
force us to such suspension of judgment: act-utilitarians are but a tiny minority and do not even amount to a substantial minority in academic (moral)
philosophy.[13] Even if act-utilitarians did amount to a substantial minority,
however—or if the numbers didn't matter—it might be that our disagreement
with act-utilitarians would not affect what we can justifiably believe.
Remember that according to,

> *Great background agreement is sufficient for peerhood.* If we should believe that
> another agrees with us about *pretty much all propositions in domain D*, then, other
> things equal, we should believe that they are our epistemic peer about (all) propo-
> sitions in domain D.

It might be that those who disagree with act-utilitarianism should not judge
act-utilitarians to be their epistemic peers about the correct normative ethical
theory because act-utilitarians—or at least signed up card-carrying full bloo-
ded non-akratic act-utilitarians—have different beliefs from them about such
a wide range of moral cases. Does act-utilitarianism yield counter-intuitive

verdicts in a sufficiently large number of cases such that act-utilitarians do not agree with non-act-utilitarians—or with you!—about 'pretty much all' moral propositions? This is not entirely clear. But it is a key issue relevant to whether non-act-utilitarians should consider act-utilitarians to be their epistemic peers about what we morally ought to do in any particular case.

6.2.7. DEEP DISAGREEMENTS

Some argue that there are limits to how peer disagreement can affect what we ought to believe that are in line with and similar to the limits that we've been discussing regarding act-utilitarianism, abortion, vegetarianism, and gender and marriage equality. Deep disagreements are: (i) disagreements between individuals that are a result of differences or conflicts in epistemic principles, that is, principles about what counts as evidence, how we should acquire and assess evidence, how we should argue and form beliefs, which such methods are reliable, and how we can gain knowledge; and (ii) disagreements in which there is no further epistemic principle that can be turned to in order to settle the disagreement in epistemic principles. One common example of a deep disagreement is between old earthers and young earthers. Most of us are old earthers who believe that the earth is millions of years old and rely on scientific methods and standards of evidence—or the testimony of those who use these methods and standards—to come to this conclusion. But some argue that the bible tells us that the earth was created by God 6,000–10,000 years ago. Young earthers think that biblical interpretation is a better guide to the age of the earth than the scientific evidence. This is a deep disagreement because it is the product of a difference in epistemological principles. And there is no further epistemic principle that parties to this disagreement could use to establish that one of them is correct in a way that the other party would accept.

Some argue that if we find ourselves in a deep disagreement with another about whether p, this does not give us reason to lower our confidence or suspend belief about whether p. Why is this? Finding ourselves in a disagreement with another that turns out to be a deep disagreement gives us no reason to believe that we made an error in our reasoning. For we already know that people who endorse different epistemic principles from our own will come to different conclusions than our own: finding ourselves in a disagreement with young earthers gives us no reason to believe that we made an error in our reasoning about the age of the earth since we already know that if you don't endorse the scientific method or the testimony of scientists, you won't believe that the earth is very old. To crudely dramatise this point a little, suppose that you mark a bunch of essays. The second-marker comes back with completely different grades. This would give you reason to doubt that you had marked them correctly. But only because you assume that they applied the same method as you did. If you came to believe that they instead adopted the method of giving marks according to the aesthetic appeal of the title or whether the thesis argued for was one that they agreed with, then the second-marker's difference of view would give you no reason to doubt that your marking was correct; you already knew that if you had adopted a method like that, you would have awarded different marks.

Some argue that if the fact that we find ourselves in a deep disagreement about whether p gives us no reason to doubt that we made an error in our reasoning regarding whether p, then the fact that we find ourselves in a deep disagreement about whether p gives us no reason to lower our confidence or suspend our judgment about whether p. One argument for this view is that what explains the truth of conciliationism is that when our epistemic peer disagrees with us about whether p, this is good evidence that we have made a mistake in our reasoning about whether p: we should lower our confidence in our belief that p when we have strong evidence that it is the product of a mistake in our reasoning or an error in one of our other faculties. For instance, in the restaurant and horse race cases that motivate conciliationism (§5.2), we gain good evidence that we made a mistake in our calculation of the bill and that our vision is mistaken. While in the cases of disagreements for which conciliationism has no implications, such as the case in which we are at dinner with two friends and one of them claims that the other is not present (§5.2), our disagreement does not provide strong evidence that we made a mistake in our reasoning. On this view the deeper epistemic rationale behind the epistemic significance of peer disagreement is the following: peer disagreement about whether p gives us good reason to believe that our belief that p is the result of an error in our reasoning or one of our other faculties (see Kappel, 2012, 2018b).

According to the view that I've been sketching, deep disagreements about whether p are epistemically insignificant. The fact that there is disagreement about whether p does not undermine or defeat the justification of our belief regarding whether p to the extent that such disagreement is deep. There seem to be some important moral epistemological implications of this view. At least some, perhaps many, disagreements about the moral status of abortion and homosexuality are deep. For some people believe that abortion and homosexuality are wrong on biblical or religious grounds. Those who disagree and do not form moral beliefs on the basis of biblical or religious interpretation find themselves in a deep disagreement about the morality of homosexuality and abortion. So neither party to these deep moral disagreements have the justification of their moral beliefs defeated or undermined by these deep moral disagreements.

Some disagreements between act-utilitarians and their opponents may also be deep disagreements. A standard methodology in normative ethics is reflective equilibrium in which we move from our stable intuitions about cases to more general principles that explain these intuitions and move back again to make particular judgments about further particular cases (see Daniels, 2003). Some act-utilitarians have argued that we should reject this methodology and seem to reject it themselves since it seems to tilt against act-utilitarianism, which has counter-intuitive implications. Some act-utilitarians have argued that we should not take our intuitions about cases epistemically seriously, or should give more weight to our intuitions about principles such as that we always ought to do what's best and that the well-being of each counts equally towards what's best. (These intuitions, when combined, favour act-utilitarianism; see de Lazari-Radek & Singer, 2012.) Opponents of act-utilitarianism disagree that intuitions about principles are more epistemically reliable than intuitions about cases. And there doesn't seem to be a way to appeal to neutral epistemic principles that all accept to settle these epistemic disagreements—since the parties to these disagreements disagree about which principles generate more reliable results.[14] So, act-utilitarians and their opponents may be locked in a deep disagreement. In this case, the view that deep disagreements are epistemically insignificant entails that the disagreement between act-utilitarians and others does not undermine the justification of the beliefs of either party.

6.2.8. EXPERTS AND SPECIALIST SUBJECTS

Suppose that you have a particular claim to expertise on a moral topic. In such a case, can you sometimes justifiably judge that others who agree with you about pretty much all other moral matters are not your epistemic peers about that particular topic? For instance, suppose that you are a world expert on the morality of drone strikes. You have spent a long time working on and formulating arguments about the wrongness of drone strikes (arguments of moral principles and values, regarding, suppose, the asymmetrical power relations involved in drone warfare, as well as other arguments).[15] Suppose that there is a substantial division of opinion about whether drone strikes are permissible or not among those with whom you agree about pretty much all other moral matters. But that all of these people have not really thought about the morality of drone strikes in detail. It seems that you can, consistent with *great background agreement is sufficient for peerhood*, judge that they are not your epistemic peers about the morality of drone strikes even though they agree with you about pretty much all other moral matters. Since *great background agreement is sufficient for peerhood* only entails that the fact that others with whom you agree about pretty much all other moral issues disagree with you about a particular moral issue should, other things equal, lead you to believe that they're your peer about this particular issue. And in this case although they agree with you about pretty much all other moral matters, you have spent far longer thinking about the morality of drone strikes than they have. In virtue of this fact, you have good disagreement-independent reason to believe that they are not your peers about the morality of drone strikes; other things that need to be equal are not equal here. Since, the asymmetry between you and them regarding the extent to which you have reasoned about drone strikes makes it the case that before finding out whether they agreed with you or not you had good reason to believe that they were not your epistemic peers about the morality of drone strikes. This shows that you have good disagreement-independent reason to believe that they are not your epistemic peers about the morality of drone strikes.

What if there is disagreement among the world's experts about the morality of drone strikes? What if there is a division of opinion among them about whether it is wrong or unjust to use drone strikes? Does this mean that you should suspend belief about the morality of drone strikes? Sometimes yes. But it might be that sometimes no.

Suppose that you have an argument that you have given to many and no one has been able to adequately respond to or make a compelling response to. And you believe your view about the morality of drone strikes on the basis of this argument. Call being in such a position being at the cutting edge of a debate with a new argument (see Rowland, 2017a, p. 10). When you are in such a position, perhaps you can judge that those who disagree with you—who do not take your argument into account—are not your peers about this issue.

This position will not be one that many, if any, are in very frequently. But it might seem that being in this position does not insulate one from the epistemic significance of peer disagreement. Some have argued that even if one should not believe that some currently existing person is or was your epistemic peer about p, the fact that there is a close-by possible world in which an epistemic peer disagrees with you about whether p could still undermine the justification for your belief that p. It might then seem that when you are at the cutting edge of a debate with a new argument, it is just a contingent matter that you are not in a position where you should believe that your epistemic peers disagree with you: sooner or later some smart moral philosopher will disagree with you, it's just your good luck that they don't currently. Non-actual peer disagreement clearly seems epistemically significant in certain cases. If the only reason why you do not encounter peer disagreement regarding your belief that p is that you have slaughtered all those who hold dissenting views, (that there would have been) peer disagreement still undermines your justification for believing that p (see Kelly, 2005, p. 181). And it may be that the fact that a recently deceased brilliant moral philosopher would have disagreed with you about the issue that you are at the cutting edge of undermines the status of your belief about this matter in the same way that actual peer disagreement does (see Ballantyne, 2014).

However, it is plausible that being in a position in which you are at the cutting edge of a debate with a new argument is in some circumstances not quite like either of these scenarios. Moral enhancement is the use of biomedical technologies or drugs to make people morally better. Suppose you have a controversial view about moral enhancement, which you have aired in print and in many other circumstances. Others who disagree with you about your view have only been able to respond in ways that you have been able to parry in a way that all those concerned have believed to be reasonable. Perhaps some brilliant dead philosophers would disagree with you if they were still around. But conciliationism should not entail that this fact undermines the justification of your belief. For epistemological scepticism seems to follow from the view that: if some brilliant dead philosopher might have disagreed with your belief that p were they around, then your belief that p is not justified. This is because for any view that one might have about anything, a great dead philosopher might have disagreed with this view if they were around. But, first, conciliationism is supposed to be a distinctive view about how peer disagreement about your view that p, rather than the mere possibility that p is false, can defeat your justification for believing that p. In order to be so distinctive, conciliationism must not take the mere possibility of peer disagreement to defeat the justification of our beliefs (see Vavova, 2014). And, second, conciliationism would seem to be implausible if it did yield a general scepticism by taking such merely possible peer disagreement into account. So, we should not understand conciliationism to entail that: if there is some possible world in which you find yourself in a peer disagreement about whether p, your belief about whether p is not justified.

There are some general lessons that it will be useful to bring out before moving on. One idea that seems attractive is that, as a heuristic, by default we should think that people who disagree with us about some small pocket of morality are our peers about it unless we have very good (disagreement-independent) reason to think that they're not. But these reasons can be provided by disagreement-independent features of the amount of reasoning we've done on an issue or the fact that others are subject to various biases or make arguments that show that they are. Call those with whom we share a great background of moral agreement, our moral tribe. Getting yourself into a position in which you can reasonably believe that the views of your moral tribe about moral issue M, which are divergent from your own, do not epistemically undermine your own view about M is very difficult. But *great background agreement is sufficient for peerhood* and conciliationism allow that if you work hard, you can have a justified belief about the morality of an action or practice even when there is significant disagreement about the morality of that action or practice among your moral tribe.

6.3. MORAL EXPERTISE, PURE MORAL DEFERENCE, AND MORAL TESTIMONY

In §1.1, we discussed pure moral disagreements. These are disagreements that are not the result of disagreements about metaphysics, epistemology, religious claims, or the empirical consequence of actions or policies. They are dis-agreements in moral principles or values that are not the result of religious or non-moral-philosophical disagreements. Disagreements about what we should do in trolley cases, disagreements between egalitarians and libertarians—like Alice and Christina's (§1.1)—and utilitarians and Kantians are pure moral disagreements (see §1.2). Some argue that we cannot be required to change our moral views in light of pure moral disagreement. This argument concerns moral deference and moral testimony. Pure moral facts correspond to who is right in pure moral disagreements: if utilitarians are right, it is a pure moral fact that we ought to do whatever will promote the best consequences; if Alice is right, then it is a pure moral fact that justice requires that we have the policies that will make the least well-off as well-off as possible.

We can gain justification and knowledge about non-moral matters via the testimony of others. We gain justification for believing, and know, that Ava was burgled just by Ava telling us that she was burgled. And we can reason-ably rely on and use her testimony. Some people can gain justified belief and knowledge on the basis of testimony about the moral facts and some people, children for instance, can reasonably rely on and use such testimony. But, according to moral testimony pessimists, we should not rely on pure moral testimony, and there is something strange, at least, about forming beliefs on the basis of testimony about the pure moral facts. Suppose that Billie, after living as a carnivore for twenty years, realises that there might be a problem with eating meat. She understands that factory farms contribute to climate change, that the animals slaughtered in factory farming are sentient beings that can feel pain. And she's also aware of the role that eating meat plays in various traditions and the pleasure that many people get from it. She doesn't have time to think about the morality of eating meat. And so she consults her friend whom she believes to be normally trustworthy and reliable about moral issues and asks her whether it's wrong to eat meat. (Her friend's not an expert in Billie's religious faith or anything like that; they're both atheists.) Her friend tells her that it is wrong. And so, she believes that eating meat is wrong.

It seems, to moral testimony pessimists at least, that Billie's reliance on her friend's beliefs about vegetarianism is puzzling, not quite justified, and/or even disturbing (Hills, 2009, p. 94). Billie defers to her friend's pure moral views in this case. But if we suspend our beliefs in light of moral disagreement with our epistemic peers, we do something very similar to deferring to the views of others: we stop having a moral belief in light of the moral views of others. Some thus ague that peer disagreement about pure moral issues could not be epistemically significant because in order for it to be significant we must be required to modify our beliefs due to pure moral testimony, and we are not required to do this.

There are two ways to respond to this argument. The first is to challenge moral testimony pessimism. I won't focus on this strategy here as it takes us too far away from issues of moral disagreement.[16] The second strategy is to argue that the features of reliance on pure moral testimony that make it puzzling and problematic are not shared by the view that peer disagreement about morality is epistemically significant. We might first argue that even if pure moral deference is puzzling, it is not puzzling for us to suspend judgment in light of finding ourselves in a disagreement with someone who is our epistemic peer or superior about a pure moral issue as conciliationism counsels. Suppose that my close long-time friend and I are both moral philosophers of pretty much the same persuasion. We both endorse the same methodology, have the same beliefs on matters that we have thought about equally, and talk about moral matters all the time. However, my friend gets a research grant to pursue the ethics of human enhancement—enhancing humans via brain enhancements or biochemical alterations—on a different continent for two years, during which time she and I will be unable to communicate. Human enhancement is a subject that neither of us has really worked on before but that we have discussed before and agreed about before she departed. On my friend's return, I find out that she now believes that human enhancement is not for the most part morally justified; and not because of its consequences, but on pure moral grounds. Whereas I still believe that human enhancement is for the most part morally justified—as she did before she departed (and she has not been indoctrinated or brainwashed during her research trip). In this case it seems that, other things equal, I ought to at least suspend judgment about the moral status of human enhancement for the time being in light of finding myself in a disagreement about it with my friend. But there seems to be nothing odd or puzzling about this at all. I might well think: if I'd had such a great research opportunity I would probably have come to the same views as she has, so I should drop my moral view until I find out more.

Furthermore, the view that we should sometimes lower our confidence in our moral beliefs or suspend them in light of peer disagreement about morality does not entail that we should sometimes defer to the moral views of others. Some argue that what's wrong with forming views on the basis of others' pure moral testimony is that moral beliefs formed on the basis of testimony lack moral understanding. But diminishing one's confidence in one's view that an action is wrong or suspending judgment about its correctness does not involve believing that this action is wrong without understanding why it is wrong. Furthermore, altering our (pure) moral beliefs in light of pure moral disagreement with others can facilitate our understanding of morality by being the first step to our gaining a better moral understanding.

Some hold that if we should sometimes defer to the moral testimony of others, then this would violate our autonomy. But we cannot be required to give up our autonomy (see Wolff, 1998, pp. 13–14). However, it seems that a requirement that we sometimes take others' pure moral views into account when forming moral beliefs does not breach our autonomy because such a requirement would only require that we modify our views in light of, rather than that we are blindly obedient to, the pure moral views of others (see Nguyen, 2010, pp. 113–127). So, it seems that, even if moral deference and reliance on moral testimony are problematic and puzzling, we should not hold that this means that pure moral disagreement makes no difference to what we should believe.

SUMMARY

Conciliationism about peer disagreement has implications for the moral beliefs that we can justifiably have. It does not yield scepticism or the conclusion that we must give up almost all of our moral views. And nor does it make it impossible to have justified beliefs about controversial topics in applied ethics. But it might imply that many of us cannot reasonably believe that it is permissible to eat animals and that those with whom we disagree about the justice of redistributive taxation are mistaken.

FURTHER READING

McGrath (2008) is an important and influential article on the epistemology of moral disagreement, which wasn't discussed explicitly in this chapter. Rowland (2017a) provides a slightly different introduction to the epistemology of moral disagreement, which discusses McGrath's argument as well as some further implications of the epistemology of moral disagreement. Decker and Groll (2013) and King (2011) respond to McGrath. McGrath (2011) responds to King's argument and Rowland (2019b) responds to Decker and Groll's argument. Sherman (2014) is an extremely detailed piece on the implications of McGrath's argument. Nguyen (2010), Setiya (2012, ch. 1), Vavova (2014), and Fritz (2018a) are important and useful pieces on whether we should accept conciliationism in the epistemology of moral disagreement. Hills (2013) is an important introduction to the debate about moral testimony. Jones (1999), Hills (2009), Sliwa (2012), Enoch (2014), Fletcher (2016), and Wiland (2017) are good next steps with thinking about moral testimony and whether it affects the moral beliefs that we can be justified in having. Nguyen (2020) brings issues regarding moral expertise together with issues about reliance on experts more generally. Fritz (2018b) is a recent piece on the relationship between moral testimony pessimism and conciliationism. Kappel (2018a) is a very helpful and readable introduction to deep disagreement and whether there are epistemic implications of deep disagreements. Kappel (2012, 2018b) are good next steps for thinking about moral disagreement and deep disagreement. Mogensen (2017) discusses the epistemic implications of disagreements in moral intuitions in particular.

NOTES

1 See McGrath (2008, pp. 103–106) and Kornblith (2010, pp. 47–51).

2 Vavova (2014, p. 305). See also Frances (2014, pp. 47–49).

3 This principle holds that *other things equal* we should believe that others who agree with us about pretty much all other propositions in a domain are our epistemic peers about a particular proposition in that domain. This is because it is at least possible that someone who agrees with you about pretty much all propositions in a domain is not your peer about particular matters in that domain. For instance, if they just parrot another peer's beliefs about some—see §5.2—then they *might* share great background agreement with you about that topic but not be your peer; see §5.2.

4 Klenk (2018) argues that great background agreement is both necessary and sufficient for peerhood at least in moral cases.

5 Cf. Kahane (2011, p. 113) and Rowland (2017a, pp. 7–8).

6 Another concern about condition (ii) is that it might not plausibly apply in cases in which the person with whom you disagree disagrees with you about the moral status of tradition. Some argue that we have good *prima facie* reason to stick to traditions; see, for instance, Feser (2003) and Gaus (2011).

7 Perhaps this epistemic advantage is best construed not as one that shows that the revisionaries need not take the traditionalists to be their epistemic peers. Rather it shows that the revisionaries have good disagreement-independent reason to believe that those who hold the status quo view are wrong and that they are right. For they have disagreement-independent reason to believe that the traditionalists hold the status quo view because it is the status quo view or have been influenced by status quo bias whereas a growing number of people who have engaged in an assessment of the issue have come to a conclusion that cannot be attributed to status quo bias; on status quo bias see Bostrom and Ord (2006) and on the implications of irrelevant influences on justification see Vavova (2018). So, even if the traditionalists are the epistemic peers of the revisionaries, it is consistent with conciliationism that they need not suspend judgment about the issue on which they disagree when they find themselves in this peer disagreement. (This reason to believe the traditionalists to be in error might be defeated by evidence showing that the traditionalists do not just hold their view because it is the status quo).

8 See §5.1 and Lackey (2013); cf. Barnett (2019a).

9 For discussion, see, for instance, Gruen (2017).

10 It might be that we are best reconsidering *tradition & bias* not as a principle for when we can downgrade someone's status as our epistemic peer regarding whether *p* but instead as a principle for when we can believe that even though they are our peer about whether *p* we have disagreement independent-reason to believe that we're right and that they're wrong; see note 7 above.

11 For discussion see Kagan (2016) and Caviola et al. (2019).

12 On consequentialism and its problems see, for instance, Shafer-Landau (2017, ch. 10) Smart and Williams (1973), and Portmore (2011, pp. 3–4).

13 See Bourget and Chalmers (2014, p. 476).

14 Although cf. McGrath (2020).

15 On such arguments see Strawser (2010).

16 For such challenges to moral testimony pessimism see Jones (1999), Enoch (2014, pp. 230–231), and Wiland (2017, pp. 60–61).

7

FROM WHAT WE OUGHT TO BELIEVE TO WHAT WE OUGHT TO DO

In the previous two chapters we discussed the implications of moral disagreement for the moral beliefs that we can justifiably have. In this chapter, we'll discuss whether the epistemic impact of moral disagreement has implications for what we ought to do: whether the fact that we cannot justifiably believe that taking an action is right in light of peer disagreement about this affects whether we ought to take that action.

7.1. OBJECTIVISM AND PERSPECTIVALISM

In their opinion in *Graham v. Connor* the US Supreme Court takes a view about when police officers may legitimately shoot people who are in fact unarmed. According to the verdict, police officers may lawfully shoot unarmed suspects if in the seconds directly prior to a shot being fired, a reasonable officer would judge that the person in front of them had a gun that might be pulled on them. Police training academies use footage from a variety of real-life incidents to teach officers how to understand and interpret this reasonableness standard. Consider one such incident. Freddy Centeno was a 40-year-old man who had gone to a woman's house with an object that he presented as a gun. She called the police. They came and shot him dead. He was in fact unarmed. His lawyers say that the police pulled up and shot him before he had a chance to respond. In the bodycam footage of the shooting, the officers tell Centeno to get on the ground. He doesn't. And if you slow the video down you can see that in the second or two before they shoot him

DOI: 10.4324/9780429491375-9

Centeno reaches into his right pocket. His hand starts to move out of his pocket. The police academy teachers ask: what would a reasonable officer do here? He appears to be pulling something out of his pocket. He said he had a gun. A reasonable person would think he had a gun. What he was taking out of his pocket was in fact a harmless garden nozzle.

The Supreme Court's decision in *Graham* implies that when officers may lawfully shoot suspects depends on their evidence. If a suspect is unarmed and the police officer in front of them either knows this or, given their evidence, should know this, then it's illegal for the officer to shoot them. But if the same unarmed suspect is in front of a police officer who has misleading evidence that they are armed, and so who reasonably believes they are armed, then it's legal for the officer to shoot them.

Some activists, incensed that police officers continue to shoot unarmed black teenagers, disagree with the Court's decision in Graham. They believe that if a police officer shoots an unarmed suspect, then that was wrong and should be unlawful even if the officer reasonably believed that the suspect was armed.

This contrasting point of view is not limited to activists. Fentanyl is an opioid that can get into your system just by your touching the skin of someone who has ingested it. Scotty Whiteman was one of two EMTs who went to an apartment building to tend to a patient who had an opioid overdose. The EMTs were not aware that people were overdosing on fentanyl or that it could be passed via skin-to-skin contact. Driving the ambulance back to the hospital Scotty passed out and exhibited the same symptoms as the patient; it turns out that in lifting the patient into the ambulance the patient's skin had rubbed onto Scotty's skin and the fentanyl that the patient had overdosed on transferred to Scotty giving him an overdose. Neither the patient, nor their friend who called the EMTs to save them, knew that fentanyl could be transmitted by skin on skin contact, and so didn't know that they could harm the EMTs by coming into contact with them. Scotty thinks that the patient and their friend who called the EMTs should be held accountable for the harm they caused; a view that seems in tension with the kind of view expressed in the Court's decision in Graham.[1]

These views map onto positions about the relevance of our evidence to what we ought to do. Perspectivalists take a view similar to the Court's view in *Graham*. They argue that what we morally ought to do is affected by our evidential situation. Objectivists about moral obligation (not to be confused with objectivism in metaethics!) take a view somewhat similar to the view of the activists and Scotty Whiteman, but a little more extreme. Objectivists argue that what we ought to do is entirely independent of our evidential situation and what we should believe about what we ought to do. Suppose that, unbeknownst to you, flipping the light switch in your hallway this evening will cause a short circuit that will trigger a further series of electrical events which will culminate in the electrocution of a worker at the power grid several kilometres away (see Thomson, 1990, p. 229). You don't know and couldn't know that this would happen. Objectivists hold that it would be wrong for you to flip the light switch in your hallway this evening. Perspectivalists hold that this is not the case, since you have no evidence at all that flipping the light switch would harm anyone.

Objectivism can seem like a crazy view. But two ideas might make it seem more plausible. First, note that if we flip the light switch, we breach someone's rights. Perhaps it is sometimes permissible to breach others' rights: it might be permissible to save a billion lives by breaching someone's property rights or their right to not have their finger dislocated by you. But the light switch case is not like this. In this case we gain very little if any benefit by seriously breaching another's rights. It seems that if by taking an action we will breach someone's rights for trivial gain, then we ought not take that action. If this is right, then it is wrong for us to flip the light switch.

Second, objectivists can hold that we're not blameworthy if we flip our light switch. There are cases of blameless wrongdoings: when we do wrong but we're not blameworthy for doing so. For instance, consider Sophie's choice's: Sophie must choose one of her two children to be killed or both will be. It's plausible that Sophie can't but do wrong here: whichever child she chooses to sacrifice, she wrongs the other. But she's not blameworthy for doing wrong by choosing one of her children to be sacrificed, since she's not responsible for being in a situation such that she can't avoid doing wrong; and now she can't avoid doing something terrible. This is a case of blameless wrongdoing. Objectivists similarly claim that flipping the light switch is not blameworthy even though it's wrong to flip it. For we can't know that flipping the switch is going to have awful consequences. We're only blameworthy for taking an action if we should've known that taking that action was wrong. And so, if we flip the switch, we act wrongfully, but we're not blameworthy for doing so.

However, there are further problems for Objectivism. Consider the following case:

> *Mineshafts.* A hundred miners are trapped underground with floodwaters rising. We are rescuers on the surface who are trying to save them. We know that the miners are in one of two mineshafts but we do not know which shaft they are in. In fact we have no reason to believe that they are in one shaft rather than the other. There are three floodgates that we could close by remote control. And depending on which gate we close the results will be as shown in Table 7.1.

Table 7.1 Mineshafts.

		The miners are in	
		Shaft A	Shaft B
We close	Gate 1	We save 100 lives	We save 0 lives
	Gate 2	We save 0 lives	We save 100 lives
	Gate 3	We save 90 lives	We save 90 lives

It seems that we morally ought to close Gate 3 in this case. Closing gate 1 or 2 would involve recklessly risking 100 people's lives. Whereas closing gate 3 would not. So, we should close gate 3 rather than gate 1 or 2. If this is right, we should accept that our evidential situation affects what we ought to do. For if our evidential situation were better and we knew which shaft the miners are in, it would no longer be the case that we should shut gate 3; if we knew that the miners are in shaft A, we should close gate 1 and save 100 lives rather than closing gate 3 to save 90 lives.

According to perspectivalism, we ought to act in line with our evidence; what we ought to do is a function of our evidence and what we (epistemically) ought to believe rather than a function of the facts that outstrip our evidential perspective. If, given our evidence, it seems that it's best to perform a particular action, we ought to perform that action, even if it's not in fact best to perform it. If we cannot justifiably believe that an action would do great good rather than great harm, and we can justifiably believe that another action would do great good rather than great harm, then we should perform the second action, even if the first action would in fact do more good. So, our intuition that we ought to close gate 3 in *mineshafts* is explained by perspectivalism. But objectivism conflicts with this intuition. For it entails that we should close the gate that would save the most lives, this is one of gate 1 or 2 rather than gate 3. So, we have good reason to accept perspectivalism (see Parfit, 2011a, p. 159; Jackson, 1991, p. 462).

Does perspectivalism entail that it is morally permissible for police officers to shoot unarmed black teenagers whom police officers could reasonably believe to have a gun and have asked to raise their arms? It does not entail this, for police officers (now) know that often such evidence is misleading. So, perspectivalism would have to be combined with the claim that one may shoot another in self-defence when one knows there is a good chance one will be shooting an innocent but when one also knows that there is a good chance they have a gun that they might use to shoot.[2]

7.2. PERSPECTIVALISM AND MORAL PRINCIPLES AND VALUES

The cases that we've been considering have been cases in which we do not have access to all the normatively and morally relevant facts. But in which we are not uncertain about moral principles or values. In *mineshafts* we do not have access to the morally relevant but non-moral fact about which shaft the miners are in. In the light switch case we do not have access to the non-moral—but morally relevant—fact that our flicking the switch will severely harm someone. Our lack of evidence seems to affect what we ought to do in these cases. It seems that we ought to perform the action that we can be most confident will have a good outcome rather than a bad outcome; in *mineshafts* closing gate 3 is the action that we can be most confident will lead to a better outcome rather than a worse one.

But does our evidential situation regarding which moral principles or values are themselves the correct ones affect what we ought to do? One way to see the force of the idea that it does is to think about the question here in terms of justified uncertainty. In *mineshafts* we are justifiably uncertain about whether the miners are in shaft *A* or *B* and this affects what we ought to do; we cannot be justifiably certain that the miners are in *A* or *B*. There seem to be similar cases of justified uncertainty about moral principles and values in which our justified uncertainty seems to affect what we ought to do. Consider the following case:

> *Dinner.* Emma is at dinner. She can either choose a beef burrito or a vegetarian tofu burrito. Suppose that according to the true moral theory, both of these options are morally permissible: animals' welfare does not matter morally and so there is no moral reason to choose the tofu over the beef. Emma knows that eating the tofu burrito would be permissible. Unlike many people (perhaps), Emma knows that she would find either burrito equally tasty and so has no self-interested reason to prefer one burrito to the other. Emma is uncertain about whether it would be wrong for her to eat the beef and she can only justifiably be so uncertain. This is because she is only justified in being uncertain about whether according to the true moral theory animals' welfare matters morally. (That is, she is uncertain as to whether we should accept the principle that for a being to matter morally is for them to experience pleasure or pain or the principle that for a being to matter morally is for them to have the capacity for moral reasoning.)

Emma is justifiably uncertain that choosing the beef is permissible, Emma is justifiably certain that choosing the tofu is permissible, and she knows that she will not be worse-off for having the tofu rather than the beef. And because of these features of *dinner* it seems that Emma morally ought to choose the tofu rather than the beef. Remember that according to the true moral theory, it's objectively permissible to eat the beef—at least putting our epistemic circumstances aside—but this fact doesn't seem to make it okay for her to eat the meat, since she can't justifiably believe that it's okay for her to eat the beef. So, it seems that her justified uncertainty affects what she ought to do. But Emma's justified uncertainty in *dinner* is justified uncertainty about which moral principles are correct: it is justified uncertainty about whether the welfare of beings like animals matters morally. So, it seems that justified uncertainty about the moral principles themselves—rather than just morally relevant empirical facts—sometimes affects what we ought to do (see MacAskill, 2014).

This case isn't a one off. Consider another:

> *Torture.* Suppose that Tina has captured a member of a terrorist network. She is unsure and is only epistemically justified in being unsure, of whether she would wrong them if she tortured them. But suppose that Tina does know that it is morally permissible for her not to torture the terrorist (because she's not in a ticking bomb scenario and because she doesn't know what information she will find out—or whether it will be reliable at all—by torturing the terrorist). In fact, although Tina is not in a position to know this, it is morally permissible for Tina to torture the terrorist in these circumstances.

In *torture* it seems that, given her evidential situation, Tina ought not torture the terrorist. And so, it seems that justified uncertainty about moral principles and values affects what we ought to do.

Call the view that our evidence/justified uncertainty regarding facts other than moral principles and values (such as those in *mineshafts*) affects what we ought to do perspectivalism^{nonmoral}. Call the view that our evidence/justified uncertainty regarding empirical facts and moral principles and values affects what we ought to do perspectivalism$^{moral\&nonmoral}$. Our intuitions about these cases give a good *prima facie* case for the view that our justified uncertainty about moral principles and values affects what we ought to do just as, though perhaps not in exactly the same way in which, our justified uncertainty about (non-moral) morally relevant facts affects what we ought to do. So, assuming that we should accept perspectivalism^{nonmoral} our intuitions about cases give us reason to accept perspectivalism$^{moral\&nonmoral}$.

One problem with the view that we should accept perspectivalism$^{moral\&nonmoral}$ and not just perspectivalism^{nonmoral} is that moral principles and values cannot be inaccessible to us in the same way that non-moral facts can be. In *mineshafts*, the empirical fact about which shaft the miners are in is inaccessible to us. But moral principles and values cannot be inaccessible in quite the same way. We cannot be physically prevented from accessing (at least most) moral principles and values in the same way that we can be physically prevented from coming to know which mineshaft the miners are in.

Why are moral principles and values not inaccessible in this way? One view is that justified beliefs and knowledge of moral principles is *a priori*, that is, independent of experience, and (typically) accessible from the armchair. Justified beliefs about the facts at issue in *mineshafts*, namely facts in the empirical, physical world of cause and effect are not accessible to us from the armchair except via some causal relationship between us and those facts (via our phone, television, testimony, other causal processes in the empirical world).[3] But it's not clear that this is a deep enough difference to establish that our epistemic relationship to moral principles and values is one that cannot make a difference to what we ought to do. Mathematical facts are not physically inaccessible to us in the way that the fact that the miners are in shaft A is and are also plausible *a priori*. But it still seems that our epistemic relationship to mathematical facts can make a difference to what we ought to do. Suppose that an evil demon gives us a choice: either we can answer question A or question B but not both. Question A is an extremely complicated mathematical question which we have no idea of the answer to and which any answer we gave to would just be a guess. And question B is, 'what is 2 + 2?' (and we know that these are the questions). The demon tells us that if we answer question A correctly, it will kill no one, but if we answer question A incorrectly, it will kill 100 people. And that if we answer question B correctly, it will kill only 10 people and if we answer question B incorrectly, it will kill 100 people (Table 7.2).

Table 7.2 The Demon's Mathematical Threat.

		Correctly	Incorrectly
We answer	Question A (complex)	It kills 0	It kills 100
	Question B (2 + 2?)	It kills 10	It kills 100

In this case, it seems very clear that we should answer question B. It seems just as clear that we should answer question B in this case as it seems that we should close gate 3 in *mineshafts*. However, mathematical truths are plausibly a priori and so it might well be that the answer to question A is not inaccessible to us. But this doesn't seem to matter. It still seems that we ought to answer question B rather than question A; to answer question A would seem to needlessly and recklessly risk the lives of 100 people.

Elizabeth Harman (2015, p. 77) argues that even if we should accept perspectivalism[nonmoral] we should not accept perspectivalism[moral&nonmoral]. She argues that

(A) If justified uncertainty about moral principles and values affects what we ought to do, then 'being epistemically justified in being certain of a false moral view is exculpatory', that is, renders one blameless for performing actions that are wrong.

But

(B) Being epistemically justified in being certain of a false moral view is not exculpatory.

And it follows from (A) and (B) that justified uncertainty about moral principles or values never affects what we ought to do.

Let's assume (A) for the time being. There is still a good case against (B). Harman's argument for (B) is from our intuitions about cases. Harman asks us to consider Max who works for the Mafia and justifiably believes that he has an obligation of loyalty to his Mafia family that requires him to kill innocents in order to protect the family's interests and so kills innocents to protect the family's interests. Harman (2015, p. 65, p. 77) claims that Max's epistemically justified certainty in this case does not exculpate him; Max is blameworthy for the wrongful killings that he commits even though he was epistemically justified in believing that conducting these killings was morally permissible.

However, consider the following case:

> Anya earns around the average income and she has a relatively comfortable life. She gives 10% of her income to charity and she ensures that that 10% goes to the most effective charities. Anya has thought long and hard about how much she ought to give to charity and she has come to believe that it is only morally wrong not to give your fair share to charity, (that is, not to give as much as it would take to lift everyone out of poverty if everyone gave the same amount). And she justifiably believes that her fair share is 10% of her income. Suppose that Anya is justified in her moral beliefs about how much she morally must give to charity. However, in fact Anya's evidence is misleading: it is morally wrong for Anya to give less than 20% of her income to charity.

Although Anya does something objectively wrong it seems that she has an excuse for having done what she did because given her epistemic circumstances she did what she reasonably thought she morally ought to do. If this is the case, then (B) is false because sometimes being epistemically justified in a false moral view is exculpatory.[4]

Can our intuitions about Max and Anya both be on-track? It might be that they can be for Anya does something (objectively) morally wrong by *omission*: Anya fails to give enough. While Max does something (objectively) morally wrong by performing an *action*: Max does wrong by actively killing others. So, it might be that our evidential situation regarding moral principles exculpates us from wrongful omissions but not from wrongful actions. If this is right, then (B) is still false: being epistemically justified in being certain of a false moral view *can be* exculpatory.

Suppose that we shouldn't think that there is a normatively important difference between actions and omissions. In this case, our intuitions about Max and Anya could not both be on-track. But if we have to hold that one of these two intuitions is off-track, we should hold that our intuition about Max is off-track. There is a good case that we do not accurately represent Max's case as stipulated. We have a lot of resistance to actually imagining Max's case as stipulated because we think that Max should've known better than to have the false beliefs about the conditions in which it is morally permissible to kill an innocent person that he had or than to kill innocent people as he did. And given that we think that Max should've known better than to have the belief that he had or than to kill innocent people as he did we don't really think that he is epistemically justified in his beliefs about the morality of killing innocent people. But we have no similar resistance to imagining Anya's case. So, other things equal, we should take our intuitions about Anya more seriously than our intuitions about Max. So, we should reject (B) in Harman's argument. So, Harman does not establish that even if we should accept perspectivalism^{nonmoral}, we should not accept perspectivalism$^{\text{moral\&nonmoral}}$.

The most popular and well-known argument for the view that we should not accept perspectivalism$^{\text{moral\&nonmoral}}$ is that it entails that we ought to be motivated by the rightness and wrongness of actions in a seemingly bad and festishistic way. For instance, if Emma should choose the tofu rather than the beef in *Dinner*, what is the reason why she should choose the tofu? Brian Weatherson (2014, esp. p. 152) claims that it's not because she values the interests of cows or their well-being or because she should value their interests or well-being, since it's not the case that she ought to value cows' interests or well-being; she ought not be more than uncertain about whether their well-being matters morally. Rather, according to Weatherson, if she ought to choose the tofu rather than the beef due to her moral uncertainty, she must choose it for the reason that she cares about morality as such, and about not doing that which is wrong and instead doing that which is right. For in her situation the only reason to plump for the tofu is the concern than by not doing so she would do wrong. But this doesn't seem to be a good reason for her to choose the tofu rather than the beef. Good people want to do what's right in virtue of features that right actions have other than their rightness, and to avoid doing wrong in virtue of features that wrongful actions have other than their wrongness: good people care about the well-being of their children, friends, and others, people getting what they deserve, honesty, justice, and equality, keeping their agreements, and not harming others; good people don't just care about doing what's right and refraining from doing what's wrong. Someone who just cares about taking the action that's right because it's right or refraining from doing what's wrong just because it's wrong isn't motivated well at all; their moral motivation is fetishistic and not morally good.[5] This is the fetishism objection to perspectivalism$^{\text{moral\&nonmoral}}$. To put this objection simply and clearly it is that:

1   If perspectivalism$^{\text{moral\&nonmoral}}$ is true, then we should sometimes be motivated to refrain from performing an action just because it might be wrong;
2   But we should never be so motivated;
3   So perspectivalism$^{\text{moral\&nonmoral}}$ is false.

One natural response to the fetishism objection is to argue that (1) is false. Suppose that she chooses the tofu rather than the beef. She can be motivated to do this for the reason that animals are sentient beings even if she is not sure that this fact makes it wrong to eat them. She can still think that this consideration is morally relevant even if she is not sure how morally relevant it is. Similarly, Tina can refrain from torturing on the basis that the fact that an action would involve severely psychologically damaging someone is a morally significant fact even if she is not entirely sure how morally significant this fact is.

Furthermore, we can be motivated to perform an action on the basis of having a credence that something is true even if we do not fully believe that it's true. For instance, suppose that I'm driving home through the city. There's a semi-final on in the city. If it goes into extra-time it will finish at 9.30. If there's a winner at the end of normal time, it will finish at 8.50. I might be motivated to avoid the city until after 10 not because I believe that the match will go into extra-time but just because I have some credence that it might. But in this case even if we do not fully believe that a consideration is morally important we can be motivated to perform an action on the basis of it because we have some credence that it's morally important. So, Emma can be motivated to eat the tofu because she (reasonably) has some credence that the interests of the cow matter (Sepielli, 2016, p. 2957).

Another way to reject (1) is to argue that although Emma's refraining from eating meat for the reason that doing so might be wrong is fetishistic, there are other close-by motivations that are not fetishistic. For instance, Emma may be motivated by the fact that she doesn't want to do something tantamount to commiting a murder and she doesn't want to severely wrong the cow. But it is not morally bad or festishistic to be concerned to not do something tantamount to murder or to try to avoid severely wronging others (Sepielli, 2016, p. 2959).

7.3. HOW SHOULD WE RESPOND TO JUSTIFIED MORAL UNCERTAINTY?

It seems that there is a good case that our justified uncertainty about moral principles sometimes affects what we ought to do. But how exactly should we respond to our justified uncertainty about moral principles and values. The most popular view is that we should

> Maximise expected value (MEV). In conditions of justified uncertainty about moral principles, we ought to maximise expected moral value.

To understand MEV, it's easiest to apply it in a particular case. Suppose that we are entirely uncertain, and can only be justified in being entirely uncertain, about whether eating meat is wrong or not. In this case we will have a (justified) credence of 0.5 that

Theory A
the moral value of eating meat is (to pick a number) −10; and
the moral value of not eating meat is 0.

And we will have a (justified) credence of 0.5 that

Theory B
the moral value of eating meat is 0; and
the moral value of not eating meat is 0.

In this case the expected value of eating meat is −5. And the expected value of not eating meat is 0. So, according to MEV, we ought to refrain from eating meat in this case because refraining from eating meat maximises expected moral value.

The most serious problem with MEV concerns the non-arbitrary conversion of all moral theories into the value maximisation framework of MEV. Suppose that we're trying to figure out whether to lie to a friend about what some people have been saying about them. We know that if we tell them the truth, this will cause them harm and no other good will come from it. And we know that if we lie, no bad consequences will result. We're (justifiably) unsure about two and only two moral views. According to the first Kantian-ish view, it's wrong to lie in this situation; perhaps it's okay to lie if doing so would stop many people from being killed, but this situation isn't like that. According to the second more utilitarian view, we shouldn't lie in general because doing so tends to cause harm. But in circumstances like this one, in which we know that lying would prevent harm at no cost, we ought to lie. We're justifiably uncertain about which of these two views holds: we have a credence of 0.5 in the first Kantian-ish view and a credence of 0.5 in the second more utilitarian view. How are we to translate the utilitarian and Kantian views into a common evaluative metric such that we can figure out what, according to MEV, we ought to do in this case?

One thing that we can't do is to, across all moral theories, assign the greatest amount of value to actions that are right, the greatest amount of disvalue to actions that wrong and neutral value to actions that are merely permissible. To see this, let's assign the value of 1 to right actions, −1 to wrong actions, and 0 to merely permissible actions. If we adopt that view, then our options in the aforementioned case are as shown in Table 7.3.

Adopting this way of assigning values is of no use, since in this case MEV would entail that lying has a value of 0 and not lying has a value of 0: the value of lying $((0.5 \times -1 = -0.5) + (0.5 \times 1 = 0.5)) = 0$ and the value of not

Table 7.3 An inter-theoretic moral value comparison.

		Value	
		Kantian-ish view	*More utilitarian view*
Action	Lie	−1	1
	Don't lie	1	−1

lying $((0.5 \times 1 = 0.5) + (0.5 \times -1 = -0.5)) = 0$. So, if we want MEV to tell us to perform one particular action in cases like this one (and there will be many such cases), then we must find another way of assigning values to actions according to different theories.[6]

Another problem with assigning values in this way is that doing so fails to fit well with certain moral views. For instance, traditional act-utilitarianism holds that (i) it's wrong both to give a toy to your child when you know that giving the toy to their friend instead would give their friend a slightly greater amount of happiness and all other things are equal; and that (ii) it's wrong to refrain from pressing a button that you could easily press when you know that pressing it would save 100 lives. But, according to act-utilitarianism, the moral difference between pressing the button and refraining from doing so is far greater than the moral difference between giving the toy to your child's friend and failing to do so. However, if we transpose the moral status of our actions according to different moral theories into a framework that can accommodate this difference, then it's unclear how we will make comparisons of moral value between act-utilitarian and deontological theories. Suppose that we hold that according to act-utilitarianism the moral dis-value of pressing the button is −1000 and the moral dis-value of refraining from giving the toy to your child's friend is −1. All lies are (equally) morally wrong on the Kantian-ish view. Should we say that the dis-value of lying according to the Kantian-ish view is −1, −1000 or somewhere in between? What would our justification be for ranking lying as −1, −1000, or somewhere in- between? Whichever we do will seem to be arbitrary. For according to the Kantian-ish view there is no gradation in moral wrong-doing; so the degree of negative moral value of wrongdoing in telling any lie is the same degree of negative moral value as all wrongdoing on the act-utilitarian picture. But on the act-utilitarian picture there are different degrees of wrong-doing. So, it seems that we cannot compare moral dis-value across these different moral frameworks; they are simply incompatible moral frameworks.

Several proposals for making inter-theoretic moral value comparisons in a supposedly non-arbitrary fashion have been proposed. But all of these proposals have been argued to be implausible, arbitrary in the end, to yield incoherent results, or to fail to genuinely capture the structure of certain ethical theories.[7]

Some have proposed views about how our justified uncertainty about moral principles and values affects what we ought to do that do not face this problem with inter-theoretic value comparisons. Jonathan Matheson (2016, p. 12) argues that we should accept the following principle:

> *Moral caution.* Having considered the moral status of doing action A in context C, if due to her epistemic circumstances regarding moral principles and values, (i) subject S (epistemically) should believe or suspend judgment that doing A in C is a serious moral wrong, while (ii) S knows that refraining from doing A in C is not morally wrong, then S (morally) should not do A in C.[8]

Moral caution fits with and explains our intuitions about cases like *dinner* and *torture* for *moral caution* entails that Emma ought to eat the tofu rather than the beef and that Tina ought not torture.

Moral caution does not face MEV's problem with inter-theoretic value comparisons. Suppose that we are (justifiably) uncertain about whether moral theory A or B holds. Theory A says that certain acts X, Y, and Z are morally wrong. Theory B says that acts U, V, and W are morally wrong. Suppose that we can either perform action X, which theory A says is wrong, or action T, which neither theory A nor theory B says is wrong. In this case, *moral caution* entails that we morally ought to perform action T. But *moral caution* does not require us to make inter-theoretic value comparisons to come to this conclusion. Rather *moral caution* only requires us to figure out which actions constitute wrongs according to the theories that we are (justifiably) uncertain regarding. Alternatively, suppose that we find ourselves in a situation in which we can only do X, which theory A says is wrong, or action U, which theory B says is wrong, and so that whatever we do will be morally wrong according to one of theory A or B. In this case, *moral caution* does not tell us to make moral value comparisons across theories A and B. Rather in this kind of case *moral caution* is silent because it only entails that we ought to perform one action rather than another in cases in which we know that one of the two actions that we could perform would not constitute a moral wrong. This feature of *moral caution*—that it does not apply to cases in which we cannot be justified in believing that any action that we can perform is permissible—does make it applicable to less cases. But this doesn't obviously show that *moral caution* is false and that justified uncertainty about moral principles and values does not sometimes affect what we ought to do.

Some worry that *moral caution* is unlikely to be a fundamental normative principle like the principles that we should promote the good of others (or maximise it), prevent harm to others, or perhaps the principle that we should never use others as a mere means to our ends (a fundamental principle according to Kantians). It seems to some that *moral caution* should be explained by a deeper principle and that principle is likely to require that we engage in inter-theoretic value comparisons.

One response to this kind of worry with a principle like *moral caution* is that it could be explained by something like a general contractualist principle not to risk wronging others (see Morgan-Knapp, 2015). It has recently been argued that the precautionary principle can be explained in this kind of way. Perhaps *moral caution* can be similarly explained. The precautionary principle is a widely accepted decision-making rule used for policy making in health and environmental matters. According to this principle, in cases of suitable risk we should take precautionary measures against an action leading to a particular harm being taken even when we do not have conclusive evidence that links this action to this harm. For instance, the precautionary principle recommends not allowing the use of new technologies even if we don't have strong evidence that they will cause a determinate harm until we have put them through a precautionary testing process. (As I write in the middle of the COVID-19 lockdown, some plausibly argue that precautionary principle style reasoning recommends the widespread use of face masks even though we do not know that they effectively mitigate harms; see Greenhalgh et al., 2020.) Matheson (2016, p. 122) notes in arguing for *moral caution* that it is in the spirit of the precautionary principle: both principles urge us to take precautionary measures against events because they might turn out to be bad even though we cannot reasonably believe that they would be bad.

Furthermore, according to Rossian deontological pluralists in normative ethics there are a plurality of fundamental ethical principles such as: don't harm others, don't break agreements with others, don't lie or deceive others, and do good to others. Pluralists hold that there is no further moral principle that is deeper than these other principles, which explains how this plurality of principles, which will sometimes conflict, should be weighed up against one another. It's not obvious that *moral caution* is a worse candidate for a fundamental moral principle than some of these principles such as the principle that we should not deceive or lie to others. *Moral caution* just says that we should not risk doing something wrong or bad when we can easily do otherwise. This seems at least as good a candidate for a fundamental moral principle as the principle that we shouldn't lie or should keep our agreements. (Alternatively, assuming that if I do something wrong I to that extent do something bad, *moral caution* might be entailed by the more general Rossian moral reason of beneficence. That is, our moral reason to, other things equal, do good or do what is better rather than what is worse; see Ross, 1930.)

Whether pluralism is a plausible ethical theory is a matter for a different time; although pluralists have recently done much to defend the view that it is and to try to answer the objections that have been put to it.[9] But *moral caution* does not entail that MEV is false; MEV might be what explains why *moral caution* is true. For proponents of MEV do also argue for principles like *moral caution* on the way to arguing for MEV (see MacAskill, 2014).

And it might be that MEV's problem with inter-theoretic value comparisons just shows that MEV holds but does not apply to cases where we must make inter-theoretic value comparisons but cannot do so non-arbitrarily. If this is right, then MEV holds but its implications are just the same as those of *moral caution*, which applies only when we do not need to make inter-theoretic value comparisons. So, it seems that a sensible policy is to suspend belief about whether MEV or some other principle explains *moral caution*. But to hold that *moral caution*, or at least some principle like it, holds. If we accept this view, then we accept that our evidence and justified uncertainty regarding moral principles does sometimes make a difference to what we ought to do, namely when we find ourselves in circumstances of the type that *moral caution* deals with.

7.4. APPLIED ETHICAL IMPLICATIONS IN CASES OF PEER DISAGREEMENT

Moral caution may seem to be extremely demanding. Suppose that Alex knows that selling her house and almost all of her possessions would promote better consequences than not doing so. But suppose that Alex cannot be justifiably certain that act-consequentialism does not hold and so cannot be justifiably certain that refraining from selling her house and almost all of her possessions is morally permissible. And Alex knows that it is permissible for her to sell her house and almost all of her possessions. *Moral caution* entails that Alex should sell her house and almost all of her possessions. Similarly, *moral caution* entails that if Beth cannot be justifiably certain that foetuses don't have a moral status, then Beth should not have an abortion in almost all circumstances. These conclusions about what Alex and Beth ought to do are extremely demanding and the fact that these conclusions are extremely demanding is seen by some as a strong reason to reject principles like *moral caution*.[10]

There are two responses to the demandingness worry. One is to argue that we shouldn't worry about whether *moral caution* or any other principle regarding what we ought to do in conditions of justified pure moral uncertainty is overly demanding. MacAskill (2014, pp. 39–42) makes this argument. He claims that problems with demandingness are factored into the acceptability of a moral theory at the first level. But *moral caution* (and MEV) is a view about what we should do once we've already considered these kinds of problems with moral theories. So, to reject a principle about how we should act in conditions of justified pure moral uncertainty because it is overly demanding would be to engage in an objectionable kind of double counting.[11]

Alternatively, we might restrict *moral caution* so that it's less demanding. For instance, we might hold

> *Moral caution**. Having considered the moral status of doing action A in context C, if due to her epistemic circumstances regarding moral principles or values,

(i) subject S (epistemically) should believe or suspend judgment that doing A in C is a serious moral wrong, while (ii) S knows that refraining from doing A in C is not morally wrong, and *(iii) S cannot justifiably believe that it is likely that her not doing A would make her significantly worse-off than she otherwise would have been*, then S (morally) should not do A in C.

Moral caution* does not entail that Alex should sell her house or that Beth should refrain from having an abortion. For Alex and Beth can reasonably believe that it is likely that their selling their house and refraining from having an abortion would be significantly costly for them.

It might seem ad-hoc to restrict *moral caution* by adding this third clause and moving to *moral caution**. But this isn't obvious. Remember the cases that motivate the view that our justified pure moral uncertainty can affect what we ought to do: *dinner* and *torture* (§7.2). In these cases it seems that the agents involved ought to refrain from performing an action because they cannot justifiably believe that performing that action would be wrong (eating beef, torturing) and there is another action which they can perform that they know is permissible (eating tofu, not torturing) and it seems that their justified uncertainty makes it the case that they should perform the action they know to be permissible. However, in both of these cases it is not significantly costly for the agents involved to refrain from performing the action they know to be permissible: in *dinner* Emma knows that she won't get any more pleasure from the beef than from the tofu; in *torture* there's no clear cost to Tina of not torturing and she's not in a ticking bomb scenario, nor does she know that she will find any useful information from torturing. So, the cases that make it seem appealing that our justified pure uncertainty about moral principles and values affects what we ought to do are cases in which our justified uncertainty about moral principles and values makes it the case that agents should perform (refrain from performing) an action that it would not be significantly costly for them to perform. In this case, it can be argued that our intuitions about these cases only favour a principle like *moral caution** that holds that our justified uncertainty about moral principles and values makes it the case that we ought to perform actions that it is not significantly costly to perform rather than a principle like *moral caution* according to which our justified pure moral uncertainty makes it the case that we ought to perform actions that it would be significantly costly for us to perform.

Moral caution* also has other attractive consequences. Suppose that Chris is attracted to only men, he is considering sleeping with another man, and it seems to him that it's definitely permissible for him to do so. But he is unluckily in a society such that many of those whom he should believe to be his epistemic peers about whether his sleeping with another man is permissible disagree with him about this. Conciliationism seems to entail that in this kind of situation, Chris cannot justifiably believe that it is permissible for him to sleep with another man. But if we accept *moral caution**, then the fact that Chris cannot justifiably believe that it is permissible for him to sleep with men does not entail that he morally ought not sleep with men—even though there is another option he could take, not sleeping with men, that he knows would be a permissible option for him to take. Since it would be significantly costly for him to never sleep with someone whom he is attracted to (see also Rowland, 2020a).

As we discussed in Chapter 6, there may be a good case that in virtue of disagreements about moral principles and values about the morality of eating meat many people cannot justifiably believe that eating meat is typically permissible. If this is right, *moral caution* and *moral caution** entail that when we can refrain from eating meat without incurring a significant cost, we ought not eat meat. However, *moral caution* and *moral caution** will not entail that testing drugs on animals should not typically be conducted due to disagreements in moral principles and values about the morality of testing drugs on animals. Many believe that we morally ought to test certain drugs on animals (e.g. potential anti-psychotics and potential treatments for cancer). For if we do not, then we will either have to test these drugs on humans—which would be worse—or not use these drugs at all—which would also be worse for it would involve passing up a chance to potentially seriously help people who need certain drugs. In this case, *moral caution* and *moral caution** cannot entail that we should never test on animals. For assuming that we should believe that those on both sides of the debate about the morality of testing on animals are our epistemic peers, we cannot justifiably believe that it is permissible to test on animals but we cannot justifiably believe that it is permissible to refrain from doing so either; for the pro-testing view is that it is wrong to refrain from testing because of the benefits of such testing (see Matheson, 2016, pp. 126–129).

Just as *moral caution* and *moral caution** have no implications for whether we ought to test on animals because there is no option that we can pursue that we can justifiably believe to be permissible, there are many other issues where *moral caution* and *moral caution** seem to have no implications. For instance, there is disagreement in moral principles and values about whether significantly taxing the rich to make the poor better-off is just and morally required or unjust and morally wrong. If disagreement about this matter should lead us to suspend belief about which side of this debate is right, then *moral caution* and *moral caution** will have no implications for what we should do; for if we should suspend belief about which side of the debate is right, then we cannot justifiably believe that taxing or not taxing is morally permissible. Similarly, if we should suspend belief about whether act-utilitarianism is correct, then it's not the case that *moral caution* and *moral caution** imply that we should sacrifice a few to save many more—when all other things are equal—or that *moral caution* and *moral caution** imply that we should refrain from doing so. For according to opponents of act-utilitarianism, sacrificing the few is wrong, and according to act-utilitarians, refraining from sacrificing the few is wrong.

What would MEV entail in these cases? This is a little bit difficult to say because of the difficulty of applying MEV due to the difficulty of making inter-theoretic value comparisons. And I won't get into complicated detailed proposals about how to do this here.[12] However, suppose that we have a credence of 0.5 in two and only two theories: a deontological view that tells us to never sacrifice one person for any greater number of lives; and an act-utilitarian view that says that we always ought to save the greatest number. Given how I explained the inter-theoretic value comparison issue in §7.3, it seems that the positive moral value of sacrificing the few to save many according to act-utilitarianism increases as the number of the many increases. But that the positive moral value of sacrificing one for the sake of saving two according to act-utilitarianism is dwarfed by the moral dis-value of sacrificing the one for the sake of the many according to the deontological view. If this is right, according to MEV we ought not sacrifice one to save two because the expected moral dis-value of doing so is higher than the expected moral value of doing so. But depending on how inter-theoretic value comparisons get made it might be the case that there is a threshold number of the many past which we should sacrifice the one for the many because of the massive dis-value of failing to do so according to act-utilitarianism.

Finally, *moral caution* and *moral caution** will have some implications for what we ought to do in light of disagreement about how much we ought to give to charity. Suppose that there is no reasonable disagreement about whether we ought to give 10% to charity A. Suppose that we both believe that we ought to give 10% to charity and currently give 10% to charity A; and that objectively we are only morally required to give 10%. But that there is peer disagreement about whether we ought to give 15% to charity: act-utilitarians say that we should, others say that doing so is supererogatory. Suppose that act-utilitarianism says that we are required to give 40% of our income to charity but no more. So, we ought to suspend judgment about whether it is wrong or permissible to refrain from giving 15% to charity. In this case, at least many of us ought to give 15% to charity rather than 10% because it is not significantly costly for us to give 15% rather than 10%. So, if we accept *moral caution* and *moral caution** it will follow that we should give more to charity than we can reasonably believe that we ought to—assuming that we are already giving—when we cannot reasonably believe that it is permissible to refrain from giving this additional amount.[13] *Moral caution** pushes us to do more than we are objectively required to do (give 10%) and to give more than we can be justified in believing that we ought to: that is to give 15% rather than the 10% we can be justified in believing that we ought to give. But *moral caution** does not require us to give as much as others believe that we ought to; it does not require us to give 40% or to split the difference and give 25%. *moral caution** requires that we go as far as we can to splitting the difference without incurring significant costs. But for issues like this one, this might not require that we go too far (Figure 7.1). This idea can probably be transposed to other scalar moral issues.

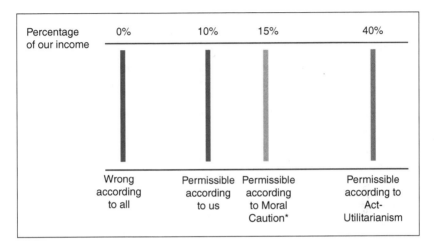

Figure 7.1 Moral margin of error.

SUMMARY

Our evidence and justified uncertainty about what we ought to do plausibly affects what we ought to do even when our evidence and uncertainty is about moral principles and values. In this case the epistemic implications of moral disagreements for what we can justifiably believe will have implications for what we morally ought to do. What these implications are will depend on the view we should accept about how uncertainty about moral principles and values affects what we ought to do. The most wide-ranging and interesting of these views face serious problems; other views face fewer problems. Whichever view we accept, however, disagreements about moral principles and values will seem to have implications for whether we can permissibly eat meat in certain circumstances and the amount that we morally ought to give to charity.

FURTHER READING

Lord (2015) and Graham (2010) are great articles that also serve as introductions to the opposing sides of the objectivism/perspectivalism debate. The debate about objectivism and perspectivalism about obligation is related to the debate about actualism and possibilism in ethics; for an introduction to the latter see Timmerman and Cohen (2019). Kiesewetter (2017, ch. 8) and Sorensen (1995) make important contributions to the objectivism/perspectivalism debate. Bykvist (2017) is an introductory overview to the debate about whether uncertainty about moral principles and values affects our obligations. Lockhart (2000) is an early book-length discussion of uncertainty about moral principles and values and its implications; Sepielli (2013) provides a response. Sepielli (2009, 2016), MacAskill (2014, 2016), Barry and Tomlin (2016), Hicks (2018), and Tarsney (2018a) are among important recent work on the topic. Many proponents of the view that moral uncertainty affects what we ought to do are consequentialists; Tarsney (2018b) provides a non-consequentialist view. Matheson (2016) is a discussion of the applied ethical implications of the view that uncertainty about moral principles affects what we ought to do.

NOTES

1 Both the decision in *Graham v. Conor* and the Freddy Centeno case are discussed at length in a fantastic episode of the podcast *More Perfect* (More Perfect, 2017). Scotty Whiteman's story is the focus of an episode of the podcast *Radiolab* (Radiolab, 2019).

2 Principles along the line of *Moral Caution*, which we discuss in §7.3–4, count against these kind of claims. Alternatively, it might be argued that adopting a norm along the lines of that adopted in *Graham* will, due to cognitive biases, inevitably lead to morally awful and racist results; cf. Bolinger (2017).

3 Cf. Hedden (2016: 122–123).

4 Roy Sorensen (1995: 254) discusses someone who deliberately diminishes their cognitive capacities to try to get themselves out of a moral obligation. Sorensen argues that such a person is still under this moral obligation. Sorensen's view is compatible with the view that justified moral ignorance exculpates in Anya's case. For it is compatible with the view that justified moral uncertainty can sometimes morally exculpate that when one has justified moral beliefs that are off the mark and one is responsible for making oneself have these moral beliefs that are off the mark, then the fact that now one has epistemically reasonable moral beliefs does not exculpate one for one's wrong-doing.

5 The fetishistic motivation argument draws on Smith (1994: 75). Hedden (2016) makes similar claims.

6 Notwithstanding that this might be the best way of so assigning values!

7 For discussion see Sepielli (2009, 2013) and Hedden (2016)

8 The principle that Matheson endorses is the same as this one except that it covers both cases of justified uncertainty about moral principles and justified nonmoral uncertainty (such as the uncertainty in *Mineshafts*).

9 See, for instance, McNaughton (1996). For a contemporary argument for Rossian pluralism see, for instance, Stratton-Lake (2011).

10 Victor Tadros originally put this point to me.

11 I don't think that we should go this way because, as I discuss below, the intuitions about cases that favour *moral caution* are cases in which we are required to do things that are not very costly.

12 But see Sepielli (2009) and MacAskill (2014).

13 The caveat that we are already giving is important due to the significance of costs beyond the current baseline on this view.

PART III

POLITICAL PHILOSOPHY

NORMATIVE INTERPERSONAL
CONSEQUENCES OF MORAL
DISAGREEMENT

8

MORAL COMPROMISE

In the previous chapter we discussed the idea that moral disagreements can affect what we ought to do because what we ought to do is affected by our evidence and our justified beliefs about what we ought to do. We focussed on how disagreement can affect our individual choices to eat meat, give a certain amount of our income to charity, have sex, or have an abortion. In this chapter we'll begin to focus on the question of whether moral disagreement affects what we collectively ought to do and the laws and policies that we ought to enact. In this short chapter we'll focus on the idea that when we are making a group decision, moral disagreement can make it the case that we ought to pursue a moral compromise.

A compromise is an agreement made by two or more parties to take a decision, do something, or enact a policy that they both agree to be second-best. Suppose that my partner and I are figuring out where to go on holiday. Her first choice is Hawaii, but I don't really care for Hawaii. My first choice is a Californian road trip, but she doesn't care for California. We'd both like to go to Greece; it's just not our first choice. We compromise by deciding to go to Greece.[1] The compromises that interest us in this chapter are compromises in which the agents involved have conflicting moral views but agree to accept a moral second-best option. And the compromises that we'll be concerned with mainly concern the pursuit of policy options.

8.1. REASONS TO COMPROMISE

In order to figure out when we ought to compromise we need to figure out what reasons there are to compromise. The most obvious kinds of reasons to

DOI: 10.4324/9780429491375-11

compromise are purely pragmatic. Sometimes we should agree to a morally second-best arrangement because if we don't, the moral consequences will be very bad. Suppose that the government (or its governing cabinet) is deciding how much aid to send to a neighbouring country, let's call it Qumar, that has been struck by famine.[2] You're a member of the government. You believe that it would be wrong not to send at least $10 million in aid. No one else will send the money. Qumar is your closest ally. And without $10 million, thousands of Qumaris will certainly die. However, the other members of the government believe that sending $10 million will decimate the domestic budget causing problems for your own people's safety, security, and well-being. The government is composed of eleven people. Five of whom propose that you send $5million. Another five are more nationalistically inclined: they think that they have been elected to serve the interests of their constituents and not of Qumaris, and partially because of this propose to send only $500,000. If the vote is tied, only $1 million will be sent. If only $1million is sent, hundreds of thousands of Qumaris will die. $5 million will ensure that only thousands die.

Table 8.1 A Pragmatic Reason to Compromise.

Outcome/option	Consequences
Tied vote: $1 million is sent	Hundreds of thousands die
Give $10 million (favoured by you)	At most, hundreds die
Give $5 million (favoured by 5 other members)	Thousands will die
Give $500,000 (favoured by 5 other members)	Over a million die

In this case, you have strong pragmatic reason to compromise: to sign up to the second-best solution, sending $5 million to save thousands of lives. In this case the only reason to compromise is that refraining from doing so would lead to awful consequences. We can call this a *purely pragmatic* reason to compromise. (Of course, sometimes pragmatic reasons will count against making a pragmatic compromise. Such as when although compromising today will benefit the lives of many it will weaken one's bargaining position— because it will make one seem less principled and stubborn to those with whom one negotiates—and thereby lead to harm in the future.)

There are, however, some clear examples of non-purely-pragmatic reasons to compromise. The value of the relationship that we bear to those with whom we are compromising can provide us with reasons to compromise and agree to something that we believe to be morally sub-optimal. Suppose that Amy and Becky have children together. But they have different moral, religious, and political views which they have not fully explored. As their children come to be of the age where they need to go to school, they realise that they disagree quite profoundly. Agnostic Amy believes that their children should go to a secular school and not have a religious identity foisted upon them, whereas believer Becky believes that their children should attend a private religious school where they will receive a proper religious education. They eventually agree to a third option: their children will go to the secular school but will regularly attend church with their parents. They agree to the third option as a second-best moral compromise solution to their moral disagreement about how to educate their children. In this case Amy and Becky have reasons to accommodate each other's goals and commitments in their joint plans which are not purely pragmatic. This is because they regard it as good in itself to have a relationship in which their collective decisions reflect both of their values. So, their reasons for compromising aren't just purely pragmatic: their reasons aren't just that compromising will make their marriage feel better or last longer, and ensure that neither party gets angry at one another. Rather they compromise because they want to be in the kind of relationship in which both of their views are equally respected in their decisions; they believe that failing to compromise is directly at odds with the nature of their relationship (May, 2011, pp. 585–586). We can think of similar examples with friendship. Suppose that I'm on holiday with my friends. I think that eating meat is wrong, but not very seriously wrong; my friends don't think it's wrong at all. I prefer eating at vegetarian restaurants to non-vegetarian restaurants because I find them at least as tasty and not morally shady. But my friends don't really like vegetarian food. The value of friendship seems to give me a reason to compromise and to eat at restaurants that serve both meat-based and vegetarian cuisine.

There may be analogous *non-purely-pragmatic* reasons to compromise when making policy decisions provided by the value of civic friendship or the value of societies, or their policy-makers, acting only on the basis of laws that all can agree to be desirable or justifiable. According to many, civic friendship is an important political value and we have reasons to only adopt policies that can be justified to all members of our society because doing so upholds civic friendship (see §9.2.4). If this is right, we have non-purely-pragmatic reasons to morally compromise on grounds of civic friendship.[3]

One popular idea is that we have (non-pragmatic) reason to compromise with others on policy matters due to the epistemic difficulties involved with assessing the morality or justice of various actions and practices. For instance, George Sher (1981, p. 369) argues that the complexity and uncertainty of a subject matter can ground reasons to compromise, and make it the case that one can permissibility make a compromise. On this view, there are sometimes epistemic reasons to compromise. Sher claims that when the issue at hand is extremely complex, and there is uncertainty about it, when there is uncertainty about the grounding of one's principles and/or one's opponents are thoughtful and intelligent and make plausible sounding arguments, then one has reason to agree to a compromise position .

There are several different lines of thought in Sher's claim. One seems to be that the complexity and uncertainty of a subject matter can itself give one reason to compromise in light of moral disagreement. Another line of thought seems to be that the epistemic credentials of those with whom one disagrees give one reason to compromise. In order to ascertain whether either factor gives us reasons to compromise we first need to distinguish between how we might be required to revise our beliefs in light of disagreement and the policies we ought to pursue in light of disagreement. There is a further difference beyond the epistemic/practical difference here. Epistemically, in response to this disagreement what we ought to do is decrease or increase our confidence in a belief; or at most suspend belief. So, if we ought to change our beliefs in response to peer disagreement about a moral issue, what we must do is what's represented in Table 8.2. If we ought to compromise and accept a different policy in response to moral disagreements, however, what we ought to do is what is represented in Table 8.3.

These two tables are different in an important way. In Table 8.2 what we're required to do post-disagreement is something that is less controversial than what we ought to do prior to disagreement. We ought to suspend judgment about whether it's right or wrong to do something. This can be said to be an epistemically humble way of responding to a disagreement. In suspending belief we are acknowledging that the person with whom we disagree is as likely as we are to be right, so we don't believe that we're right and they're wrong and nor do we hold that they're wrong and we're right. Instead we come to stop taking a stand. But in Table 8.3 this is not what we do if we compromise. Rather we pursue a policy that is neither the position that we nor those with whom we disagree thought we ought to pursue prior to disagreement.

Simon May (2005, p. 339) claims that this difference shows that moral disagreement cannot require us to compromise in response to disagreement,

Table 8.2 What we ought to believe in response to disagreement.

	Believe that p	Suspend belief about whether p	Believe that ~p
Pre-disagreement	A		B
Post-disagreement		A; B	

Table 8.3 What policies we ought to pursue in light of disagreement.

	Pursue policy 1 (e.g. left-wing policy)	Pursue policy 2 (compromise policy)	Pursue policy 3 (e.g. right-wing policy)
Pre-disagreement	A		B
Post-disagreement		A; B	

since any compromise position will be just as controversial as the non-compromise positions. This is different from the epistemic case where suspending belief that p does not seem to be controversial in the same way.[4] Furthermore, according to May, if the controversial nature of a policy topic gives us reason to doubt our own position, the complexity of the policy topic will also give us reason to doubt a compromise position. For example, suppose that we are part of a government considering whether to change immigration restrictions. Our grouping is in favour of lax restrictions, everyone else who is part of the government is in favour of very stringent restrictions. There are some reasons to think the issues are complex here if there is overwhelming popular support for more stringent restrictions; in this case we might ask: how do the economic benefits of immigration and the rights of potential immigrants stack-up against the rights to self-determination of communities? A compromise position—that allows some but not as much immigration—will be at least as controversial as either a very lax or a stringent position; since no one, in our imagined case, holds the compromise position. Complexity would seem to count against the compromise position as much as the lax and stringent positions for the compromise position takes a stand on the complexities at hand in just the same way that the lax and stringent positions do; so either complexity counts against the compromise position just as much as it counts against the non-compromise positions or it counts against no positions at all.

Daniel Weinstock (2013, esp. pp. 545–546) argues that May is mistaken that compromise positions are just as controversial as non-compromise positions. He first argues that we should distinguish between integrative and substitutive compromises. Integrative compromises combine elements of the deliberating parties' initial views. For instance, the compromise between marriage partners to send their children to a secular school but to a church on the weekend incorporated elements of both partners' initial views. Substitutive compromises instead seek to move past disagreement by proposing something completely different that addresses the motivations for the non-compromise positions. Consider discussions over Britain's exit from the EU in Spring 2019. One side argued that the UK should leave as soon as possible with no deal, no customs union or single market agreements in place. Another side argued that the UK should make a deal with some form of customs union or single market agreement in place. A substitutive compromise policy was discussed, namely the policy of putting these two options back to the British people in a (second) referendum. This substitutive compromise did not involve parts of the two positions under debate exactly—as the marriage partners compromise does—but it aimed to speak to the motivations of both of the non-compromise positions. Weinstock argues that although substitutive compromises are just as controversial as non-compromise positions, integrative compromises are not.

Is Weinstock right about this? The answer seems to be that some integrative compromises are less controversial than non-compromise positions. In the marriage/children case the integrative compromise seems to be less controversial than the non-compromise positions. But we can imagine a version of this case where this integrative compromise is as controversial: suppose that both partners are dogmatic and are just as opposed to the compromise position as they are to their partner's non-compromise position.

Let's consider a different case: centrist political policies. In certain circumstances these might seem to offer a kind of integrative compromise. Libertarians say that any tax over that required for the minimal state is akin to forced slavery; socialists say that we should equalise the income of all, and so say that we should tax 100% of earnings above the average income (say £30,000). Suppose that socialists and libertarians are trying to agree on a taxation policy. A (more) centrist policy taxing 50% of everyone's income which is above the average income to support the least well-off would seem to take seriously the seeming conflict of liberty and equality here. Such a centrist policy takes seriously the idea that taxation constricts liberty because it holds that we shouldn't tax above 50%, but also takes seriously the egalitarian idea that we are required to support the least well-off. Is this integrative compromise less controversial than the non-compromise positions? Intuitively, no, since, it's just an alternative taxation policy that both socialists and libertarians are against! However, the centrist policy may be importantly less controversial than alternatives in a certain way. Suppose that you're one of the socialists. And suppose that you should believe that the libertarians you disagree with are your epistemic peers about which taxation policy justice requires. So, you should suspend belief about whether justice requires 100% taxation above £30,000 or 0%. In this case, you should suspend belief about the conception of justice according to which equality is a value that requires this 100% taxation. And you should no longer believe that the conception of justice according to which all taxation is forced slavery is mistaken. Instead, you should increase your credence that justice requires taking certain kinds of liberties, or certain conceptions of liberty seriously, and you should reduce your credence, but still have a significant credence in, the idea that equality requires 100% taxation over £30,000. The non-compromise positions only take 1/2 of *these values*—liberty and equality—that one now should have *strong credence* in seriously: the socialist proposal caters to equality but not liberty; the libertarian proposal caters to liberty but not equality. But the compromise position takes account of both of these values. So, although the proposal itself may be just as controversial, its rationale is in a sense less controversial. So, there is a way in which, if we take the epistemic credentials of those with whom we disagree seriously, we should take up the compromise position (see Weinstock, 2013; Kappel, 2018c, p. 81, pp. 88–89).

So, in principle, an epistemic argument can be made for making principled compromises; and this epistemic argument gives us non-purely-pragmatic reasons to compromise. Two caveats though. First, of course, this argument only works if we should judge those with whom we disagree to be our epistemic peers, if we should revise our beliefs in light of peer disagreement, and if what we ought to do is (partially) a function of what we ought to believe or how we ought to apportion our credences. (To get something like the latter conclusion it seems we will need an epistemic/practical linking principle like one of those discussed in the previous chapter). Second, this kind of case is very simplified. It becomes more complicated as soon as we add in the fact that socialists and libertarians have their own conceptions of liberty and equality, and that, of course, our society is full of people with other views.

8.2. COMPROMISING ABOUT ABORTION LAWS

Some philosophers and political theorists argue that we should adopt a compromise position regarding abortion law on the basis of the epistemic reasons for compromise discussed in the previous section. On this view, the issues pertinent to the legal status of abortion, such as the moral significance of potential personhood, are extremely complex and difficult and no irresistible arguments for either the view that foetuses (in the 1st–2nd trimesters) have a moral status or that they do not have been made (Sher, 1981, pp. 369–370). Getting into the details of the abortion debate would take us too far afield here. So, let's grant the claim that the moral status of the foetus and potential persons is a difficult very complex issue; let's just suppose with the philosophers who think we should adopt a compromise position on abortion that this claim is true and see where it leads—we will come back to this claim a little later. In this case the epistemic reasons to pursue a compromise discussed in the previous section may come into play regarding this issue and we want a reasonable and workable compromise position.

Philosophers have argued for two different compromise positions on abortion: (i) pro-lifers and pro-choicers should agree to keep abortion legal but should agree to withdraw state funding of abortions; (ii) pro-lifers and pro-choicers should agree to keep abortion legal but pro-lifers should not have to pay for abortions.

George Sher (1981 p. 371) argues for the first position. He argues that this compromise should be accepted because, first, any government funding of abortions would draw upon taxes collected from those who believe abortion to be morally wrong, and so would put those who are anti-abortion in the position of actively supporting abortions. And, second, state funding of abortions amounts to an implicit collective endorsement of abortions, which conflicts with the moral view of those who believe that abortion is wrong.

Amy Gutmann and Dennis Thompson (2014, pp. 88–90) argue for the second position: they argue that abortions should be funded on the basis of voluntary tax contributions that tax payers can opt-out of making. They agree

with Sher that we should do all we can to ensure that pro-lifers are not finan-
cially supporting abortions. But they claim that we can do this without stopping
state funding of abortions entirely by adopting the second proposal, which is
preferable to the first because it does not impinge on the right to have an abortion of those who cannot afford to pay for one themselves.

Simon May (2005, esp. p. 336) argues against both of these proposed
compromises. He argues against the rationale behind both of them: that we
should pursue a compromise that ensures that pro-lifers are not complicit in
abortions. May argues that complicity in an activity is a moral problem only
if that activity is really unethical; the fact that some citizens believe an activity to be immoral does not give their government reason to ensure that they
do not contribute towards that activity taking place.

However, this seems to me to be a mistake. Social security or welfare pay-
ments are often now conditional on recipients applying for jobs and taking jobs
that are offered to them. But this conditionality does not require that recipients
take jobs that they are morally opposed to doing: vegetarians are not required
to work in abattoirs and those who believe that sex-work is wrong are not
required to work as bar staff, chefs, cooks or security for strip clubs.[5] This seems
entirely right. And these exemptions don't seem right just because we agree with
the moral views involved: I think that the view that sex-work is wrong is entirely
misguided; but I don't think that people who disagree should have to take jobs
that make them complicit in sex-work. So, *contra* May, we do have some reason
to try to ensure that those who believe that a practice is wrong do not have to
positively support that practice. There are questions about the limits of such
exemptions, however. Libertarians believe that redistributive taxation is mistaken, but this doesn't exempt them from taxation. Whether pro-lifers have a
case for such an exemption from their taxes being used to support abortions
may depend on what would happen if they were afforded such an exemption.

The second compromise position, proposed by Gutmann and Thompson, is
preferable to the first proposed by Sher because it offers a compromise that
minimises both the complicity of pro-lifers while still securing at least a good
degree of access to abortions for those who need them.

There are two different ways that we could understand Gutmann and
Thompson's proposed compromise:

> *Voluntary pro-choice contributions.* Abortions should be funded only via voluntary
> contributions made by only pro-choice taxpayers;
> *Compulsory pro-choice contributions.* Abortions should be funded by the mandatory
> taxation contributions of only pro-choice taxpayers (See May, 2005, p. 330).

May argues that neither of these positions are good or reasonable compromises. He argues that if we adopt *compulsory pro-choice contributions*, then

pro-choice tax dollars that currently fund other government programs would be diverted and used to pay for abortions; with pro-life tax dollars making up for the shortfall regarding the governmental programs that the pro-choice tax dollars funding abortions were taken from. May (2005, p. 338) claims that this solution would be a 'convoluted yet entirely cosmetic modification of the original public funding policy'. And because of this could not be the basis of a good and reasonable compromise on the laws regarding abortion. We can reasonably challenge this claim of May's however. First, pro-lifers may not share May's attitude towards this compromise. Second, this policy would reduce their complicity. And when a change of policy reduces someone's complicity without a change in the outcome, this seems to mark an important difference. For instance, if one of A or B must kill C, A's killing C is importantly different (for A and B) than B's killing C even though the outcome is the same.

On the other hand, May (2005, p. 337) argues that *voluntary pro-choice contributions* would be unfair: it is unfair for the financial burden of abortions to fall only on pro-choicers. It does seem that this would be unfair. Similarly, it would be unfair for the financial burden of the foreign aid budget to fall only on the morally motivated—that is only on those who believe that it is wrong for us to allow people to starve in faraway countries while we are well-off. However, it's not clear that this unfairness counts decisively against the proposed compromise. For it's also unfair for the burden of homelessness in Western countries to fall only on those who are willing to contribute to homelessness charities. Yet we currently seem to accept political arrangements where this is exactly what happens. Perhaps these arrangements are not in fact the result of a reasonable compromise; perhaps these arrangements are unreasonable. But the unfairness of the financial burden falling on pro-choicers' is only as bad as the situation we currently have in which the financial burden of homelessness falls on those who are motivated to give to homelessness charities. And the unfairness of *voluntary pro-choice contributions* is in one respect not as bad since there is a reason to accept it, namely that it would ensure that pro-lifers are not complicit. Furthermore, one way of mitigating the unfairness of *voluntary pro-choice contributions* would be to temper it somewhat by making only most of the burden fall on pro-choicers. Such a policy would require pro-lifers to contribute some but less, thereby making pro-lifers less complicit than they would be if they contributed as much as pro-choicers.[6]

It seems that May's arguments against proposed compromises on abortion fail. If we accept (or should accept) that those with whom we disagree about the moral status of abortion are our epistemic peers about this—or that this is a very difficult and complicated issue—then we may well be forced to conclude that some form of legal compromise that reduces the tax liability for state funded abortions of pro-lifers is a reasonable compromise. We might instead resist the idea that those with whom we disagree about the moral status of abortion are our epistemic peers about this; there are reasons to resist this idea, which we discussed in Chapter 6 (especially §6.2.2).

SUMMARY

We can have pragmatic, epistemic, and relationship-based reasons to take a compromise action in light of moral disagreement about which action we ought to take. In some circumstances, compromise policies are less controversial than non-compromise policies, but these circumstances are less common than they may seem. However, if abortion is a very complicated issue that there is peer disagreement about, we will have strong reasons to accept a compromise policy on abortion.

FURTHER READING

May (2013) is an introduction to the topic of our reasons to compromise in light of disagreement. Wendt (2016) is a thorough book-length discussion of disagreement and compromise. The papers in Wendt (2013) as well as May (2011) and Kappel (2018c) are good next steps. Margalit (2009) and Gutmann and Thompson (2014) are book-length discussions of our moral and political reasons to compromise which focus on very specific applied policy proposals.

NOTES

1 For a plausible more specific account of what it is to make a compromise see Wendt (2016, p. 33).
2 Qumar is a fictional country in *The West Wing*.
3 See also Wendt (2016, esp. ch. 13).
4 There is, however, a question about this for in one sense it is just as controversial: some believe that one should have a positive view and not suspend; so in one sense suspension is a controversial position.
5 See, for instance, Hansard (2014, column 267W).
6 A second issue with *Voluntary Pro-Choice Contributions* is that it seems that a major consequence of this policy would be that there is less funding for abortions. The extent to which this is a problem with such a compromise position depends on the extent to which the view that those who cannot afford abortions themselves have a right to have an abortion can be appealed to in this context; for discussion see Gutmann and Thompson (2014, pp. 88–90) and May (2005, p. 332, p. 335).

9

PUBLIC REASON, LEGITIMATE STATE ACTION, AND JUSTIFIABILITY TO ALL

Much of the most important 20th-century work and debate in political philosophy has been about *justice*. Rawls argued that a society and its institutions are just only if any social and economic inequalities in that society make the least well-off members of that society better-off than they would be without such inequalities. Nozick argued that societies and their institutions can be just even if they contain vast social and economic inequalities that do not benefit the least well-off so long as those inequalities are the result of non-coerced free transfers of resources. This debate about justice between Rawls and Nozick was a debate between a developed quite radically liberal egalitarian account of justice and a radically right-libertarian account of justice. But much of political philosophy is also concerned with questions about the *legitimacy* of particular policies, decisions, and states.

One widely held view is that states can be legitimate without being just. Suppose that I wash up on a desert island with 49 other people. We make decisions about how inequalities in goods obtained from the island and ocean around it are to be redistributed. We agree that an equal amount of food and other resources will be taken from each person such that everyone has enough food to survive and other resources to allow them to live minimally well: we will collectively ensure that each has a basic minimum. But all other inequalities between the 50 of us—in food, housing, clothes, materials, other tradeable goods, etc—will be left as they are. There was a long collective discussion between the 50 of us about this basic minimum proposal and other proposals such as Rawlsian and Nozickian proposals. After this discussion we

DOI: 10.4324/9780429491375-12

each secretly voted for our favoured redistributive arrangement. According to one view of legitimacy, the distribution and redistribution of resources in this desert island society is legitimate for it was brought about by a process in which we all collectively agreed to this redistributive arrangement. But if we suppose that Rawls—and other egalitarians—are right about what justice requires, this desert island society is not a just one. For it allows inequalities that are not to the benefit of the least well-off. So, this desert island society's political arrangements are legitimate but not just. Legitimacy is therefore a less demanding virtue of a society and its institutions than justice.

But what makes a state or law legitimate? One idea is that a law is legitimate if it is democratically agreed to. We will discuss the relationship between democracy and legitimacy in Chapter 10. In this chapter we'll discuss public reason accounts of legitimacy. Public reason accounts hold that the fact that a law was democratically enacted is not sufficient for it to be a legitimate law. This is because even in a democracy, substantial minorities may reasonably morally disagree with the majority who vote for a law.

9.1. PUBLIC REASON, JUSTICE, AND LEGITIMACY

We might hold that a law is legitimate so long as it promotes better consequences than any alternative law or having no law. Or we might hold that a law is legitimate just in case it is right for a state to make this law, or so long as this law will make people do what they morally ought to do. But views like these can seem to fail to take moral disagreement seriously enough. For according to these views, a state may take a particular account of what's right and wrong, or what consequences we should be aiming to promote, and then coerce its citizens in line with this view. Suppose that, against the wishes of its people, a state decided to make all its policies in line with act-utilitarianism, spending most of its budget on donating to the Against Malaria Foundation and instigating a mandatory organ transplant lottery among its citizens (where if your number comes up, you must sacrifice all your organs—and so your life—so that 5 or more others can live). Even if act-utilitarianism were the correct moral view—and if the majority voted for such a policy—many political philosophers claim that a state that decided to act in this way would be illegitimate. For it would not take seriously the fact that many of its citizens reasonably hold that act-utilitarianism is false. On this view truth, rightness, or even justice, is not sufficient to establish legitimacy.

The polar opposite to a truth-based account to legitimacy is a consent-based view according to which a state is legitimate only if all those over whom it claims authority consent to it. This view takes any moral disagreement with a law to render it illegitimate. This would seem to entail that all current states are illegitimate. For it seems that no state in current existence attains the consent of all those over whom it rules.[1]

Public reason accounts attempt to take a middle ground between a consent-based approach to legitimacy and a truth-based approach which holds that states are legitimate just so long as they do what's right or just.[2] According to public reason accounts, in order to be legitimate a state's laws must be justified in a particular way to all its citizens. That is, these laws must be justified to all citizens even assuming their diversity of moral views about the right and the good. We can call this type of justification public justification. Low rates of taxation cannot be publicly justified to egalitarians on the basis that such laws protect libertarian rights of self-ownership; but lower rates of taxation can be publicly justified to egalitarians if the view that such laws would be better for the least well-off can be justified to them. (For the rest of this chapter, I will refer to public justifications just as justifications).[3]

A law can be (publicly) justifiable to someone even if they don't accept or consent to it. For instance, suppose that I believe that act-utilitarianism is true and provides the correct criterion of justice. I might still not consent to a law requiring all citizens to participate in a utilitarian organ lottery. (For I might care more about not being killed for the sake of saving the lives of others than about morality and justice). But if I accept act-utilitarianism, such a law could still be justified to me. So, public reason accounts take a position in between consent-based and truth-based accounts of legitimacy.

Public reason accounts normally constrain the set of citizens to whom laws must be justified in order for these laws to be legitimate. We have justifications for non-racist laws. But we can't justify non-racist laws to Nazis if justification to another involves justification in light of their current moral views. So, proponents of public reason accounts restrict the set of citizens that a law must be justified to in order to be legitimate. This set of citizens—what is sometimes referred to as the constituency of public reason—is specified in various ways. According to some views, it is 'reasonable' citizens. According to others, it is 'normal' citizens. But this set of citizens is always specified in a way that rules out Nazis. So, we can understand public reason accounts most generally as holding

> *Public reason (PR).* A law (or set of laws) L is legitimate iff it can be (publicly) justified to all those who fall into the constituency of public reason (e.g. reasonable or normal citizens depending on the account) who are also citizens (or residents) in the jurisdiction that L is proposed in.

We'll discuss different accounts of the constituency of PR, and other differences between different accounts of PR in §9.3–4. In §9.5 we'll discuss the self-defeat objection to public reason; this objection is analogous to the self-defeat objection faced by conciliationism, which we discussed in §5.4. First, we'll discuss motivations for PR.

9.2. MOTIVATIONS FOR PUBLIC REASON

Why should we accept PR?

9.2.1. INTUITIONS ABOUT CASES

One argument for PR is that it fits with and explains our intuitions about certain cases. Suppose that Catholicism is the one true religion and the Pope has a direct line to God. So, the Pope knows what's right and wrong, good and bad, just and unjust. Aimee is a 30-year-old atheist. Her catholic state forces her to go to mass every week as the Pope believes to be right; the state will fine her $10,000 if she fails to go to mass every week. In forcing Aimee to go to mass her state makes her do what's right and stops her from doing wrong. For, in this case, we are all—Catholic and non-Catholic—morally required to go to mass at least once a week (and it is right for the state to force us to do this). The law requiring Aimee to go to mass every week still seems illegitimate. Our intuitions about this kind of case might seem to give us reason to accept PR rather than the view that laws that are not justifiable to all can be legitimate just because they make us do what is morally right.[4]

However, this law has two features that make it seem illegitimate. And these two features are not shared by all laws requiring us to act rightly in ways which cannot be justified to all. First, we do not believe that all Catholics and non-Catholics are morally required to go to mass at least once a week or that it's morally right for a state to force us to do this. Second, a state that required us to do this would seem to breach our basic liberal rights to freedom of conscience and association by forcing us to attend Catholic ceremonies. We might think that a law can be legitimate if it makes us do what's right, even when this law cannot be justified to us, so long as it does not breach our basic liberal rights of freedom of conscience and association. Consider a case without these features. Suppose that it's right for everyone to give 7% of their post-tax income to the most effective charities. If everyone in our state gave 7%, the lives of thousands of people in faraway countries would be saved by them. Suppose that, against the views of a significant minority, our state forces us to give 7% of our post-tax income to the most effective charities. It's not so intuitively obvious to me that a law forcing us to give 7% of our post-tax income to the most effective charities would be illegitimate.

But our intuitions about cases may still favour PR. First, perhaps it is intuitive to you that such a taxation policy would be illegitimate. Second, it might be that the taxation for charity policy has features that ensure that it satisfies PR. We can all agree that there are reasons to give to effective charities: according to all plausible moral views, we have reason to give a modest amount of money to others who would be greatly helped by this. So, even though it is not right to force everyone to give some of their income to charity according to all moral views, there is a sense in which we can justify to each person a policy that forces all to do so. If this is all right, then we should hold that the law forcing us to give 7% to charity can be justified to all and so passes PR. And so our intuitions about this case do not push in the opposite direction from our intuitions about the Catholic mass law. It should be noted, however, that it may reasonably be claimed that the 7% taxation cannot be (publicly) justified to libertarians for although (at least many) libertarians hold that there are moral reasons to give to charity they hold that there are no moral reasons for the state to force us to do this. This is because these reasons are extinguished by the fact that it's doing so would violate our rights. So, our intuitions may favour PR, but this is not quite as clear as it may initially seem.[5]

9.2.2. ANTI-PATERNALISM

A second motivation for PR is anti-paternalism. Paternalistic actions are actions that try to improve the well-being of particular people motivated by a negative judgment about these people's ability to manage their own well-being. (E.g. a mother who pays her daughter to do her homework acts paternalistically because she does not believe that she will make a responsible choice on her own; Quong, 2011, p. 80.) The idea that anti-paternalism favours PR is attractive because the idea behind PR is that legitimate laws are neutral between citizens' diverse conceptions of the right and the good rather than being based on such conceptions. Alternatives to PR that do not aim to be neutral regarding diverse conceptions of the good may license the enactment of laws that aim to promote a conception of citizens' well-being that is not shared by those citizens. So, some proponents of PR argue that

(a) Paternalistic state action is always *prima facie* morally wrong; and
(b) If a state can legitimately adopt policies that outstrip those licensed by PR, it can legitimately act paternalistically.

If (a) and (b) are right, and the rightness of these claims can be justified to all those in the constituency of PR, then it follows that alternatives to PR allow states to act wrongfully. But should we hold (a) and (b)?

Jonathan Quong (2011, ch. 3, esp. pp. 87, 101–102) makes a case for both (a) and (b). His case for (a) is that paternalistic actions involve treating people as having an inferior status; since they involve treating people as if they are worse at pursuing the good life than those taking the paternalistic action. And it is always *prima facie* wrong to treat others as having a lower status than you.

However, *A*'s paternalistic action towards *B* need not involve the thought that she (*A*) is better at pursuing the good life than *B*: it can merely involve the thought that *B* has a blind spot, which perhaps she (*A*) has too, or that both she and *B* are equally bad at pursuing what's good for them, they just both need a little help. For instance, suppose that my partner will make donations to alt-right groups on my behalf if I renege on my promise to stop smoking and I will make donations to men's rights activist groups if she reneges on her promise to stop smoking. In this case we both act paternalistically towards one another but I do not view myself as better at pursuing the good than my partner or vice versa. This could easily be true of the state too. A state might well adopt anti-drinking, anti-smoking, and pro-saving-for-the-future laws on the basis that it's really tough for everyone (the members of the government included!) to not get drunk all the time, refrain from smoking, and save adequately.

There are reasons to reject (b) too. Some 'perfectionist' alternatives to PR hold that it is permissible for states to adopt laws based on controversial views of the good that are not shared by all its citizens. For instance, according to certain perfectionist views, states may legitimately devote large amounts of funding to the Opera even if doing so is not justifiable to all its citizens. Quong is concerned to argue that such perfectionist alternatives to PR license paternalism. But it's not clear that even these views need license paternalism. Such a state could fund the Opera purely on the basis that it is better for those who love the Opera that it is funded or that they want it to be publicly funded. Such state action is not paternalistic for it is not based on a negative judgment of anyone's capacity to pursue the good. So, perfectionist alternatives to PR need not license paternalism.

9.2.3. RESPECT

A third, somewhat related, argument for PR is that coercing another in a way that cannot be justified to them disrespects that person's capacity for moral agency. For to coerce another in this way is just to treat them as an obstacle that must be forcibly dealt with rather than someone to whom justification is owed in virtue of their rational and moral capacities (Lister, 2016, p. 59). This rationale might provide us with reason to often prefer policies that satisfy PR. But when a state stops one of its citizens from doing something morally wrong it often bypasses their agency and doesn't treat them as anything more than an obstacle. For instance, when a state stops people from killing or assaulting others it overrides their agency and does not treat them as anything more than an obstacle. But it seems perfectly legitimate for a state to act in this way (ibid., pp. 59–81).[6] However, this just shows that states should treat their citizens as more than mere obstacles except when their prospective actions do not accord sufficient respect to other citizens; that is, when they do not act towards others in ways that bypass their agency and breach others' basic rights.[7]

A different problem with this rationale, however, is that it's not clear why in order to treat its citizens with respect and treat them as moral agents rather than mere objects, a state must only enact laws that can be justified from those agents' moral and evaluative perspectives. For instance, suppose that many of a state's citizens are libertarians. And a redistributive tax is levied on all citizens to ensure that citizens receive an income equivalent to their earning a living wage regardless of whether they try to work or not. This tax cannot be justified to these libertarians (assuming their libertarian views).[8] So such a tax to fund a living-wage-level basic income may be illegitimate according to PR because such a tax cannot be justified to these libertarians (in the relevant sense). Suppose that the tax is put to a referendum and despite a campaign against the tax, which was heavily funded by the libertarians, the tax is approved by a large majority. Does the state treat its libertarians as mere objects to the extent that it imposes this tax? It is not obvious that it does, for their views were taken into account equally in deciding whether to implement that tax.

It might seem that this tax can be justified to libertarians because the view that we should adopt all laws that are a product of democratic decisions can be justified to them. However, libertarians believe that they have a basic right not to be taxed for the sake of allowing others not to work—they argue that such taxation is akin to slavery. And many believe that we should not have referenda on, nor accept the results of referenda on, basic rights. For instance, if put to a referendum, the death penalty would return to the UK; many believe that this issue cannot legitimately be put to a referendum. And many Australians believe that it was right to legalise same-sex marriage, but it was wrong to put this issue to a referendum, or to do something very similar, as Australia did in 2017; because we should not have referenda on citizens' basic rights.[9]

9.2.4. CIVIC FRIENDSHIP

A fourth motivation for PR is that it makes civic friendship possible despite seemingly intractable disagreements in moral principles or values. According to this view, if a society only acts in ways that can be justified to all, this enacts a valuable form of relationship between citizens. And a community's only acting in ways that can be justified to all enables them to act together (through their governing processes). For a community that acts only in ways that can be justified to all its members always acts on its members' behalf in a way that a community that acts in ways that cannot be justified to all its members does not. This commitment to act only in ways justifiable to all (reasonable) persons is a commitment to only act in ways that all can, in a sense, get on board with. So, a society involves a valuable form of civic friendship only if it lives up to PR's standard of legitimacy (Lister, 2016, p. 106).

This is plausible for it seems valuable in itself for a community to come together to do something good. Similarly, friendship seems good in itself (see

Helm, 2005, §2.1). And if these things are valuable in themselves, then it is plausible that civic friendship is too. But the view that such things are valuable in themselves is a controversial evaluative view that hedonists, desire-satisfaction theorists, and others will deny (see, for instance, Shafer-Landau, 2017, ch. 1–4). This is problematic for proponents of PR, since PR is not supposed to be based on controversial views of the right or the good.[10]

However, civic friendship also seems to be instrumentally valuable. For we do not fear that those who are committed to making political decisions with us in a way that is consistent with civic friendship would try to adopt laws that cannot be justified to us if they obtained power (without us): so long as they maintain their commitment to civic friendship, they would not take such steps even if they acquired power. So, civic friendship can contribute to the stability, and sense of stability, of a society and its political constitution.[11]

It is not entirely clear how strong the civic friendship-based motivation for PR is. If civic friendship is valuable in itself, and proponents of PR may invoke this value, then it's value may still be outweighed when breaching the norms of civic friendship is the only way to stop a grave injustice. Furthermore, although civic friendship may generally have the instrumental benefits of contributing to stability, it may in some cases be better to breach civic friendship to better mitigate an injustice; doing so may sometimes not seriously undermine stability. So, although PR may enable civic friendship it is not entirely clear that this shows that laws are legitimate only if they satisfy the requirements of PR.[12]

9.3. RAWLSIAN AND GAUSIAN PUBLIC REASON

There are two importantly different versions of PR: the Rawlsian account and the Gausian account. The Rawlsian account has been developed by those who hold views in political philosophy similar to John Rawls's, and are heavily inspired by his work. What I call the Gausian account continues to be developed by Gerald Gaus and several of his students and colleagues. Gaus's account is also inspired by Rawls's work but departs from it in several important and interesting ways.

Rawlsian PR holds that a law is legitimate iff it is justified by reasons that all reasonable persons can accept and see as justifying that law. 'Reasonable' here is a more minimal term than that of being epistemically reasonable. One can be reasonable in the sense that Rawlsians are interested in without holding most of the moral beliefs than one ought to hold (For discussion see, for instance, Lister, 2016, p. 8). Reasonable people in the Rawlsian sense are people who are morally motivated, are willing and able to reason sincerely with others about what is good, right, just, and true, and accept that society is a cooperative venture between free and equal persons. They are people who accept what Rawls calls the 'burdens of judgment'. That, is they accept that it is very difficult to come to the correct views about the right and the good because of the complexity of the evidence, conceptual vagueness, and influence of diverse life experiences on the normal functioning of the cognitive faculties of morally motivated people (at least within relatively free liberal societies).[13] In this case, if we accept the burdens of judgment, we accept that:

i   moral judgment is difficult in virtue of these features of our epistemic situation; and
ii   in virtue of (i), people who are minimally reasonable will quite understandably and through no fault of their own come to different moral views and views of the good life; but
iii   such reasonable people with different moral views must still be cooperated with politically for the purpose of establishing legitimate laws.[14]

Rawlsian reasonable persons can hold a wide range of substantive views of what is right and good. For instance, liberal Muslims, utilitarians, and Catholics can all continue to hold, with full certainty, their view of what is right, good, and just, while still holding that for the purposes of assessing whether a law is legitimately authoritative more must be taken into account than their own conceptions of the right, the good, and the just.

Rawlsian PR holds that a law is legitimate only if it is justified by reasons that can be accepted by all reasonable persons. Suppose that a state is going to make a law regarding sex-work: it's going to either make buying and selling sex legal or illegal or make only buying sex illegal. In this case certain justifications for various laws are irrelevant to whether these particular laws are legitimate; justifications for laws regarding sex-work that trade on views that cannot be accepted by all reasonable persons, such as religious or other views about the wrongness of selling sex, are considerations that cannot justify a legitimate law regarding sex work.

What are the considerations that can be agreed to be reasons by all reasonable persons? Some examples are reasons that speak to the freedom and equality of individuals, and considerations of fairness and economic efficiency. For instance, suppose that a city has a portion of its budget that it can either spend on constructing a football stadium or a modern art gallery. Some reasonable citizens hate football, other reasonable citizens hate modern art. There is a set of reasons that all reasonable persons could see as favouring building either the stadium or the gallery. Suppose the city already has a modern art gallery but no football stadium. In this case one reason that could justify constructing the stadium would be that fairness favours constructing a stadium rather than another gallery. For the art lovers already have a gallery but the sports fans don't have a stadium. This is a justification that all reasonable persons could accept as such. Suppose that the construction of the stadium would also benefit the city's economy because it would serve as a new

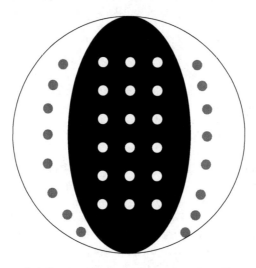

■ Reasons that all reasonable persons see as justifying φ-ing
□ Reasons that some reasonable persons see as justifying φ-ing
● Reasons for φ-ing

Figure 9.1 Reasons that all reasonable persons share vs those that only some reasonable persons share.

home to a professional team (whereas adding another gallery would not add additional economic revenue). It would also be legitimate to choose to construct the stadium rather than the gallery for the reason that there are greater economic benefits to choosing the stadium; for all reasonable persons could see this as a reason to favour the construction of the stadium.[15]

Gausian PR contrasts with Rawlsian PR in two salient ways. First, Gausian PR holds that a law is legitimate only if it can be justified to all citizens who are normal moral agents rather than all citizens who are reasonable in the Rawlsian sense. Normal moral agents have conceptions of the right, the good, and the just within 'the common human horizon' of such conceptions. Libertarians, socialists, Marxists, and anarchists have conceptions that are within this common human horizon, as do those with religious conceptions of the right, the just, and the good. Not all of these people are necessarily Rawlsian reasonable persons. Some libertarians, for instance, do not see people with left egalitarian political views as people who should be cooperated and compromised with politically and some left egalitarians and some Marxists don't believe that reasonable people can disagree with them that justice requires high levels of redistribution from the rich to the poor. But, according to Gaus, people only motivated by one (strange) goal, such as those whose one and only goal is to count blades of grass all day do not count as within the common human horizon. And nor do egoists as such agents are not morally motivated, and so are not moral agents. It is natural to see the contrast here as between Rawlsian PR, which just requires that laws be justifiable to relatively liberal citizens, and Gausian PR which requires that laws be justifiable to citizens beyond those who are relatively liberal (see Gaus, 2011, pp. 263, 268).

Second, Gausian PR allows that a law can be legitimate if it is justified to all on the basis of different reasons: it does not require that a law must be justified by reasons that all normal moral agents can see to be reasons. Whereas Rawlsian PR requires consensus on the reasons that justify a law among its constituency (reasonable persons); Gausian PR just requires that its constituency (normal moral agents) have justifications that converge on the view that that law is justified. For example, consider a system of laws with taxation only for a libertarian minimal nightwatchman state that only provides its citizens with a military, police, and court system that protects them from aggression, theft, breach of contract, and fraud. Libertarians have sufficient reason to accept this system of laws because they believe that any further taxation is akin to forced labour. But suppose that in our particular context egalitarians also have reason to accept this system of laws because (in this context) any higher taxation would result in many businesses moving abroad and less jobs and a weaker economy, which would be worse for the worse-off. In this case egalitarians and libertarians have different reasons for accepting this system of laws. Libertarians don't see the fact that it would be good for the worst-off as a reason to accept that system of laws, so this is no reason for them. And egalitarians don't believe that further taxation policies would constitute forced labour so this is no reason for them. But both libertarians and egalitarians still have sufficient reason to accept this system of laws. In this case the convergence model Gausians favour holds that the system of laws is justified but the consensus model favoured by Rawlsians holds that it is not.[16]

Table 9.1 Rawslian and Gausian public reason.

	Constituency	Reasons
Rawlsian public reason	Reasonable (liberal) persons	Reasons for acceptance must be shared (consensus)
Gausian public reason	All (normal) persons (not just liberals)	Reasons for acceptance need not be shared (convergence)

9.4. WHICH PUBLIC REASON ACCOUNT IS BETTER?

Rawlsians give at least three reasons for preferring their view to Gausian PR. First, we can justify something to another only if we have a common moral framework with them. Jonathan Quong (2011, p. 181) puts this point in the following way: 'justification, as Rawls says, is reasoning addressed to others, and as such, it requires some common ground from which the reasoning can begin. But ... there is, by definition, little common normative ground with unreasonable people.' In which case laws can only be justified by and to agents that share a common framework: a justificatory community is needed for the justification of laws to take place. So, only citizens with a shared commitment to a broadly similar set of values can justify laws to one another.

Quong might be right that we need to have some degree of normative or evaluative overlap with people in order to be able to justify things to them. However, it might seem that Rawlsian reasonable persons can have normative/evaluative overlap with those who do not qualify as Rawlsian reasonable persons. For instance, in order to qualify as a Rawlsian reasonable person one must accept the burdens of judgment. But two people can hold the same moral and evaluative framework without both accepting the burdens of judgment. David Enoch (2015, p. 121) argues that 'pretty much any epistemologist working in the field today' will reject the burdens of judgment and so turn out to be unreasonable according to Rawlsian public reason. And many on the left and the right who seem relatively reasonable and otherwise agree about what's good and right may hold that certain political issues are not difficult, as the burdens of judgment imply they are, and that there cannot be reasonable disagreement about them. For instance, many on the left hold that it's not difficult to figure out that its unjust and unfair for a society to permit the super-rich to get richer while the poor live off next to nothing; and that they are not in a reasonable disagreement with those on the right about this. Similarly, many right-libertarians hold the converse view. But these people can hold otherwise very similar moral and evaluative frameworks, so it's not clear that they cannot justify moral claims to one another. (For a similar issue and point see §6.1).

Rawlsians' other two reasons for accepting their view rather than the Gausian alternative are more promising. First, they argue that Gausian PR is too ambitious. If a law is legitimate only if it can be justified to all reasonable and non-reasonable normal moral agents, then no laws are legitimate because no law can be justified to all. Second, they argue that a state that only acts if its actions can be justified to all (on consensus) is more stable than a state that acts on justifications that can only be shared by some (on convergence). For such a state's laws are based on more than a merely temporary convergence of its citizens views: rather such a state is based on a moral agreement among its citizens.

However, if we reject Gausian PR and prefer Rawlsian PR on these grounds, we need to explain why it is not ad-hoc to only be concerned with justifying laws to Rawlsian reasonable citizens. And we need to explain why a view that holds a law to be legitimate if it can be justified to such citizens is a view that really gets us what we want from an account of legitimacy: an account that takes moral disagreement seriously but does not take it so seriously as to require consent from all those who are bound by a law for legitimacy.

Quong (2011) argues that the aim of Rawlsian PR is the less ambitious aim of rendering liberalism coherent. Liberals accept that a free liberal society is one in which it is inevitable that people will have a diverse variety of conceptions of the right and the good. According to Quong, the project of Rawlsian PR is to figure out whether it is coherent to believe that there can be legitimate laws in such a liberal society. That is, whether there can be laws that bind citizens of a liberal society who sign up to liberal values but also hold diverse thorough conceptions of the right and the good (e.g. liberal Catholics, liberal utilitarians, etc.) If we accept this view of the project of Rawlsian PR, then there is a clear rationale for accepting the Rawlsian constituency of PR; for restricting the constituency of PR to reasonable persons in the Rawlsian sense. For it is only such reasonable persons who accept liberal values and so justification to whom we must be concerned with when ascertaining the coherence of a legitimate liberal society.

However, this can seem extremely unambitious. It seems very close to the view that the project of Rawlsian PR is to ascertain whether laws that enact Rawlsian PR are justifiable to those who already accept such laws. To many, moral disagreements among Marxists, libertarians, liberal egalitarians, and those who believe that religion should have a greater role in politics, motivate PR's search for legitimate laws: PR views are supposed to give an account of legitimacy that takes account of these disagreements without yielding anarchism. On Quong's account this is not the case (see Enoch, 2015).

Andrew Lister (2016, ch. 5) argues that we should accept Rawlsian PR because only reasonable persons are committed to living by principles that are grounded in justifications that one another can accept. Given that society is a co-operative venture between free and equal persons it makes sense to only be concerned with justifications that can only be accepted by others who accept this idea; it is only those who also accept this idea who are willing to compromise their principles for the sake of living in such a society. We cannot expect to find common ground with those who are not similarly committed to such a cooperative venture. But this restriction does not illegitimately exclude anyone. For all that someone needs to do in order to become part of the set of persons to whom the justification of a law is owed for it to be legitimate is to take up a commitment to living with others on terms that a variety of free and equal persons with different views of the right, the good, and the just can accept.

Lister's rationale seems less like it involves the claim that Rawlsian PR is concerned with justifying liberal laws to those who are already committed to them. However, it will still entail that Rawlsian PR does not take as its aim justifying laws to many libertarians, Marxists, and many of those who wish religion to play a greater role in political life who hold that those with who they disagree do not have reasonable or intelligible views. For many libertarians, Marxists and people who wish religion to play a greater role in public life do not believe that those with whom they disagree have reasonable or intelligible views and that those with whom they disagree should be co-operated with to come to an agreed conclusion; Rawlsian PR will still entail that a law can be legitimate even if it cannot be justified to any of these people. If you believe that PR should be concerned with justifying laws to such people, you'll be more interested in the Gausian approach to PR.

The main concern with Rawlsian PR is explaining why its restriction of the constituency of PR to reasonable persons does not betray the motivations of the PR account. The main problem for the Gausian account is showing that an account without such a restriction does not yield anarchism: does not entail that no laws are legitimate. According to Gausian PR a law is legitimate only if all normal moral agents have sufficient reason to accept it. (Where, remember, for one to having sufficient reason to accept something in the relevant sense is to have sufficient reason to accept it assuming one's current moral/evaluative views). Gaus's (2011, p. 538) argument that his view does not yield anarchism starts with the idea that whether we have sufficient reason to accept a law is always a comparative matter. When we're assessing whether we have sufficient reason to accept a particular law we must ask what the alternatives to accepting it are. Suppose that we're considering proposals for the building of a new road. Thrill seeking drivers want there to be no speed limit on the road. But there being some road is of more value to them than there being no road at all. So, they have sufficient reason to accept the proposal to build the road with a significant speed limit given that others will not accept the building of a road with no speed limit. Gaus believes that once we see that what laws we have sufficient reason to accept is an essentially comparative matter, we see that Gausian PR does not yield anarchism. For although we all have very different moral and evaluative views, most can agree that a state that protects our rights is better (by the lights of our moral standards) than no state at all; according to Gaus, the moral and evaluative standards of all normal moral agents dictate that such a state is better. So, we have sufficient reason to accept some state rather than no state at all.

A classical liberal state secures basic civil rights and liberties for all (freedom of thought, conscience, assembly, etc.), protects its citizens from violence, attacks, and theft (via a police and army), and secures strong private property rights. But the classical liberal state does not engage in redistributive taxation for the purpose of reducing inequalities or funding museums and art galleries (see Gaus, 2011, p. 533). Gaus argues that his version of PR entails that a classical liberal state, and only a classical liberal state, is legitimate.

According to Gaus (ibid., pp. 386–387), all normal moral agents, inclusive of their diversity of views about morality and the good, have reason to endorse laws that protect their basic civil liberties of freedom and protection from harm, manipulation, and invasion in virtue of the fact that these laws give each individual person a sphere in which their moral and evaluative standards have authority. And Gaus gives empirical arguments for the view that extensive private ownership of capital goods and finance is a prerequisite for a state that protects such civil liberties; Gaus claims that 'there has never been a political order characterised by deep respect for personal freedom that was not based on a market order with widespread private ownership in the means of production' (ibid., pp. 513–514).[17] But all agents have a fundamental claim not to be coerced by the state unless the benefits of such coercion are extremely high (ibid., pp. 479–502). So, all of us have sufficient reason to accept some set of laws rather than none, and to accept strong property rights and protections of civil liberties. But laws mandating heavily redistributive taxation for the purpose of equalising citizens' opportunities are not legitimate. This is because such laws cannot be justified to some people who would, given their moral and evaluative frameworks and desires and goals, reasonably prefer very few laws rather than such heavily redistributive laws (ibid., p. 52).

However, it can be questioned whether Gaus really succeeds in showing that only classical liberalism is legitimate given his version of public reason. For although it is true that classical liberals prefer no egalitarian redistributive laws at all to any such laws, classical liberals do prefer some extremely redistributive laws to there being no state at all; just as socialists may prefer classical liberalism to no state. So, it's unclear why classical liberal and socialist laws can't both be legitimate according to Gausian PR.[18] But even if Gaus is mistaken that Gausian PR entails that only a classical liberal state is legitimate, this would not undermine his argument that Gausian PR does not yield anarchism. However, in order for his argument that on his view any state is legitimate to succed, his empirical arguments for the benefits of a minimal state to anarchism have to be justifiable to all—including anarchists.

I do have my doubts about whether these claims can be so justified. But if Gausian PR yields anarchism only on the assumption that anarchism is no worse than a minimal state, this strikes me as the right conclusion: if anarchism really were no worse for most people than a minimal state, then it would be hard to see how a minimal state could be justified to anarchists.

There is one final reason to be worried about the constituency of Gausian PR however. Gaus (2011, p. 281) claims that Nazis are not normal moral agents. This is because Nazis' commitment to genocide indicates that they do not conceive of many of those with whom they disagree as reasonable and intelligible. But if this is why Nazis do not count as normal moral agents, then the constituency of Gausian PR seems to be closer to that of Rawlsian

PR than it seemed. If in order to be a normal moral agent in the Gausian sense one needs to view those with whom one disagrees as reasonable and intelligible, then many anti-capitalists, libertarians, and Marxists may fail to count as normal moral agents. For many anti-capitalists do not believe that pro-capitalists or libertarians are reasonable; and many libertarians do not believe that socialists or Marxists have reasonable or intelligible views. The fact that many libertarians and Marxists seem to fall outside the constituency of Rawlsian PR was a reason to reject Rawlsian PR and accept Gausian PR instead. But if we make the conditions for being a normal moral agent in the Gausian sense more lax, then Nazis may count as normal moral agents. And if Nazis count as Gausian normal moral agents, then laws guaranteeing equal rights and freedoms for all are illegitimate. Since, on at least some Nazis' moral views it is presumably not better for there to be no laws than for there to be laws guaranteeing equal rights and freedoms for all; for they believe that it is of central importance that certain people are not treated as having equal rights and freedoms. It's unclear to me whether this problem with Gausian PR could be fixed by holding that normal moral agents are moral agents who do not explicitly deny the equal rights and liberties of other moral agents.

One unexplored way of solving this problem for Gausian PR is to hold that those who form the constituency of Gausian PR are those whom we should judge to be our epistemic peers about a variety of moral and political issues. It seems that making this move would ensure that Nazis are not part of the constituency of Gausian PR. For, as we discussed in §6.1, we should not judge that moral monsters are our epistemic peers about moral and political issues. And appealing to epistemic peerhood in the constituency of PR would not be ad hoc, since we might argue that we should only take the moral judgments of our epistemic peers (and superiors) seriously (see Chapters 5–6).

However, there are two problems with this strategy. First, this way of carving out the constituency of Gausian PR may seem to render very conservative or religious persons not part of the constituency of Gausian PR. For, as I explained in §6.2.2–3, we may lack sufficient reason to believe that very conservative or religious people who disagree with us on a vast range of moral topics are our epistemic peers about those topics (and similarly they may lack reason to believe that we are their epistemic peers about these moral topics). Proponents of PR may not be, and probably should not be, happy with this result. And it seems that if we should want laws that can be justified to all within our society, we should want laws that can be justified to conservative Christians and Muslims too. Second, this view would seem to have the result that if Nazis became 51% of a population in a particular jurisdiction, then liberals would no longer be part of the constituency of Gausian PR for that jurisdiction. For, as we discussed in Chapter 6, the reasons that make it the case that we should not judge that Nazis are our epistemic peers about moral issues also make it the case that they should not judge that we are their epistemic peers about these issues.

Another way to put this issue is the following. On this view, A is a member of the constituency of Gausian PR only if some agents B should judge them to be their approximate epistemic peers about moral and political issues in general. But who are these agents B? And why is it that their epistemic position and whom they should judge to be their epistemic peers is what matters and determines legitimacy? Perhaps this issue for restricting the scope of Gausian PR via epistemic peerhood can be solved. More work on how epistemic peerhood might relate to determining the constituency of PR is needed to figure out whether this is a viable strategy.

9.5. PUBLIC REASON AND THE SELF-DEFEAT PROBLEM

PR may seem to be self-defeating. Here is one way of putting this objection. PR holds that a law or set of moral and/or political rules is illegitimate and lacks authority if those laws cannot be justified to those to whom they apply. But PR is a moral or political rule. So, if moral/political rules must be justified to all to whom they apply in order to be legitimate, then PR must be justified to all to whom it applies. But PR cannot itself be justified to those to whom it applies. This is because both normal moral agents and people who will qualify as reasonable Rawlsian persons reject PR. Many liberals who believe that we should take moral disagreement seriously, who accept Rawls's burdens of judgment, and who hold that we should adopt liberal laws that treat all individuals as free and equal citizens and enable citizens with diverse moral views to live with one another reject PR; for instance, philosophers such as Joseph Raz and David Enoch, reject PR.[19] These philosophers have different justifications for a broadly liberal set of laws that tolerates much diversity and disagreement. Philosophers who do not accept PR can still accept that we should have liberal disagreement tolerating laws for other reasons, such as for the reason that such laws promote autonomy or liberty; the liberalism of Mill (1978) and Raz (1998) holds that liberal laws for these kinds of reasons. Some argue that PR is self-defeating because it entails that we should accept it only if it can be justified to reasonable Millian and Razian liberals. And it cannot be.[20]

There are two types of responses to the self-defeat objection that have been made. The first response argues that PR does not apply to itself. Remember that in §5.4 we discussed the self-defeat objection to conciliationism, a view about how we should respond to peer disagreements that holds that we should reduce our confidence in a view when we realise that we are in a peer disagreement about it. Conciliationism is subject to a self-defeat worry because there is peer disagreement about conciliationism. We discussed responses to this self-defeat worry that argue that conciliationism should not apply to itself. At least *prima facie,* these responses seemed ad-hoc: there is no obvious reason why an epistemic principle that entails that we should reduce our confidence that p when we find ourselves in disagreements about whether p should not apply to disagreements about epistemic principles. And this makes it hard to argue that conciliationism should not apply to itself. In contrast, PR is a view about what it takes for a law or set of laws to be legitimate. PR, though, is not a law, set of laws or state. And, given that it is neither a law, set of laws, nor a state, it's not clear that PR is the right kind of thing to be legitimate or illegitimate.

PR is, however, a moral/political principle. And laws that claim legitimate authority claim to have a similar status to moral/political principles. Since they claim to ground genuine moral obligations to follow them. So, how does PR differ from these laws? Laws sanction coercion, but PR sanctions coercion when that coercion can be justified to all. Laws are used to legitimate coercion, but PR can be used for this purpose too: the fact that a law satisfies PR legitimates it. One difference between laws and PR is that PR is sometimes understood to be a constraint on legitimate coercion or the laws that can legitimately coerce. Laws are not constraints on legitimate coercion. However, if PR is understood as a constraint on legitimate coercion, then it seems to sanction a default of no coercion. Many proponents of Rawlsian PR have concerns about this way of understanding PR: mainly because such an understanding seems to tilt PR towards exclusively legitimising smaller states. But, such an understanding of PR may seem perfectly amenable to proponents of Gausian PR, since they explicitly argue from Gausian PR to the view that only smaller states are legitimate. However, Rawlsian PR operates as a constraint on the reasons that can justify a law. A view about the reasons that can justify a law is distinct from those laws that such a constraint applies to. So, Rawlsian PR can also be distinguished from the laws that it regulates.[21]

But it is possible to setup a law that either (a) acts as a constraint on legitimate coercion or (b) acts as a constraint on the reasons that can justify a law. For instance, a parliament could pass a law forbidding the passage of any laws on the basis of a certain set of reasons or forbidding the passage of laws that coerce in particular ways. If PR is a view about the legitimacy of laws, then it should be a view about the legitimacy of these laws too. So, it is unclear that the fact that PR operates as a constraint on legitimate coercion or a constraint on the reasons that can be used to justify a particular law really distinguishes PR from the laws to which it applies. So, it is unclear that these responses show that PR is not self-defeating if it cannot be justified to all reasonable or normal persons.

A second way of responding to the self-defeat objection is to argue that PR is not self-defeating because it does in fact satisfy its own criteria: PR can be justified to all (reasonable) persons. Here is one way of responding to the self-defeat objection in this vein. A law, set of laws, or whatever satisfies Rawlsian

PR iff it is based on a justification that can be shared by all liberal reasonable (in the Rawlsian sense) persons. According to Quong (2011, ch. 7), a justification can be shared by all liberal reasonable persons so long as it is grounded in an interpretation of a value that all liberal reasonable persons share. Suppose that values X, Y, and Z are the only values that are shared by all reasonable persons that have a bearing on whether a particular law prohibiting φ-ing is legitimate. A prohibition on φ-ing is proposed and is justified on the basis of reasonable interpretations of X, Y, and Z. In this case, the prohibition of φ-ing is legitimate. If this understanding of Rawlsian PR is correct, then we may be able to show that Rawlsian PR is not self-defeating. All Rawlsian reasonable persons will believe in the idea that society is a cooperative venture between all members of society. If society is a cooperative venture, then we should all have some say in the laws that our society has. And that means that the laws we have (or the procedure for adopting them) must be justifiable to all those to whom these laws apply. In this case it seems that PR will be an interpretation of the idea of society as a cooperative venture that all Rawlsian reasonable persons share. In this case, Rawlsian PR will not be self-defeating because it is an interpretation of this value that all those in the constituency of Rawlsian PR share.[22]

However, the constituency of Gausian PR is all normal moral persons inclusive of libertarians, Marxists, those who believe that religion and religious ideals should play a greater role in politics, and even egoists. Many of these people do not see those with whom they disagree as people who should be cooperated with politically; many Marxists do not think that we should try to politically cooperate with rich libertarians for instance. So, it is not clear that all those in the constituency of Gausian PR see society as a cooperative venture in any non-trivial way that could amount to their sharing values. Generally, Gausian PR attempts to provide a route to establishing state legitimacy even in light of wholesale disagreements in moral principles and values. And it is not clear that there is an interpretation of a value that all normal moral agents share that could justify PR. So, the self-defeat objection may be more problematic for Gausian PR than Rawlsian PR.[23]

In §5.4 we discussed the self-defeat objection to conciliationism about peer disagreement. One of the most promising responses that we considered was John Pittard's (2015). Perhaps we can model a promising response to the self-defeat objection to Gausian PR on Pittard's response. Remember that Pittard argues that if we should be conciliationists this is because we should defer to epistemically well-credentialed thinkers in a way that is proportionate to their epistemic credentials: conciliationism is grounded in the idea that we should be appropriately deferential to well-credentialed others. Suppose that I have a credence of 1 in conciliationism but I realise, for the first time, that an epistemic peer, Amy, disagrees with me about conciliationism. According to Pittard, my decreasing my credence in conciliationism exhibits no greater deference than remaining steadfast in my conciliationism. Suppose that I decrease my credence in conciliationism to 0.5. According to Pittard, if I do this, my credence is deferential because it gives weight to Amy's view, but my reasoning that gets me to lowering my credence in conciliationism is not deferential to Amy's view; for my reasoning depends entirely on conciliationism rather than to any extent on Amy's steadfast view. Similarly, if I stick to my guns and do not modify my credence in conciliationism, then my reasoning can be deferential for it can be based on the reasoning of Amy's steadfast view even though my credence in conciliationism is not deferential for it does not take into account Amy's different view. Given that whatever I do either my reasoning or credence (but not both) will fail to be deferential, I can satisfy the idea that conciliationism is based on and be appropriately deferential to well-credentialed others by sticking to my guns and not lowering my credence in conciliationism. Even though when I find myself in a peer disagreement about a topic other than conciliationism I cannot so satisfy the appropriate deference requirement by being steadfast in my confidence about this topic.

Perhaps a similar argument can be made regarding PR. When we find ourselves in a peer disagreement about conciliationism, sticking to our guns about conciliationism involves no less deference than not so sticking to our guns. Similarly, perhaps when we find ourselves in a disagreement with (normal) others about PR, acting as PR requires us to at least often involves doing something just as justifiable to those with whom we disagree as acting in ways that PR does not require. Suppose that there are fifty of us, who are all normal persons, attempting to come to an agreement on a set of laws. 30 of us accept Gausian PR and otherwise have similar moral and evaluative views, suppose that we are liberal egalitarians. The other 20 (i) do not accept Gausian PR and (ii) have different moral and evaluative views from us. Regarding (i), they instead believe that we should simply vote on alternative proposed laws and not worry about whether different proposed laws can be justified to all given their different moral and evaluative perspectives. And, regarding (ii), they prefer a libertarian ultra-minimal state. We 30 liberal egalitarians believe that laws are legitimate and should be implemented if they are both (a) voted on by a majority and (b) are justifiable to all. And the 20 minimal staters believe that laws are legitimate if they meet (a). Now if we 30 drop Gausian PR in line with the views of the minimal staters, we will adopt liberal egalitarian policies, and because we are the majority we will not adopt policies which are justifiable to the 20 for they are libertarians. But we will not act in line with Gausian PR, and our not acting in line with Gausian PR is justifiable to the 20 for they reject it. If we act in line with Gausian PR and refrain from adopting liberal egalitarian policies and instead adopt policies that are justifiable to the 20, we will act in a way that is justifiable to the 20. But we will also act on a principle that is not justifiable to them; for Gausian PR is not justifiable to them. In this case, our acting on Gausian PR is just as justifiable to the 20 as our not doing so.

But what happens when the numbers change, when there are 30 opponents of Gausian PR and 20 proponents of it? Well suppose that there are three policy options: (i) liberal egalitarian laws; (ii) ultra-minimal state laws; (iii) a third alternative that can be justified to all, perhaps laws that instigate a small but not ultra-minimal state. Now if the 20 liberal egalitarians vote for (iii) on the basis that this can be justified to all and (i) and (ii) cannot be, then they will be acting on the basis of their view that Gausian PR is correct and trying to only promote policies that can be justified to all. If they vote in this way they do not take into account the disagreement they have about PR with the 30. But they do take into account the first-order disagreement they have with the 30 about justice. If instead, the liberal egalitarians voted for (i), on the basis that the 30 with whom they disagree about justice also disagree with them about PR, then they would be taking into account their disagreement about Gausian PR but not their disagreement with the 30 about first-order matters of substantive justice. So, their voting for a policy that they believe to be legitimate, given PR, would demonstrate no less of a concern for justifiability to others than their not taking what is legitimate according to PR into account. So, it seems that a response to the self-defeat objection inspired by work on the epistemology of peer disagreement may help Gausian PR avoid problems with self-defeat. According to this response, Gausian PR is not self-defeating because when we disagree with others about PR our acting in line with PR involves our doing something no less justifiable to them than our not acting in line with PR.

SUMMARY

Public reason holds that laws are legitimate only if there are reasons for all (reasonable) persons to accept those laws. There are a variety of reasons to accept public reason. But it is not clear that these reasons show that laws are legitimate only if they conform to public reason's standard. Public reason faces a variety of objections. But one of the main objections that has been levelled at it involving self-defeat seems to be surmountable. Rawlsian public reason understands reasonable persons as liberal-inclined persons. One worry about Rawlsian public reason is that its view that only reasonable persons need to be able to accept laws in order for them to be legitimate seems to betray the motivations of public reason. In contrast, Gausian public reason holds that laws are legitimate only if they can be justified to all normal persons. Gausian public reason faces problems giving a non-ad-hoc account of what makes citizens normal while simultaneously rendering some laws (rather than no laws) legitimate.

FURTHER READING

Quong (2013) and Vallier (1996) are useful first stops for thinking in greater detail about public reason. Rawls (1996) started the contemporary discussion of PR. Freeman (2007) is an incredible resource for understanding Rawls's work. Lister (2016) is a very clear and accessible book length defence of Rawlsian public reason. Quong (2011) is an extremely thorough defence of a Rawlsian view of public reason. Gaus (2011) and the debate between Enoch (2013) and Gaus (2015) is a good next step in understanding his particular account of public reason. The literature on public reason is enormous. I recommend looking at the references in Quong (2013) and Vallier (1996) to figure out exactly what to look at next depending on your interests. Enoch (2015) is an accessible and plausible critique of public reason.

NOTES

1 See, for instance, Huemer (2013, ch. 2).
2 Quong (2017, §1), Otsuka (2013, pp. 89–113), and Simmons (1999).
3 An astute reader might realise that this sense of justification is in line with Williams's (1981) internal reasons or justifications. Gaus (2011, pp. 221–263) makes a case that internal reasons are the reasons relevant to whether a law is legitimate or not.
4 See Estlund (2009, p. 5) and Enoch (2015, p. 114). See also Quong's (2011, pp. 108–118) examples.
5 Quong (2011, ch. 7) argues that laws—perhaps like this one—can be justified to others if they are based on interpretations of values that they share. He argues that a variety of different laws on abortion can be justified to others who oppose them because they are based on interpretations of values—such as those of the freedom and equality of persons—that they share. This might be a plausible view of what public justification involves. But it may mean that PR loses its intuitive appeal. For a highly restrictive abortion policy seems just as unjustifiable to many of us as the forced Catholicism policy discussed above.
6 Cf. Gaus (2011, pp. 479–490).
7 It might also be argued that all persons would agree to a law prohibiting persons from killing one another if asked.
8 Although cf. note 5 above.
9 Ireland did have a straightforward referendum on this issue in 2015.
10 However, cf. Lister (2016, p. 2) who says that he is providing a communitarian version of PR.
11 A concern for stability is also part of what motivated Rawls (1996) to argue for PR. See Lister (2016, pp. 115–118). For Lister's full articulation of this rationale for public reason see ibid., pp. 106–127. See also Wendt (2016).
12 See also Quong (2013, §1.4). Gaus (2011) makes a further argument for PR based on the relationship between legitimate laws and what it is to have a normative reason to accept a law.
13 See Lister (2016, p. 8) and Rawls (1996, pp. 36–37, pp. 55–57).
14 This way of understanding the burdens of judgment and the epistemological commitments of Rawlsian PR are not shared by all, and are especially not shared by some critics of Rawlsian PR; see Enoch (2015, 2017), van Wietmarschen (2018, pp. 489–490), and §8.1.2.
15 This is Quong's (2011, p. 280) example.
16 See, for instance, Gaus (2011, p. 278); although cf. note 5 above.
17 For Gaus's response to Rawlsians' arguments that private property regimes limit political liberty see Gaus (2011, pp. 515–519).

18 Assuming with Gaus that life without a state would be bad or that we have reasons to believe this; for an argument against this view see, for instance, Huemer (2013, part 2).

19 See Enoch (2015, pp. 120–126) and Raz (1998).

20 See Quong (2013, §7.2) and the references therein.

21 See Lister (2016, pp. 21, 124–126).

22 For a problem with this idea of Quong's see note 5 above.

23 We also might worry about Quong's interpretation of shared values strategy more generally, see note 5 above.

10

DEMOCRACY AND DELIBERATIVE RESTRAINT

In Chapter 9 we discussed public reason (PR) accounts of the legitimacy. In this chapter we'll discuss two further related constraints on the legitimacy of laws and how moral disagreement is related to them. In §10.1 we'll discuss the idea that laws are legitimate only if they are deliberated about on the basis of reasons that all (reasonable persons) agree to be reasons and voted for on the basis of such reasons. In §10.2 we'll discuss the idea that laws are legitimate only if they are the product of a democratic process and how disagreement relates to this idea.

10.1. PUBLIC REASON AND DELIBERATIVE RESTRAINT

At the end of the previous chapter we discussed a case in which people voted in line with their view that PR holds. Much of the debate about public reason has been about what the public reason approach to legitimacy requires of individual citizens and legislators in their deliberations and voting. This is because public reason is discussed as both a view about (i) the legitimacy of laws and as a view about (ii) how laws may be legitimately argued for.[1] In the previous chapter we discussed (i), which we specified as PR in §9.1. (ii) is a view that we'll call deliberative restraint. It is a view that is normally endorsed by proponents of Rawlsian PR, and is the view that when engaged in political deliberation or action deliberators must (only) invoke and/or act on reasons that other reasonable persons (in the Rawlsian sense) can see to be reasons; these are referred to as public reasons. Religious reasons, as well as other

DOI: 10.4324/9780429491375-13

controversial metaphysical and epistemological claims are not public reasons (Freeman, 2007, p. 387). However, settled scientific theories and standards of evidence that are generally accepted by the relevant experts in the relevant fields do constitute public reasons. And values shared by all reasonable persons such as freedom and equality (for all), fairness, economic efficiency, equality of political and civil liberty, equality of opportunity, economic reciprocity, and the common good are liberal public values and so are public reasons; for all reasonable persons (in the Rawlsian sense) hold these values.[2] According to proponents of deliberative restraint, a law is legitimate only if deliberative restraint was exercised in its adoption; if non-public reasons played a role in deliberation or argument for a law, it is not legitimate.

Deliberative restraint holds that not all considerations bearing on the truth, rightness, or justice of a law are relevant for deciding whether it should be enacted. According to this view, we should screen-off certain considerations when considering and deliberating about particular laws. This idea can seem quite intuitive. It doesn't seem that the fact that drinking alcohol is outlawed by most interpretations of Islam should be taken into account by all societies when they consider what laws to adopt regarding drinking. (Though the fact that some of its citizens are Muslims who believe in this prohibition should be so taken into account). This screening-off move is familiar from other contexts too. In criminal trials not all the evidence bearing on whether a defendant is guilty is admissible in the court room. For instance, evidence that is obtained illegally is not generally admissible in courts in the United States. This evidence is sometimes known as fruit of the poisonous tree. One example is illegal recordings of conversations. Some jurisdictions require two-party consent for a recording to be legally made, others only require one-party consent. So, if a recording was made in a jurisdiction with a two-party consent rule (such as California or Florida), and one of the parties did not know about the recording, then this recording is illegal and inadmissible. This means that if a secret incriminating recording of someone was made in California of someone confessing to a murder, then this evidence is inadmissible in Californian courts. This evidence does bear on the guilt of defendants but it is screened off from jurors (because it is 'fruit of the poisonous tree'). Moreover, if this evidence is heard by jurors, they must not take it into account when considering whether the defendant is guilty: they must take a view about whether all the evidence apart from the inadmissible evidence establishes the guilt of the defendant.

In this section, we'll discuss several versions of deliberative restraint. But what exactly is the relationship between deliberative restraint and PR? Proponents of PR may understand deliberative restraint as necessary in order for a society to be stably making laws that are legitimate according to (Rawlsian) PR. For laws must be made by someone. And if those making the laws do not make any effort to justify the laws with reasons that all other reasonable persons can see as justifying them, then it's hard to see why the laws that are being made would end up being laws that can be justified to all reasonable persons.[3]

10.1.1. STRONG AND WEAK RESTRAINT

There are several different versions of deliberative restraint:

> *Strong restraint.* Citizens may only invoke, appeal to, and act on public reasons when deliberating about political issues.
>
> *Moderate restraint.* Certain citizens, such as legislators and judges, may only invoke, appeal to, and act on public reasons when deliberating about political issues. Other citizens must appeal to public reasons when deliberating about political issues but may also invoke and act on non-public reasons.
>
> *Weak restraint.* Citizens must appeal to public reasons when deliberating about political issues but may also invoke and act on non-public reasons.

According to *strong restraint*, those engaged in political discussion, deliberation, and advocacy in public political forums must only appeal to public reasons in arguing, campaigning, or justifying particular political claims or views.[4] And, furthermore, individual citizens may only vote for political representatives and public officials on the basis of public reasons.[5]

Why should we accept *strong restraint*? Rawls argues that (i) if we accept it, no one is forced to act for the sake of values or religious, metaphysical, or epistemological doctrines that fundamentally conflict with their own. And, (ii), in virtue of (i) if people in a society embrace and follow strong restraint, this will enable all citizens to achieve their political autonomy by making it the case that citizens can always endorse all the laws of their society. At least in the sense that they can always agree that the reasons discussed, on the basis of which laws and policies were enacted, do favour those laws and policies, even though they might disagree with the weight put on particular reasons that justify particular laws and policies.[6] Other proponents of *strong restraint* make a further argument: they argue that *strong restraint* is trust-building, encourages public-spirited justifications, extends imagination and empathy, and promotes free discussion and debate.[7]

However, these arguments for *strong restraint* do not seem to give us reason to accept it rather than a more lax version of deliberative restraint; it might seem that *weak* and *moderate restraint* have all of these virtues that have been claimed for *strong restraint* to the same extent (Vallier, 2015, pp. 148–149). For instance, it might seem that the requirement that we cite public reasons— even if we may also cite other reasons—encourages public-spirited justifications and extends imagination and empathy just to the same extent as the requirement that only public reasons may be cited.

Furthermore, Kevin Vallier (2015, esp. p. 145) argues that in the absence of a very strong argument for *strong restraint* we should accept a weaker version of deliberative restraint. Rawlsians are keen to argue that they are not advocating for the enforcement of *strong restraint* via legal sanctions (see Freeman, 2007, p. 412). But this does not mean that a requirement to conform with *strong restraint* cannot be enforced by other means. If we should conform with the requirements of *strong restraint*, then these requirements can and should be enforced by the normal mechanisms that moral and other norms are normally enforced by. Namely, via the mechanisms of criticism, disapprobation, blame, praise, guilt, shame, etc, that is, the moral reactive attitudes. Some argue that even if we are not legally prohibited from φ-ing, our liberty to φ can be restricted by the acceptance of a social moral rule that prohibits φ-ing. For if it is a social moral rule that people not φ, then those who φ are subject to moral reactive attitudes for φ-ing. And being subject to moral reactive attitudes if we φ does interfere with our individual liberty to φ because being subject to the reactive attitudes for φ-ing deters us from φ-ing. (For example, men's liberty to wear mascara in public in, for instance, the 1950s was restricted because they would have been shamed and shunned for wearing it see Mill, 1978, p. 63). According to Vallier, Rawls held, and we should accept, a presumption against legal restrictions on our liberty as well as a presumption against restrictions of our liberty due to subjection to reactive attitudes. So, we should prefer versions of deliberative restraint that are less restrictive of citizens' liberty to those that are more restrictive.

Jeffrey Stout (2009, esp. pp. 69–70) provides further reasons to reject Rawlsian strong restraint. He argues that Rawls' requirement of strong restraint entails that slavery abolitionists and Martin Luther King were wrong to utilise religious oratory in public forums as they did to advocate for the abolition of slavery and for civil rights. So, we should reject strong restraint because King and certain abolitionists' speeches are paradigms of public discursive excellence. This argument favours *weak restraint*; as *weak restraint* allows all—including governmental officials—to cite non-public reasons in their argument.

More lax versions of deliberative restraint may also secure benefits that strict restraint cannot secure. Hélène Landemore (2017, pp. 98–103) draws on the mathematical work of Lu Hong and Scott Page (2004) to argue that greater cognitive diversity, and a greater range of perspectives in deliberation, yields epistemic benefits and so is to be welcomed in deliberation because it leads to better problem solving. If this is right, then we can argue that a more lax deliberative restraint that enables citizens to offer non-public reasons in their deliberations, would make greater cognitive diversity, and a greater number of perspectives, presented and represented in deliberations. In which case weak or moderate restraint would seem to make deliberation better in a certain way—which all can accept—than strong restraint. So, there are benefits to accepting weak and moderate restraint rather than strong restraint (see Vallier, 2015, p. 149).

If we really want to secure these epistemic benefits, however, perhaps we should favour the view that citizens need not offer public reasons at all in deliberation. Requiring citizens to offer public as well as non-public reasons when advocating for views may deter some from contributing to the discussion at all because they only have non-public reasons to offer. But if it is significantly beneficial to deliberations that they involve a diversity of moral perspectives, then we should not want to deter people from offering their perspective in this way. There is an analogous non-epistemic rationale here too: requiring all citizens who contribute to public discussions to contribute public reasons may have the effect of excluding some citizens from discussion who cannot think of such public reasons; and it might be that this exclusion affects primarily disadvantaged groups of citizens who might not have been taught how to come up with such public reasons. So, the epistemic (and moral) benefits of having cognitive diversity in deliberation might seem to favour our accepting no deliberative restraint at all.

It might be argued, however, that weak or moderate restraint is a good compromise between strong restraint, which entirely sabotages cognitive diversity in public decision-making, and no restraint. If no principle of restraint were adopted, this would undermine the goals that Rawlsians cite when arguing for strong restraint such as the goal of ensuring that no one is forced to act for the sake of values or religious, metaphysical, or epistemological doctrines that fundamentally conflict with their own; for without some principle of restraint some laws may be enacted that force some people to act for the sake of values that conflict with their own.[8] (And this might undermine Rawlsian PR too, for in this case some laws may be enacted that some reasonable liberal persons cannot accept; see Chapter 9).

10.1.2. EPISTEMOLOGICAL MOTIVATIONS AND PROBLEMS

R. J. Leland and Han van Wietmarschen (2012) make an epistemic rationale for accepting

> *Strong restraint.* Citizens may only invoke, appeal to, and act on public reasons when deliberating about political issues.

Their concern is with establishing what citizens need to accept to accept *strong restraint*. This is important for in order for *strong restraint* to hold, it must be that citizens can internalise and act on it. In order to understand their argument, we have to remember that public reasons are considerations that all reasonable persons accept to be reasons. They argue that a citizen is reasonable (in the relevant political sense) if and only if: (a) they accept central liberal democratic political values and expect all others to do the same; and (b) they believe that even the most epistemically competent reasonable persons disagree with them about their non-public convictions and political views—that is, their political convictions and values that extend beyond those held by all democratic liberals (Leland & van Wietmarschen, 2012, pp. 731–732).

In this case, all reasonable citizens can appeal to liberal political values as reasons, but are prohibited from appealing to non-public values as reasons in deliberation. According to Leland and van Wietmarschen (ibid., p. 733), accepting (b) commits 'reasonable citizens to a strong form of intellectual modesty about their non-public views: they believe that all their non public views are disputed by the most competent people, including people who are equally or more competent than they are themselves'.

They argue that if we accept their view that reasonable persons must accept (a) and (b), then we could be justified in asking people not to invoke their non-public reasons in deliberation. Suppose that Sarah is a pro-lifer. She endorses the view that human life is ensouled at the moment of conception and the intentional killing of ensouled human beings is impermissible. *strong restraint* asks Sarah not to appeal to these views about ensoulment and abortion in deliberation. And this is asking a lot. But we can see why we might be justified in asking Sarah not to invoke these reasons if we accept that persons are reasonable if and only if (a) and (b) hold of them. Suppose that Sarah is reasonable and thereby, *ex hypothesi*, (a) and (b) are true of her. In this case, if Sarah appealed to her views about ensoulment—and so appealed to non-public reasons—in political decision-making, this would show that 'she would be willing to make fundamental political decisions by appeal to a consideration she recognises that the most competent judges disagree about'. And, according to Leland and van Wietmarschen (2012, p. 735) 'such willingness is straightforwardly at odds with the requirement that fundamental political decisions should be justifiable to all reasonable citizens'.

Leland and van Wietmarschen's argument explains how and why a reasonable liberal citizen who is fully convinced of their own controversial moral, religious, and evaluative views might restrain themselves from appealing to all of these views in political deliberation and decision-making. One interesting and important feature of their view is how the claim that reasonable persons must accept (b) rather than close-by alternatives does a lot work. Suppose that instead of their account of a reasonable person we held that a citizen is reasonable (in the relevant political sense) if and only if: (a) they accept central liberal democratic political values and expect all others to do the same; and (b*) they believe that *moderately epistemically competent* reasonable persons disagree with them about their non-public convictions and political views. Leland and van Wietmarschen (2012, p. 737) argue that if (a) and (b*) holds of one, one may well invoke non-public reasons when the political decisions being made are high stakes decisions. For if the decision is high stakes and only (a) and (b*) holds of one, one may well hold that the most epistemically competent others agree with you, and conclude that, given that the matter is high stakes, one should act in line with what the most epistemically competent believe. So, it seems that we have a motivation for *strong restraint* if all democratic liberals should: (i) accept central liberal democratic political values; (ii) expect all others to do the same; and (ii) believe that even the most epistemically competent reasonable persons disagree with them about their non-public convictions and political views.

However, there are problems for this epistemic argument for *strong restraint*. Elsewhere van Wietmarschen (2018) argues that agents who satisfy (a) and (b) either do not have justified non-public moral and political views or are not justified in their belief that people at least as epistemically competent as themselves have non-public moral and political convictions that are in conflict with their own. His argument for this view is quite straightforward. If conciliationism about peer disagreement is true (Chapters 5–6), we cannot justifiably believe that p if we do or should believe that a significant number of our epistemic peers (about whether p) disagree with us about whether p. But if we believe that reasonable persons at all levels of epistemic competence disagree with our non-public moral and political views, then we believe that a significant number of our epistemic peers (regarding these matters) disagree with us about them. In this case, it cannot be that we are simultaneously justified in our non-public moral and political beliefs and in our belief that reasonable persons at all levels of epistemic competence disagree with us about these moral and political matters are . Van Wietmarschen (2018, p. 500) further concludes that in this case no one can coherently maintain these non-public moral and political beliefs and maintain the belief that these beliefs are subject to peer disagreement.[9]

Leland and van Wietmarschen usefully bring out what seem to be the epistemic commitments of citizens who accept *strong restraint*. But, as we've been discussing, these commitments seem problematic. And to the extent that PR accounts require operationalisation via something like *strong restraint*, these epistemic problems are problems for PR accounts too. Can PR accounts be operationalised without citizens accepting *strong restraint*? Perhaps Rawlsian PR cannot be. For Rawlsian PR holds that only laws that can be justified on the basis of public reasons are legitimate. And without *strong restraint* some proposals that do not meet this standard may become laws; and there may be pressure to make proposals that do not meet this standard into laws. However, Gausian PR does not hold that a law is legitimate only if it is or can be justified by public reasons. And so, Gausian PR does not require *strong restraint*.

10.2. DEMOCRACY AND MORAL DISAGREEMENT

Consider to the following principle:

Democratic legitimacy condition. Laws (or certain kinds of laws) are legitimate only if they are agreed to by a majority of those in the jurisdiction where that law applies or are agreed to by their legitimately elected representatives.

This view can either be added to PR or adopted without PR. Moral disagreement plays a key role in arguments that attempt to justify this condition and in arguments against alternatives to this view. In the rest of this chapter we'll discuss this legitimacy requirement and the role that disagreement plays in arguments for it.

Before we discuss these arguments, I'll clarify two features of it. First, what does 'certain kinds of laws' refer to in the *democratic legitimacy condition*? There is debate among proponents of this condition about whether it extends to all laws rather than just almost all laws. Jeremy Waldron (2001), for instance, argues that it applies to all laws. Thomas Christiano (2008, p. 285, pp. 299–300) argues that it does not apply to basic liberal rights and freedoms such as freedom from assault, freedom of speech and freedom of association, as well as laws guaranteeing a basic minimum to all. This is because the democratic legitimacy condition is justified by everyone's interests in having laws that treat all equally and the same justification favours having unconditional guarantees of basic liberal rights and a basic minimum of resources and/or opportunities for welfare.

Second, there is an issue about the relationship between citizens and their representatives. One view is that citizens define the aims of society via general elections. And legislators implement and devise the means to achieve these aims. An alternative to such a representational division of labour is direct democracy, according to which all laws must be agreed to by a majority in order to be legitimate. Proponents of the representational division of labour argue that (a) direct democracy is too difficult to implement for it to be a requirement on a law's legitimacy that it be enacted by a direct democratic process. And that (b) direct democracy would be hijacked by elites who have the time to engage with it; for most people would not have time to vote on every law (see Christiano, 2008, pp. 104–105). In which case direct democracy would in fact represent the views of members of that community worse than representative democracy.

10.2.1. INTRINSIC JUSTIFICATIONS OF DEMOCRACY

Some argue that the democratic legitimacy condition is justified due to features that are intrinsic to democracy: features of what democratic processes necessarily are and necessarily do. Others—instrumentalists—argue that the democratic legitimacy condition is in large part justified instrumentally: it is justified because of the good consequences of democratic decision-making.

Christiano argues that the condition is intrinsically justified and argues against instrumental justifications. Against instrumentalists, he argues that there is too much disagreement in moral principles or values about what consequences are good ones or what justice is for us to justify democracy on the basis that it produces better or more just results than alternatives to democracy.[10] Christiano also makes a positive argument that the legitimacy condition is justified non-instrumentally. He argues that democratic decision-making ensures that all individuals are treated as equals, and this is how all people deserve to be treated; anyone not given a vote or a say via a representative would be treated as less than an equal. There are many political arrangements that treat individuals as equals in particular ways: egalitarian distributions of resources treat everyone as equals by giving them equal amounts of things. But Christiano argues that given facts about moral disagreement, democracy is the best that can be done to make sure that society advances the interests of each equally. This is because there is too much moral disagreement about all supposed further criteria a society must meet in order to treat all its citizens as equals. For instance, one suggestion is that a society treats its citizens as equals if it gives each of them an equal amount of resources. But there is moral disagreement about whether it is just to give people these things and whether doing so treats others (whom resources are redistributed from) as equals: libertarians, utilitarians, some egalitarians and classical liberals argue that it is not just to do this; and that doing so is not a good way of treating people as equals (Christiano, 2008, p. 96). So, we cannot hold that a society is legitimate only if it gives an equal amount of resources (or equal opportunity for such equal resources) to all.

This argument of Christiano's can seem particularly plausible if thought about in the context of public reason's requirement on legitimacy discussed in the previous chapter. According to this requirement, a law is legitimate only if it can be justified to all assuming their current moral and evaluative views. Suppose that democratic decision-making procedures can be justified to all and other decision-making procedures cannot. In this case, it will seem plausible that even if a particular law can be justified to all in principle, if it has not been enacted by a democratic decision-making procedure, then the law's enactment at this time is not justifiable to all. If we think of Christiano's idea in this way, then his claim is not that, necessarily, laws that treat people as equals that go beyond democratic decision-making cannot be justified to all. It's just that if they are not enacted in a democratic way, then they cannot be justified to all.

However, it does not seem that Christiano's intrinsic justification of the democratic legitimacy requirement succeeds. If we just consider the intrinsic features of democracy alone, then democracy is not the only way of treating everyone as equals to which we can all agree. A random lottery in which each individual is given an equal shot at being one of 50 people who form the government treats everyone equally. And such a process doesn't involve a substantial and controversial view about what it is to treat people equally or justly, and so can be accepted by all (see Estlund, 2009, p. 6).[11]

Democracy may seem to necessarily provide all citizens with an equal chance to influence politics. For everyone has a chance to take an active role in democratic politics, argue for their preferred views, or attempt to become a democratic representative. A random lottery does not have this intrinsic feature that democracy has. However, alternative systems to democracy can provide similarly equal opportunities to influence politics. For instance, a system in which laws are chosen by throwing darts at a board where all the laws are difficult to hit with a dart—but can be hit by those who have cultivated their dart throwing skills—gives citizens an equal chance to influence policy choice. Since everyone has the opportunity to cultivate their dart-throwing skills just as everyone has the opportunity to cultivate their skills at exerting political influence.[12]

Christiano (2008, p. 110) holds that citizens have an interest in engaging in the egalitarian deliberation and negotiation that happens in ordinary democratic procedures. But both the dartboard and random lottery alternatives do not ensure that such deliberation and negotiation will take place prior to lawmaking. However, requirements of deliberation and negotiation could be added to the random lottery and dartboard proposals without making these processes into democratic processes. For instance, deliberation and negotiation could be required among those who win the lottery or could be built into the process of ratifying policies chosen by the best dart-throwers. Yet it seems that choosing policies by political argument is better than choosing policies by throwing darts. But better how? What we really seem to think is that this process is better because it leads to better results, better political policies. But to accept this view is to abandon an intrinsic justification of democracy and instead accept an instrumental justification.

10.2.2. INSTRUMENTAL JUSTIFICATIONS OF THE DEMOCRACY

David Estlund (2009) proposes just such an instrumental justification. Estlund models his instrumental justification of democracy on the instrumental justification of trial by jury. Jury trials seem to have legitimacy. If someone was convicted of a crime by a jury—and they have exhausted their appeals—it seems that we are justified in holding that they committed that crime (and treating them as if they did). Relatedly, it can seem that if someone was exonerated of a crime by an aptly chosen jury, then others have a moral duty not to punish them for that crime. But the jury trial would not have this justificatory significance and moral standing if it were not for its epistemic features: the evidence uncovered, discussed, and ensured to pass certain standards for admissibility; the testimony of witnesses and experts; cross-examination of those testifying; the adversarial equality ensured to defendant and prosecution; and the collective deliberation by the jury. These features of the jury trial make it more likely to convict people only if they are guilty and less likely to set criminals free. And these features of the jury trial convey legitimacy on decisions produced by juries even when they are incorrect. We disagree about what the best decisions are (in politics and in jury trials). And, accordingly, we disagree about who, if they were empowered to make binding decisions, would make the best decisions. But we can all agree that a jury trial on the whole produces better decisions than alternatives in virtue of its epistemic features, which allow it to get at the truth more often than many alternative procedures (Estlund, 2009, pp. 6–7).

Similarly, Estlund argues, democratic decision-making has epistemic features that make it to some degree a reliable means of coming to correct verdicts about justice and what we ought to do. These features don't make democracy more reliable than all possible alternatives. Suppose that Rawlsians are right about what justice requires. In this case their beliefs about justice are more reliable than others and the epistemically best procedure would be to let Rawlsians make decisions about our society. But there is enough reasonable moral disagreement about whether Rawlsians are right about what justice requires and so whether they make the best decisions about justice to make the procedure of letting the Rawlsians make political decisions illegitimate. The fact that there is reasonable disagreement about the rightness of a Rawlsian account of justice establishes that a law empowering Rawlsians to make laws based just on their own views would not pass public reason's legitimacy condition on laws discussed in the previous chapter. And Estlund (2009, esp. p. 168) argues that a democratic decision-making procedure has epistemic features that make it more reliable than any alternative other than those that will fail to pass the legitimacy requirements of public reason.

What are these epistemic features of a democratic decision-making process? Estlund first asks us to consider a hypothetical ideal democratic deliberation procedure. In this procedure, decisions about whether to adopt a policy or law are made by majority vote after discussion in a forum in which everyone deliberates about the virtues and vices of these laws and policies. In this ideal process, everyone has full and equal access to the deliberative forum. Everyone has the same chance to speak as everyone else. People only say things that they believe will help others to appreciate reasons to hold one view or another. All those whose interests are at stake are either present or a have an effective spokesperson. Everyone has as much time to speak as they wish. Everyone has equal bargaining power. Everyone equally credits and attends to the contributions of all others. Everyone recognises or tends to recognise a good reason when they see one. Participants consider devils advocate positions. And participants vote at least partly for principled reasons (see Estlund, 2009, pp. 175–176). This ideal hypothetical democratic procedure has epistemic features that we can all agree would lead it to make just and desirable decisions more often than a random procedure and more often than the random lottery and dartboard procedures discussed in §10.2.1. How can we know this? Well, all reasonable persons can agree that there are a set of harms and injustices such as war, famine, economic collapse, political collapse, epidemic, and genocide. These are things that all reasonable people want to avoid in their own country (and in others too; ibid., pp. 163–164). This ideal procedure would be better at making decisions that avoid these harms and injustices than a random procedure because all reasonable persons want to avoid these things and this process enables individuals to collectively pool their knowledge and understanding and galvanise together to ensure that these things are avoided.

Estlund claims that if this ideal democratic procedure is more reliable than a random procedure at coming to decisions that enable a society to avoid these harms and injustices, then this is reason to believe that our real world democratic processes will be better than alternative law-making procedures at coming to decisions that avoid these things. However, it is unclear that real world democratic procedures are close enough to the ideal to produce the epistemic benefits that Estlund claims they can produce. For voters are subject to a variety of biases such as self-serving biases, and biases to favour the views of people they perceive to be more attractive. And in real world democracies people do not have equal bargaining power and do not give equal credit to the contributions of all participants. It is also unclear that voters tend to recognise good reasons when they see them rather than tending to recognising good reasons given by people whom they believe to be on their side and recognising good reasons for policies and proposals that they are already attracted to or are in favour of.[13] In this case, it seems that Estlund's argument only establishes that the democratic legitimacy requirement *would hold* if we were not inevitably subject to biases and if we voted on the basis of good reasons.[14]

Hélène Landemore (2017) argues that democracy has epistemic benefits on the basis of Hong and Page's (2004) theorem. According to this theorem, under the right conditions group cognitive diversity can be more important to a group's effectiveness at solving problems than the group's overall ability level. Landemore argues that Hong and Page's theorem shows that there are epistemic benefits to having a democratic decision-making procedure. One problem that some have raised with this claim is that Hong and Page's theorem doesn't show that it's better to have *all* adult citizens participate in the decision-making process but only that it's better to have more citizens participate in the decision-making process to generate greater cognitive diversity: the theorem does not hold that maximal cognitive diversity is better than some degree of cognitive diversity (see Brennan, 2017, p. 184). So, this justi-fication for democracy doesn't show that a democratic decision-making pro-cess involving all citizens (in some way) is better than one involving a large diverse group of citizens.

However, even if these objections to Landemore's argument are on the mark, her argument might still allow us to argue that the democratic legiti-macy requirement holds on the basis of a combination of the instrumental and intrinsic features of democracy. Remember that the problem with Chris-tiano's intrinsic justification of democracy was that it did not show that laws must be enacted via democratic processes rather than via a lottery or dart throwing process in order to be legitimate. But, assuming that Hong and Page's theorem is right, making decisions in a way that harnesses all the per-spectives of a diverse group is better than making decisions via a random procedure. And making decisions in this way is also better than making decisions via a process that empowers individuals who happen to have culti-vated their skills at picking policies via dart-throw. In this case we can argue: democracy can be agreed by all to be appropriately egalitarian unlike all other political decision procedures except the random lottery and dart throwing decision-procedures discussed in §10.1.1. But it's also epistemically better than the random lottery and dart throwing procedures. And this combination of features that democracy has makes it the case that laws are legitimate only if they are the result of a democratic process.

10.2.3. EPISTOCRACY AND DELIBERATIVE DEMOCRACY

The view that the democratic legitimacy requirement holds at least in part because of the instrumental benefits of democracy opens up the possibility that alternatives to democracy will produce better, more just, and/or more egalitarian outcomes than democracy. But does moral disagreement under-mine the legitimacy of all such alternatives, as Christiano argues?

Epistocracy is rule by the few rather than by everyone. Jason Brennan (2017) argues that some form of epistocracy will lead to better results than democracy. His main argument for this view is that a wealth of empirical research shows that voters lack a stunning amount of political knowledge and that the mean level of political knowledge among voters is extremely low. Brennan details many ways in which voters are ignorant and incompetent in the US. For example, most citizens can't identify the congressional candidates in their district, citizens generally don't know which party controls congress, and most Americans don't know even roughly how much is spent on social security. MostAmericans also lack relevant historical knowledge. For instance, only 40% of Americans know who the US fought in World War II. In general, voters are ignorant of how much is spent on what, what in fact is happening in their country (e.g. how many immigrants there are), and what the economic and social consequences of various policies are. These facts about policies, and the relevant social science and economics, are extremely important when assessing policies regarding trade, immigration, and employment. And knowing these things about these policies is extremely relevant for considering which party, president, or member of parliament or congress to vote for. Furthermore, highly informed citizens have very different policy preferences from less informed citizens. So, this knowledge does seem to make a difference to the policy preferences that we have. In this case many, perhaps most, voters have no idea what they are voting for or which policies are good ones. So, according to Brennan, democracy puts us at serious risk of enacting bad and unjust policies because of the (completely understandable) ignorance of average voters (Brennan, 2017, ch. 2).

Brennan argues on this basis that some form of epistocracy would produce better results than democracy. There are several forms that epistocracy could take: citizens could acquire the right to vote and run for office only if deemed sufficiently well-informed; or those citizens deemed better informed could have additional votes. An epistocracy can maintain many of the institutions, decision-making processes, procedures, and rules that are found in the best and most esteemed democracies such as parliaments, contested elections, free political speech open to all, and the existence of a variety of deliberative decision-making fora (Brennan, 2017, p. 208).

There are two natural concerns about epistocracy. First, many argue that epistocracy communicates the judgment that some citizens are worth less than others and doesn't communicate a commitment to equality. But holding that some are better informed than others regarding social science, economics, the policies we currently have, and how much particular policy options would cost only involves holding that some citizens are worth less than others to just the same extent that holding that expert plumbers are better at plumbing than those of us who are not expert plumbers involves holding that some citizens are worth less than others: that is not at all. Holding that some are expert plumbers and others are not involves holding that some have a particular type of knowledge and skill that others do not. And, analogously, holding that some have politically relevant knowledge that others lack involves holding no more than this: that some have a particular type of knowledge and skill that others do not; those others may well have valuable knowledge and skills that those with politically relevant knowledge lack. Furthermore, societies can express their commitment to equality in a variety of different ways that don't exclude epistocracy such as by educating all their citizens about equality and/or by having public egalitarian motifs and statues (as well as by having other egalitarian policies!).[15] So, epistocratic societies can still express a commitment to the equal status of their citizens without giving all equal voting rights.

A second concern is that disenfranchising voters who pass competency tests for social science and economics would have the effect of disproportionately advantaging already advantaged groups and disadvantaging already advantaged groups (especially given that the competency tests would presumably be written and administered by those who are already privileged). Or that, at any rate, it would result in a homogeneous electorate of only those who have had a particular kind of education.

However, certain forms of epistocracy do not have this consequence. For instance, consider an enfranchisement lottery. This lottery has two stages. First, everyone other than a random representative sample of the population is disenfranchised. Those in the random representative sample are not automatically given the vote however. Instead, these pre-voters are assumed insufficiently competent to vote prior to engaging in a competence building process in small groups designed to optimise their knowledge of the issues that they are going to vote on. This process could take different forms. For instance, it could involve small group deliberation, information sessions, opportunities to ask questions of the relevant experts and to be led through the relevant literature in a relatively neutral way. Those pre-voters who engaged in the competence-building process would then be eligible to vote.[16] This enfranchisement lottery is a form of epistocracy because it involves rule by the few and does not enfranchise all. However, it overcomes the problem of disenfranchising minority groups. Since its random representative sample ensures that these groups have the chance to vote (proportionate to their size—or the view could be altered to ensure that certain - e.g. traditionally marginalized - groups have a greater chance to vote than that warranted by their size).

The case for epistocracy faces a problem with moral disagreement. Even if it's right that many potential voters are ill-informed about empirical issues relevant to policy matters, many matters relevant to law- and political-policy-making are not empirical matters but rather matters of moral principles and values. For instance, libertarians, classical liberals, socialists, and Rawlsians disagree in moral principles and values and not just about issues of economic policy; and many democrats and republicans and labour and conservative voters disagree about these matters too (see §1). For instance, some believe that we shouldn't redistribute (a great amount) from the rich to the poor even if doing so would in fact be (slightly) better for the economy; and, vice versa, some believe that we should even if it would have (slightly) worse economic consequences. Similarly, some voters believe that we should not allow as many immigrants into our country as we currently do even if immigration in fact has very beneficial economic consequences. But it doesn't seem that we have grounds that all can reasonably accept to claim that any of us are badly informed about moral principles or values (as we discussed in Chapter 6 and §2.3.2).[17] It might be that we cannot justifiably judge that those with whom we disagree about moral issues very broadly and deeply are our epistemic peers about moral issues (see §6.2). But those with whom we disagree so broadly and deeply similarly will not be able to reasonably believe that we are their epistemic peers about moral issues. So, we cannot justify the claim that we are more informed than them about the relevant moral principles or values to them and neither can they justify the claim that they are more informed to us. And the moral principles and values relevant to redistribution and immigration as well as a host of other moral issues are pertinent to the policy and governmental preferences that we have and that we think are right and just. Shouldn't everyone have a say about what the right moral principles or values are given that we have no grounds to say that any individual is worse informed about what the right moral principles and values are than others? (Or at least no grounds on the basis of which we can justify our claim to higher competence to those whom we claim have less competence).

However, the enfranchisement lottery discussed a few paragraphs ago is one way of avoiding the disagreement problem for epistocracy. Since in that scenario everyone has an equal chance of becoming a voter and so no one's moral views are treated as superior to others. Some proponents of epistocracy are not particularly supportive of the enfranchisement lottery form of epistocracy (see Brennan, 2017, ch. 8). Part of the reason for this is that this view is one that deliberative democrats are attracted to: the enfranchisement lottery procedure is both an epistocratic procedure and a deliberative demo-cratic procedure. For it attempts to build the competence of a random selec-tion of citizens via deliberative competence building mechanisms. According to deliberative democrats, deliberation builds the competence of those involved and yields better decisions than decisions made by non-deliberative procedures. But some proponents of epistocracy are sceptical of the idea that engagement in group deliberation about an issue can really lead people to become better informed about that issue.

However, there is good reason to believe that engagement and deliberation about an issue can lead us to become better informed about it. In James Fishkin's deliberative polls a random representative sample of a particular population come together to deliberate about a particular policy issue. For instance, in the first deliberative poll a representative sample of UK partici-pants deliberated about whether the best response to crime is to put more people in jail and to build more prisons. Prior to the poll, participants are given information about the issue, rigorously vetted to ensure neutrality. Par-ticipants deliberate with one another in small groups about the issue in ques-tion for one or two days. And participants have a chance to ask questions of those with expertise on the topic. Participants are anonymously polled about their views on the issue both before and after the deliberation (Fishkin, 2011). Fishkin presents a wealth of empirical evidence for the view that participants in his deliberative polls are more informed post-deliberation. There have been a lot of deliberative polls and so there is a lot of data. But to take one example, in a deliberative poll about Northern Ireland's education system, only 22% of participants answered the information questions presented in the poll correctly in the pre-poll, whereas 50% answered them correctly after deliberation. And in the first deliberative poll on crime in the UK in 1994 there was a statistically significant gain in information between the pre-deliberation and post-deliberation polls. For some questions the knowledge gains were very significant. For instance, 80% of people knew which country had the highest rate of imprisonment in Western Europe after the deliberation, only 50% knew this beforehand (ibid., pp. 8, 134, 140).[18]

The epistocratic/deliberative democratic procedure of the enfranchisement lottery treats everyone as equals and may well have greater epistemic benefits than those of democracy. Given that in order to justify democracy it seems that we need to make reference to the beneficial consequences that democracy generates, it may be that certain forms of epistocracy and democracy can both be justified.[19] In which case laws can be legitimate even if they are not democratically enacted. However, other forms of epistocracy do not seem to be plausible competitors to democracy because we cannot justify the view that some are epistemically better equipped regarding moral principles and values than others.

SUMMARY

Proponents of public reason often argue that we should exercise restraint in public political deliberations and only invoke and act on reasons for decisions that all agree to be reasons. There are problems with such a strong principle of restraint. Weaker principles that do not require all to only cite such reasons, or that allow us to cite other reasons as well that all do not agree to be reasons, face fewer problems. But the stronger principles of restraint may be necessary for the stable implementation of Rawlsian public reason. Moral disagreement plays an important role in arguments about what justifies democracy and is important for assessing alternatives to democracy such as epistocracy. However, because democracy must be partially instrumentally justified this opens up the possibility than other alternatives may be justified at least as well as democracy. And some forms of epistocratic/deliberative democratic hybrids may be as well justified as democracy.

FURTHER READING

The essays in Estlund (2001a) are a good next step regarding debates about the value and justification of democracy. Landemore (2017) is a book length argument for the epistemic value of deliberation. And Estlund and Landemore (2018) is a shorter accessible article on the topic that is also state of the art. Gutmann and Thomson (1998) and Fishkin (2011) are substantive but also accessible and informative introductions to the theoretical and practical issues surrounding deliberation and its (democratic) benefits. The articles in

Bächtiger et al (2018) dig a lot deeper into a vast range of empirical and theoretical issues surrounding deliberative democracy. For a book-length discussion of political legitimacy including a discussion of democracy, epistemic arguments for democracy, and public reason see Peter (2007). Freeman (2007, ch. 9) is a good introduction to Rawlsian public reason's idea of deliberative restraint. Vallier (2015) offers a thorough and useful counter-point from a perspective more in line with Gausian public reason. Enoch (2017) is perhaps the most sustained evaluation of the epistemic commitments of public reason. The topic of political legitimacy might make a reader wonder about the relationship between disagreement and toleration; McKinnon (2007) is a book-length introduction to this topic.

NOTES

1   See Rawls (1996, p. liv, n. 28), who conceives of public reason as both (i) and (ii).
2   See Freeman (2007, p. 388) and Rawls (1996, p. 139).
3   For an opposing view see Gaus and Vallier (2009).
4   See Rawls (1996, pp. 215–216) (1999, p. 575).
5   See Freeman (2007, p. 386). Most proponents of *strong restraint* follow Rawls (1996, p. 214, p. 227) in holding that it should apply only to deliberations and voting about 'constitutional essentials and matters of basic justice' rather than to all public political matters, policies, and laws, and all discussions of these. Quong (2011, ch. 9), however, holds that it should apply to a more capacious set of deliberations.
6   See Freeman (2007, pp. 400–401).
7   See, for instance, Freeman (2000 p. 383), Goodin (2008, p. 263), Fearon (1998, p. 55); and see Vallier (2015, p. 148) for discussion.
8   Deliberative restraint has often been associated with the view that only rational arguments can be made in public political forums. However, principles of deliberative restraint can and should be understood so that they do not entail that giving a public reason in a public forum must take the form of giving a rational argument rather than reporting a personal experience, telling a story, or utilising rhetoric. See, for instance, Polletta and Gardner (2017, pp. 72–76).
9   For discussion of whether it is really true that we cannot maintain our practical commitments (rather than our beliefs) in light of peer disagreement see Barnett (2019b), Rowland and Simpson (2021), and Rowland (2020a).
10 See Christiano (2008, p. 102) and Estlund (2001b, p. 6).
11 For Christiano's response to this line of argument see Christiano (2008, pp. 108–111).
12 See Estlund (2009, pp. 95–96).
13 For a recent useful summary—and discussion of some of the philosophical upshots—of the empirical literature on these topics see McKenna (2019).
14 Estlund (2009) claims that since it is possible that individuals could behave and vote partially on principle and in a way that avoids these biases, they should. And so the democratic legitimacy requirement holds. But if a decision-making procedure would be better than alternatives if everyone acted as they should, this doesn't establish that this decision-making procedure is legitimate on those grounds when we know that people will not act as they should. See also Brennan (2017, esp. ch. 1–2).
15 See Brennan (2017, pp. 118, 121).
16 This is López-Guerra's (2014, ch. 1–2) idea, discussed in Brennan (2017, pp. 214–215).
17 See McGrath (2008). Moral philosophers might know more about how to link very different moral cases and principles together, but it is far from clear that they are better informed about

the moral principles and values relevant to, for instance, whether we should favour more redistribution than less (for its own sake). See also McGrath (2011) and §2.3.2.

18   For a less sympathetic account of the empirical data regarding deliberative fora see Mendelberg (2002). For state-of-the-art data and discussion see Bächtiger et al. (2018).

19   There may be other problems with epistocracy; I've just been discussing whether moral disagreement justifies the democratic legitimacy condition, not trying to defend the view that we should only accept a tempered version of this condition.

PART IV

METAETHICS AND DISAGREEMENT'S NORMATIVE IMPLICATIONS

11

METAETHICS AND THE NORMATIVE IMPLICATIONS OF MORAL DISAGREEMENT

In the last two parts of the book we've seen that moral disagreement has epistemic and practically normative implications. We saw that moral disagreement makes a difference to what kind of political decision-making procedures and laws are legitimate. We saw that moral disagreement can imply that we should give (more) money to charity, not eat animal products, and pursue moral compromises. And we saw that moral disagreement can impact on what we may reasonably believe, especially about controversial moral issues where it may often imply that we should suspend our moral beliefs. In this chapter we'll discuss whether these practical and epistemological implications of moral disagreements should lead us to further question the objectivity of morality. We will investigate whether the normative upshot of moral disagreement has implications for metaethics.

In §11.2–3 we'll discuss how the normative implications of a lack of moral convergence may yield metaethical consequences. In §11.4 we will discuss how some have argued that the epistemic consequences of moral disagreement are relevant to assessing whether evolutionary debunking arguments that purport to undermine objectivist views in metaethics succeed. But, first we will look at metaethical arguments based on faultless moral disagreement and (reasonable) moral intransigence—and how these arguments link up to work on the normative implications of moral disagreement.

DOI: 10.4324/9780429491375-15

11.1 FAULTLESS DISAGREEMENT AND MORAL INTRANSIGENCE

In Chapter 3 we discussed the following view:

> *Framework relativism.* The moral judgments that we make are all standard-relative. No one judges that an action is right or wrong *tout court* only that it is right relative to a particular moral standard or framework.

On this view, Christians who judge that polyamory is wrong just judge that it is wrong-relative to the moral standards of Christianity rather than wrong more generally, and utilitarians who judge that polyamory is permissible only judge that it is permissible-relative-to-utilitarianism. Once we understand the correct semantic theory for judgments about right and wrong we see that what it is to make a judgment that an action is right or wrong is to rank it according to a particular standard or framework, and we cannot make moral judgments that are not relativised to any such standards or frameworks. We also discussed:

> *Truth relativism.* Whether our moral claims are true or false is determined by the particular moral standards that we hold.

If we accept this view, then Kantians are correct that it is wrong to push the heavy man off of the footbridge in the footbridge trolley case. What makes their claims correct is that their claims are made true or false by the Kantian moral standards that they hold. But act-utilitarians are also correct that it is right to push the heavy man because their judgments are made true/false by the act-utilitarian standards they hold and it is true-relative to act-utilitarianism that it is right to push the heavy man off of the bridge. As we discussed in Chapter 3, we can be truth relativists without being framework relativists: for framework relativism involves a claim about our moral *judgments* that truth relativism does not involve (that our moral judgments are always standard-relative). Objectivists deny both forms of relativism, I'll refer to objectivists who deny these claims as objectivist non-relativists for the time being.

11.1.1. FAULTLESS DISAGREEMENT

Some argue that we should accept relativism because otherwise we will be forced to hold that there are no faultless moral disagreements.[1] A disagreement between A and B is faultless when A and B disagree but neither make a mistake or are at fault. Suppose that I judge that everyone should give 10% of their income to charity but you judge that everyone should give 11%. In this case we disagree and if realism holds and there is an objective fact of the matter about how much we ought to give to charity, only one of us can be right. But it might seem that neither of us is at fault for holding the views that we hold.

Both forms of relativism seem able to explain this. If framework relativism holds, then my judgment is relative to my standards, and your judgment is relative to your standards. There is no fault here, we are just employing different standard-relative moral judgments. And what's right according to these standards differs: according to my standard we each owe 10%; according to yours we each owe 11%. Truth relativism can similarly hold that there's no fault here. For even if we are not making relativised moral judgments, the truth of our moral claims are determined by our differing moral standards, so my claim that we ought to give 10% is correct and your claim that we ought to give 11% is correct too. But if there is a standard-independent objective fact of the matter about who's belief is correct, our judgments and claims are about this objective matter, and whether our claims are true is determined by the objective standard-independent truth about how much we ought to give, then it seems impossible for neither of us to be at fault. Suppose that I judge that everyone should give 10% but that I am mistaken and everyone should give 11%. In this case I make a mistake and my beliefs would be better if I believed the truth. But if this is right, then our disagreement is not faultless: I am at fault for having the moral belief that I have.[2] So, if there are faultless moral disagreements like this one, this would seem to favour relativism.

Assuming that we share these intuitions that this disagreement is faultless, whether this argument counts in favour of relativism really depends on how we should understand faultless disagreements. Max Kölbel (2004), author of a seminal paper on faultless disagreement as a general phenomenon, gives several different characterisations of a faultless disagreement, namely:

i A disagreement is faultless if neither of the parties (who have inconsistent beliefs) has made a mistake;
ii A disagreement is faultless if both of the parties have exactly the views they ought to have and neither party would improve their beliefs by adopting new ones;
iii A disagreement is faultless if neither party is in error and further investigation by either party is not called for;
iv A disagreement is faultless if each party is blameless for having their differing beliefs.

Now whether objectivist-non-relativism implies (or can fit with the view) that disagreements like the one that we've been discussing about how much we should give are faultless in the sense of (ii) depends on what we mean by an improvement. If my evidence favours the conclusion that we ought to tax the rich more to help the poor and your evidence favours the conclusion that we ought not, then even if objectively we ought not tax the rich more, in a sense my view would not be improved if I came to believe that we ought not tax the rich more. Since my evidence favours the view that we ought to tax the rich more. (Similarly, in a sense of (i) I have not made a mistake for I have the view that my evidence favours.)

Similarly, whether disagreements like the one we've been discussing about much we should give are faultless in the sense of (iii) depends on how we should respond to disagreements and further details about the case. If conciliationism about peer disagreement is true (Chapters 5–6) and we should regard one another as peers, then perhaps we should suspend belief about whether we ought to give 10% or 11% of our income to charity. But perhaps those whom you and I, in this case, should judge to be our epistemic peers are slightly different such that what we should do after taking all peer disagreement into account is slightly different in this way: I should judge that we ought to give 10%; you should judge that we ought to give 11%. Or perhaps we should not regard each other as epistemic peers in this case. In either case, neither of us are in error because we have different evidence, and given that only one person disagrees with us—and do not disagree a great deal—perhaps we are not required to investigate further. And if this is right, we are blameless for having different beliefs and so are faultless in the sense of (iv) too. So, objectivist non-relativism may seem consistent with there being faultless disagreements however we understand such disagreement's faultlessness.

This response to the argument from faultless disagreement seems to generalise to other cases. Suppose that Alyssa has been raised in a meat-eating family and culture and Brie has been raised in a vegetarian family and culture. Alyssa judges that eating meat is permissible and Brie judges that it's not. Some claim that this disagreement is or may be faultless (see Hills, 2013, p. 413). I struggle to share this intuition. But even if this disagreement is faultless, at least part of the response that I've been making to the faultless disagreement argument is generalisable to moral disagreements like this one. Non-relativists can plausibly hold that we can have quite different evidence regarding many moral issues: different intuitions, different non-moral information and testimony, access and understanding of different arguments. In this case, because we can have different evidence (and ethics is hard) two people—like Alyssa and Brie—can (a) have inconsistent but reasonable moral judgments, (b) be blameless with regards to their different judgments, and (c) have assessed the evidence in a reasonable way (not erroneously or mistakenly). Suppose that Brie is objectively right and Alyssa is objectively mistaken. Even in this case, Alyssa's adopting Brie's judgment wouldn't constitute an improvement or be a better response to her evidence. So, it is plausible that in a wide range of cases non-relativists can hold that there are faultless disagreements in the sense of (iv) and in an interpretation of the sense of (i), (ii), and (iii). Perhaps the phenomenon of faultless disagreement does favour relativism. But it seems that there are somewhat reasonable responses that non-relativists can make to this argument.

11.1.2. REASONABLE MORAL INTRANSIGENCE

Mark Kalderon makes a somewhat related argument from moral disagreement to non-cognitivism. Remember that according to non-cognitivism, moral judgments are desire-like states rather than belief-like states: to judge that stealing is wrong is to disapprove of it in a particular way or to adopt a certain kind of plan to not steal, see Chapter 3.

Kalderon (2005, p. 9, p. 15, p. 21) makes the following two claims:

(A)   Suppose that A believes that p. A doesn't know anyone else's view about whether p. Then A comes to know that B believes that not-p. A knows that B has the same evidence as her, believes that there is perfect epistemic symmetry between her and B, and believes that B is otherwise rational and reasonable. In this case, if A and B's disagreement is a cognitive one, that is one in which they have different beliefs, A has reason to re-examine her grounds for accepting p.

(B)   If the disagreement between A and B is a disagreement in moral principles or values it is reasonable for A to have no motivation at all to re-examine her grounds for accepting p.

A claim along the lines of (A) will follow from conciliationism about peer disagreement, which we discussed and found to be a plausible view in Chapter 5. Kalderon gives some examples to support (B). He supposes that Edgar and Bernice disagree about the morality of abortion. They take one another to be otherwise rational, reasonable, well-informed individuals who share evidence and hold coherent views about the morality of abortion. Edgar holds that abortion is morally permissible but Bernice believes that it is wrong. It makes sense to imagine that Edgar unflinchingly insists on his liberal view of abortion even after realising that Bernice disagrees with him—and even if she is the first person he has realised to be his epistemic peer on this issue. And according to Kalderon,

> nor is Edgar alone in this. I suspect that we too would be unmoved by such a disagreement. Our own persistence in liberal morality would be unflinching as well. We too would be intransigent in the sense of lacking a motivation to inquire further into the grounds of moral acceptance. In normal circumstances, we are under no obligation to re-examine the foundations of moral claims that we accept as unproblematic even if they are disputed by otherwise rational and reasonable, informed, and interested people who coherently accept reasons that, if genuine, would undermine them.
>
> (Kalderon, 2005, p. 35)

(A) and (B) seem to imply that moral judgments are not belief-like mental states but are rather non-cognitive desire-like mental states. The idea here is that we ought to further investigate the content of our judgment when we find ourselves in a peer disagreement about its content and our judgment is a cognitive, belief-like judgment about objective facts in the world. But this is not the case for disagreements in moral principles or values. So, moral judgments are not beliefs.

There are at least two ways of responding to this argument. One is to deny (A) by holding that we should accept a steadfast view rather than con-ciliationism.[3] However, this view does face the problems that we discussed in Chapter 5. Perhaps the most popular response to Kalderon's argument is simply to deny his intuitions about cases such as the Edgar and Bernice case. Many moral philosophers including Henry Sidgwick (1981, p. 342) and Derek Parfit (2011b) have argued that we precisely should investigate further in light of such disagreements with our epistemic equals. And as we discussed in Chapters 5–6, the view that we should further investigate and conciliate in response to disagreements in moral principles and values is a plausible one. Matthew Kramer (2009, p. 186) takes up this kind of response to Kalderon. He claims that although the intransigence demonstrated by people like Edgar is tiresomely familiar, this does not make such intransigent behaviour reasonable or rational.

11.1.3. INTELLIGIBLE MORAL INTRANSIGENCE

Kramer's response to Kalderon involves the claim that such intransigence, although not reasonable, is completely intelligible since we see it so frequently. Such intransigence in light of peer disagreement about moral issues does seem intelligible even if it is not reasonable. Consider the following case:

> *Anti-torture advocate.* Anna is a moral philosopher who also spends a lot of time doing humanitarian work for torture victims and engaging in anti-torture advocacy. She has a strong conviction that it is always wrong to torture. But Anna comes to believe that at least half of those who have spent their lives open-mindedly con-sidering, thinking about, and writing arguments about the moral status of torture, and whose moral capacities, sensitivity, and reasoning skills she respects, judge that there are some circumstances in which torture is morally permissible. So, Anna finds herself with a conviction about the moral status of torture that she knows is at odds with the beliefs of half of those whom she believes to be her epistemic peers about the moral status of torture.

It seems intelligible for Anna to maintain her judgment that torture is always wrong while also carrying on judging that half of those whose moral reason-ing capacities she respects and who have spent their lives thinking about the moral status of torture are her epistemic peers about the moral status of torture. It would not be that surprising if she didn't change her strong anti-torture judgment even if she acknowledged that many of her epistemic peers about this issue disagree with her.

However, elsewhere I've argued that if such moral intransigence is intelligible, then this supports non-cognitivism (Rowland, 2018). This is because if it's intelligible for our moral judgments to be entirely intransigent in light of perceived peer disagreement, then there is a good *prima facie* case that moral judgments are not beliefs. To see this, consider the following principle:

> *Beliefs track perceived evidence.* If one gains what one believes to be new evidence that bears on whether *p*, and one's judgment regarding *p* (whether *p*) is a belief, then either (i) one adjusts one's judgment regarding *p* in light of and in line with this evidence or (ii) one adjusts one's judgment that what one gained was in fact evidence bearing on whether *p*.

Tamar Gendler argues that this claim fits well with and explains our intuitions about cases such as the following:

> I used to believe that stomach ulcers were caused primarily by stress and diet; but when Warren and Marshall's research on the *Helciobacter pylori* bacterium became widely known, I revised my belief to reflect this information. Williamson's 'N.N.'—'who has not yet heard the news from the theatre where Lincoln has just been assassinated'—believes that Lincoln is President; but as soon as he learns that Lincoln has been shot, he will make the corresponding adjustment in his belief.
>
> (Gendler, 2008, pp. 565–566)

And the view that *beliefs track perceived evidence* is also entailed by the widely held view that beliefs are necessarily transparent to the truth, that is, that 'the deliberative question whether to believe that *p* inevitably gives way to the factual question whether *p*'.[4] According to this view, (a) if we believe that *p*, this just means that we see *p* as being true, and (b) we cannot but form beliefs that correspond to the evidence that we think we have.

It's widely agreed that when one comes to believe that a significant number of others one believes to be one's epistemic peers regarding *p* disagree with one regarding *p*, one comes to believe that there is (strong) evidence against one's view regarding *p* that one did not previously have. To believe that half of those who are as likely to be right about a (cognitive) matter as you are disagree with you about it just is to believe that you have strong evidence that you made in your reasoning (or assessment of the evidence) regarding this matter. This evidence is higher-order evidence, that is, it is evidence that one has made an error in one's understanding or interpretation of the evidence regarding *p* or one's reasoning regarding whether *p* more generally. But such higher-order evidence regarding one's belief that *p* is still evidence regarding whether *p*. For such evidence regarding one's reasoning about *p* affects how you see your evidence regarding whether *p*; it can, and should, lead you to see your reasoning regarding whether *p* as not establishing that *p*, or not providing as strong evidential support for *p*. And to find that a large number of one's epistemic peers disagree with one about whether *p* is to find that there is such higher-order evidence that one has made a mistake regarding one's reasoning about whether *p*. [5] In this case, if our principled moral judgments can be intelligibly completely intransigent in light of perceived significant peer disagreement regarding *p*, then these moral judgments intelligibly do not track perceived evidence. In this case, given *beliefs track perceived evidence*, moral judgments are not beliefs.

11.2 WOULD THERE BE CONVERGENCE IN IDEAL CONDITIONS?

The rest of this chapter will focus on moral disagreement as a problem for objectivist views in metaethics. In Chapter 2 we discussed two objectivist views. First,

> *Robust realism.* There are truths and facts about right, wrong, good and bad, and what we morally ought to do. And these facts are not constituted or grounded by what we, or our society, do or would believe in any particular circumstances.

For instance, according to robust realism, slavery would be wrong even if everyone thought it was right, and even if (after engaging in the best reasoning process about morality) people in moral ideal conditions could coherently think that slavery is permissible. According to robust realism, moral facts and truths are as objective and independent of our current attitudes as facts about physics, biology, and mathematics.

We also discussed what I called

> *Constructivism.* Moral facts and truths are constituted by the views about right, wrong, and justice that we would come to if we engaged in the best reasoning process about these topics.

According to many, there is no alternative to reasoning about morality other using wide reflective equilibrium reasoning. When we engage in wide reflective equilibrium reasoning we take the moral intuitions and judgments that we are greatly confident in and which persist over time (e.g. that slavery is wrong, homosexuality is permissible, it is often wrong to break promises, etc.) and we try to find moral principles that explain these intuitions and judgments. For instance, the Kantian view that an action is wrong iff it involves harmfully using someone as a mere means to yours or others' ends could explain why slavery is wrong—for slavery uses people in such a way—and why homosexuality is permissible, for homosexuality does not involve such use. In a search for wide reflective equilibrium we consider modifying these principles in line with any of our stable considered judgments with which they clash and modifying any judgments with which these principles clash to fit with more general and simple principles. We try to refine our intuitions and the principles that explain them until we have a strong consistency, or equilibrium, between these principles and judgments. And we try to ensure that these principles and judgments mesh with the best theorising in other domains such as sociology, economics, epistemology, etc.—if the reasoning in these other domains makes a difference to what the right moral principles are![6]

According to constructivism, the true moral theory is the one that we would accept if we engaged in the very best reasoning process about morality, which we might think of as a kind of ideal wide reflective equilibrium reasoning process. In such an idealised wide reflective equilibrium process agents are fully informed of all the relevant empirical non-moral facts, are fully rational, are unaffected by cognitive biases, and don't hold any conflicting beliefs. Constructivists say that what *makes* the correct moral theory the correct one is that if we engaged in the very best reasoning process about morality, we would accept it. Constructivists of the form that I have in mind hold that, in general, facts about what's right, wrong, just, and unjust are constituted by the views about rightness, wrongness, and justice that we would come to if we engaged in the best reasoning process about these topics. In contrast, robust realists hold that our best reasoning about morality can get us to understand which moral theory is the true or correct one but that this truth is independent of our reasoning about morality (see §2.1).

Suppose that everyone engaged in the idealised best reasoning process about morality, call such circumstances moral ideal conditions. Many philosophers including John Rawls (1974), Michael Smith (1994, pp. 5–6), and Crispin Wright (1995, p. 223) claim that if there were still moral disagreements in such moral ideal conditions, this would undermine objectivist views such as robust realism and constructivism. We'll discuss whether this is the case in §11.3. But first, should we accept that there would be moral dissensus in moral ideal conditions?

11.2.1. ACTUAL DISAGREEMENT AND DISAGREEMENT AFTER ENGAGEMENT IN A REFLECTIVE PROCESS

Stephen Stich (2007), John Doris and Alexandra Plakias (2008a), and Ben Fraser and Marc Hauser (2010) argue that there would be dissensus in moral ideal conditions on the basis of the large amount of widespread *actual* disagreement in moral principles or values that we find; as we discussed in §1.2

there is a large amount of such disagreement. However, Simon Fitzpatrick argues that such arguments from actual moral disagreements for the view that there would be moral dissensus in idealised conditions do not support this conclusion. Fitzpatrick (2014, p. 180) argues that most people's ordinary moral judgments

> are culturally entrenched as a result of the fact that we, as humans, automatically and unconsciously internalize the prevailing norms of our social group, rarely, if ever, reflect on the judgments these internalized norms give rise to, and thus rarely bring them into contact with the rest of our beliefs. This leaves open the possibility that such disagreements [as the actual disagreements discussed in §1.2] may be resolved were the parties to the disagreement to consciously reflect on their brute moral intuitions, bring them into contact with their non-moral beliefs, and engage in the pursuit of wide reflective equilibrium.

If this is right, we cannot so straightforwardly claim that there would be moral disagreement in moral ideal conditions just because there is widespread actual moral disagreements in moral principles and values. This is because parties to these disagreements have not engaged in the reflective moral reasoning process that would be engaged in idealised conditions. Fitzpatrick concludes that we just have no evidence either way regarding whether there would be moral convergence in idealised conditions.

In §2.3.2 we discussed the fact that there is widespread disagreement among moral philosophers. Should this lead us to conclude that there would be moral disagreement in idealised moral conditions?[7] It is not obvious that this is the case. For it may be that there are incentives propelling moral philosophers to so disagree: papers get published for disagreeing with other papers not for agreeing with them and philosophy as a discipline in general prizes conflict and disagreement, or so it might seem.[8] Furthermore, although moral philosophers do often come to moral judgments after employing an extensive moral reasoning process such a process will not be an ideal one in which they are free from cognitive biases and irrationality, have knowledge of all the relevant non-moral facts, and have conducted the most thorough search for wide reflective equilibrium—that is, the most extensive revision of intuitions and principles in light of one another—possible.

11.2.2. THE INTRANSIGENCE OF MORAL JUDGMENTS

Moral ideal conditions are very different from actual conditions. But we might think that the fact that there is widespread moral disagreement gives us good reason to believe that there would be a disagreement in moral ideal conditions because many of our judgments of moral principles and basic moral values are intransigent: these judgments are extremely resistant to change. As we discussed in §11.1.2–3, it seems that many people's moral judgments do not change when they recognise that their epistemic equals disagree with them.[9] And, as we discussed, Kramer (2009, p. 186) claims that it is a 'tiresomely familiar' fact that some people are entirely intransigent in their moral views in the face of compelling counterarguments. Furthermore, many of the moral judgments that we make in disagreements of moral principles or values are judgments that we might class as moral convictions: they are resilient central moral beliefs or views that are strongly motivating such that we are disposed to speak out to some extent on the issue about which we have a conviction and take some proactive measures in service of this conviction (see Pianalto, 2011, p. 382). But such moral convictions are important to our identities and sense of self (ibid., p. 383). For instance, my views on just immigration and asylum laws and distributive justice issues are strongly connected to my sense of self: they are things that I've cared about for a long time. And I find it hard to conceive of myself as having a complete change of view or inclination and disposition about these issues.

However, some preliminary empirical evidence seems to show that moral judgments are not quite as intransigent as they might seem. David Killoren and I conducted an event very similar to the deliberative polls discussed in §10.2.3 but on moral issues.[10] We recruited 114 (majority non-philosophy) student participants.[11] We constructed an overview document on the trolley problem that was vetted for neutrality by several moral philosophers. Participants were given this document prior to the deliberative event. They were then asked to anonymously give their views about the footbridge and switch trolley cases prior to the beginning of the event (see §1.1). The event consisted of 4 hours of (lightly moderated) small group discussions and two sessions in which participants had an opportunity to ask questions of moral philosophers about the issues raised by the trolley problem. At the end of the day participants were again given a survey about the switch and footbridge cases. 39% of participants reported different moral judgments about the footbridge trolley case post-deliberation about it. That is 39% of participants changed their view from one of the following three options to another option: (i) the person in the footbridge case ought to push the heavy man; (ii) they ought not push the heavy man; (iii) I don't know. (We conducted a second deliberative event on a similar issue and found similar results.)[12]

So, it seems that less than seven hours of reasoning and deliberation, not even in perfectly idealised conditions, was sufficient in our studies for a great number of our participants to change their principled moral judgments. Perhaps this result would not be replicated for all controversial moral topics; more research is needed here. Perhaps it would not be replicated by people who have extremely strong views on the issues in question—though such people might be argued to have biases regarding the relevant topics or to be driven by irrationality in a way that would not be present in moral ideal conditions. Regardless, it is clear that we cannot argue that just because some people are intransigent in their moral judgments in everyday life, this would imply that they would be so intransigent in moral ideal conditions.

11.2.3. INEVITABLE DISAGREEMENTS IN WIDE REFLECTIVE EQUILIBRIA

Thomas Kelly and Sarah McGrath (2010, esp. pp. 338–340) have argued that if the very best reasoning process about moral issues is a search for wide reflective equilibrium, then there would be no moral convergence in moral ideal conditions.

Ideal Bayesian reasoners use only one belief-revision rule—Bayesian conditionalisation—to come to their beliefs. (It doesn't matter if you don't know exactly what this is for the point that Kelly and McGrath make) Ideal Bayesian reasoners can start with different views about what is probable and will accordingly have different beliefs in virtue of these different initial views. Mathematical results known as the swamping of the priors results show that for a wide range of prior probability distributions (or prior views about what's probable), 'initial differences [among ideal Bayesian reasoners] are washed out over time: as individuals are increasingly exposed to common evidence, their initial differences become increasingly insignificant, and they converge on a common view' (Kelly & McGrath, 2010, pp. 338–339). However, these results show that for many prior probability distributions, idealised Bayesian reasoners reasoning from those prior probability distributions would never converge even if they shared all the same evidence. So, there is no convergence among all ideal Bayesian reasoners in ideal conditions. The question is whether ideal moral reasoners are more or less likely to converge than ideal Bayesian reasoners. As Kelly and McGrath point out, if anything, idealised moral reasoners are less likely to converge than ideal Bayesian reasoners because Bayesian belief revision is governed by a solitary norm, conditionalisation, which leaves no room for judgment; the judgments made by reasoners engaged in reflective equilibrium can be governed by multiple, different, conflicting norms.

Kelly and McGrath make their argument as part of a discussion of whether wide reflective equilibrium is the very best reasoning process about normative ethics. You can engage in wide reflective equilibrium no matter what your moral starting points (e.g. one person could engage in this process with the starting point that lying is always wrong, another could have the opposite view as a starting point; we could have the intuition that pushing the heavy man off of the bridge is wrong as a starting point, or the intuition that it is right as a starting point). So, if wide reflective equilibrium is the very best reasoning process about morality, their argument would seem to give us reason to believe that there would be dissensus in moral ideal conditions.

Kelly and McGrath argue, however, that this argument shows that engagement in wide reflective equilibrium is insufficient for moral justification, one must have the right starting points. This argument does not show that there would be no convergence in moral ideal conditions if those in such conditions engaged in a search for wide reflective equilibrium from the same moral starting points.

11.2.4. MORAL DISAGREEMENT IN IDEAL CONDITIONS AS A SALIENT POSSIBILITY

Elsewhere I've argued that it is a salient possibility that there would be moral disagreement in ideal conditions. I make two arguments for this claim. First,

a Many of those with the greatest claim to expertise about whether there would be convergence in moral ideal conditions claim that there would be dissensus.

John Rawls (1999, p. 290, p. 301), Bernard Williams (2006, p. 136), Terence Horgan and Mark Timmons (2009, pp. 231–232), Bart Streumer (2011, pp. 330–334), Nick Zangwill (2000, p. 284), John Doris and Alexandra Plakias (2008a), and Stephen Stich (2007) believe that there would be no moral convergence in idealised conditions. But

b Non-salient merely logically possibilities are not possibilities that are believed by many of those with the greatest claim to expertise about the relevant matter.

For instance those with the greatest claim to expertise about the matter do not *positively* hold that we are brains in vats that seem to be experiencing an external world (only that we might be). This marks this out as a merely logical rather than salient possibility. (a) and (b) seem to entail that it is a salient possibility that there would be disagreement in moral ideal conditions.
Second,

c Many such as John Rawls (1971), Michael Smith (1994, p. 40–41), T. M. Scanlon (2003), and Derek Parfit (2011a) hold that, and we have positive reason to hold that, the most thorough search for wide reflective equilibrium is the very best reasoning process about normative ethics. This shows that we have positive reason to believe that the most thorough search for wide reflective equilibrium is the best reasoning process about ethics.

But as I've just been discussing we also have good reason to believe that

d   The most thorough search for wide reflective equilibrium will not produce convergence.

And

e   If we have positive reason to believe that p, then it is a salient possibility that p.

(c–e) similarly imply that it is a salient possibility that there would be a lack of moral convergence in ideal conditions.[13]

11.3 PEER DISAGREEMENT AND MORAL CONVERGENCE

If there are moral disagreements in moral ideal conditions about a vast range of moral topics, such as those that we currently disagree about—abortion, war, euthanasia, distributive justice, trolley-related issues, all the topics discussed in the applied ethics literature and §1—this would seem to be a problem for constructivism. Since constructivism seems to imply that if there would be disagreement about whether abortion, euthanasia, pushing the heavy man, heavily taxing the rich etc., is wrong in moral ideal conditions, then there is no truth of the matter about whether it is right or wrong to do all of these things. So, if there would be such moral disagreement, constructivism implies that there are very few moral truths. But we clearly think that there is a right answer to these ethical questions, otherwise we would not be disagreeing about them: pro-lifers and pro-choices think that one of them are right and one wrong; socialists and libertarians think that there is a right answer about whether we should tax the rich as well as holding their own views. So, constructivism seems to entail that there are too few truths or correct moral claims. This decreases its plausibility. And if it's even a salient possibility that there would be such a large level of disagreement in moral ideal conditions, this would seem to cause trouble for constructivism. In this case, it is a salient possibility that constructivism yields the counter-intuitive consequence that there are no truths of the matter about the controversial moral issues that we disagree about. And this consequence is at odds with our moral practice.[14]

Although a lack of moral convergence seems to undermine constructivism, many including Rawls (2013, p. 290, p. 301), Smith (1994, pp. 5–6), and Wright (1995, p. 223) claim that if there are moral disagreements that would survive in moral ideal conditions, this undermines robust realism too. But why would this be the case? Suppose that there were disagreement about whether we have free will among agents who are fully informed of all the relevant facts—except the fact of the matter regarding whether we do/don't have free will—are unaffected by cognitive biases, don't hold any conflicting beliefs, and have engaged in the very best reasoning process about whether we have free will. Would this undermine the view that there is an objective fact of the matter about whether we have free will? It doesn't seem so. Such disagreement would at most show that we cannot be justified in believing that we do (or do not) have free will. So, why would a lack of moral convergence in ideal conditions undermine moral realism? In the rest of this section, I'll explain why considerations regarding peer disagreement seem to imply that disagreement in moral ideal conditions is as much of a problem for realism as for constructivism.

11.3.1. ACCESSIBILITY, REALISM, AND PEER DISAGREEMENT

Elsewhere I have made an argument for the view that if there is a significant amount of moral disagreement in ideal conditions, this undermines realism. This argument relies on views about the epistemological impact of moral disagreement, which we discussed in Chapters 5 and 6, and views about the practical implications of this impact, which we discussed in Chapter 7.

I first argue that

> *Accessibility requirement.* If φ-ing has a moral status, then the moral status of φ-ing is accessible to some possible agent.

To understand my argument for this claim we need the notion of a fact making a difference to what an agent ought to do. For a fact F to make a difference to whether an agent ought to φ is for F to provide a reason that bears on whether they ought to φ or otherwise play a normative role in making it the case that an agent ought or ought not φ.[15] The essence of my argument for the *accessibility requirement* is that:

(i)   Facts about the moral status of an action φ—φ-ing's being right/ wrong/permissible—essentially make a difference to what agents ought to do.

For example, φ-ing is wrong only if the fact that φ-ing is wrong makes a difference to what some agent ought to do by, for instance, making it the case that they ought not φ. But

(ii)   A fact F makes a difference to what some agent ought to do only if that fact is accessible to some possible agent.

(i) and (ii) entail the *accessibility requirement*. (i) is intuitive enough.[16] (ii) is less obviously plausible. I argue that if we should accept perspectivalism$^{\text{moral\&nonmoral}}$ about our obligations, which, as we discussed in §7.2, is a plausible view, then we must accept (ii). Why is this? Well, remember that one of the motivations for accepting perspectivalism that we discussed in Chapter 7 was that it explained our intuitions about cases like the following:

> Mineshafts. A hundred miners are trapped underground with floodwaters rising. We are rescuers on the surface who are trying to save them. We know that the miners are in one of two mineshafts but we do not know which shaft they are in. In fact we have no reason to believe that they are in one shaft rather than the other. There are three floodgates that we could close by remote control. And depending on which gate we close the results will be as shown in Table 11.1.

Table 11.1 Mineshafts.

		The miners are in	
		Shaft A	Shaft B
We close	Gate 1	We save 100 lives	We save 0 lives
	Gate 2	We save 0 lives	We save 100 lives
	Gate 3	We save 90 lives	We save 90 lives

It seems that in this case what we ought to do is close Gate 3 even though there is a fact of the matter about which shafts the miners are in. But because this fact of the matter is inaccessible to us, it does not make a difference to what we ought to do in this case. If we accept this idea, we accept that facts that are inaccessible to us do not make a difference to what we ought to do. And, as we discussed in §7.2, if we should think that if a non-moral facts' inaccessibility means that it does not affect what we ought to do, we should similarly think that if a moral fact is inaccessible to us, this means that it does not affect what we ought to do.[17] So, there is something of a case that

> Accessibility requirement. If φ-ing has a moral status, then the moral status of φ-ing is accessible to some possible agent.

I then argue that we should accept

> No convergence, no access. If there would be disagreement about the moral status of φ-ing in moral idealised conditions, then no one has access to the moral status of φ-ing.

First note that the conciliatory views about peer disagreement discussed in Chapters 5–6 seem to entail that if idealised reasoners A and B hold conflicting beliefs about the moral status of φ-ing, know this, and know that they are idealised reasoners, then neither A nor B are justified in holding conflicting beliefs about the moral status of φ-ing; A and B are only justified in suspending belief about the moral status of φ-ing. For instance, a plausible form of conciliationism holds that if we should believe that there is a substantial division of opinion among our (approximate) epistemic peers regarding whether *p*, then, other things equal, we should suspend belief about whether *p* (§5.2). Even if we do not accept conciliationism, it seems plausible that we should accept that A and B should suspend belief in this case. For unlike in most cases of disagreement with someone whom you should believe to be your epistemic peer, in A and B's case *they both know that they are idealised reasoners* who have the same non-moral beliefs and who have engaged in the very best reasoning process about normative ethics. In this case, A and B do not have access to the moral status of φ-ing since they can only reasonably suspend belief about the moral status of φ-ing. So, if there is disagreement about the moral status of φ-ing among idealised reasoners, they do not have access to the moral status of φ-ing.

But if even idealised reasoners do not have access to the moral status of φ-ing, I argue, no one has access to the moral status of φ-ing. This is because we should hold that

> *Access entails immunity to defeat.* A has epistemic access to *p* at time T only if there is a justification R that A can justifiably believe *p* on the basis of at that time that is such that A's belief that *p* on the basis of R would not be defeated in more ideal or ideal conditions. (Where one way in which a belief can have its justification defeated is by its justification being defeated via peer disagreement defeating it.)

To see the plausibility of this claim consider some cases. Suppose that Anna justifiably believes that it is 8 a.m. because her clock tells her that it is 8 a.m. But although it is in fact 8 a.m., unbeknown to Anna, her clock has stopped. Suppose that Anna has no other way of knowing what time it is other than by looking at her clock; she is locked in a room with no windows for instance. In this case, Anna does not know that it is 8 a.m. even though she has a justified true belief that it is 8 a.m. But nor does it seem that Anna has access to the fact that it is 8 a.m. This is because there is a defeater for the only justification that Anna has access to for the belief that it is 8 a.m.: the fact that her clock has stopped working is a defeater for her justification for believing that it is 8 a.m. because her clock says that it is 8 a.m. So, this justification would be defeated in more ideal and ideal conditions. So, if there would be disagreement about the moral status of φ-ing in idealised conditions, then neither we nor idealised reasoners have access to the moral status of φ-ing. So, we should accept the principle that:

> *No convergence, no access.* If there would be disagreement about the moral status of φ-ing in idealised conditions, then no one has access to the moral status of φ-ing.[18]

But, as I explained, it seems that we should also accept the principle that

Accessibility requirement. If φ-ing has a moral status, then the moral status of φ-ing is accessible to some possible agent.

And the combination of this claim and *no convergence, no access* entails the principle that

No convergence, no moral facts. If there would be disagreement about the moral status of φ-ing in ideal conditions, then φ-ing does not have a moral status.

No convergence, no moral facts seems to entail that robust realism has the same consequences as constructivism if there would be a great amount of moral disagreement in ideal conditions. As I explained above, if the moral disagreements that we currently have about controversial moral issues would survive in ideal conditions, then this would be a problem for constructivism for it would imply that there are no right answers about all of these controversial moral issues. If *no convergence, no moral facts,* holds then robust realism faces this problem to just the same extent that constructivism does too.[19]

Should we accept my argument? Obviously I think we should. But I do want to point out what I think are the largest problems with it. One problem is with conciliationism. Robust realists might just stand firm and argue that we should reject conciliationism and instead hold a steadfast view about the epistemology of disagreement (see §5.3). Or they could hold that although peer disagreement undermines the justificatory status of our non-moral beliefs it never undermines the justificatory status of our moral beliefs; this is a position that moral testimony pessimists may be inclined to take up (see §6.3).[20] There are costs to taking these kind of positions but realists might claim that these costs are not as severe as the costs of accepting that most of the actions and practices that we disagree about the moral status of have no moral status.

A second line of attack would be to hold that knowing that yourself and another are in these ideal moral conditions regarding the moral status of φ-ing is insufficient to be in a position to justifiably believe that this other person is your epistemic peer about the moral status of φ-ing; in order to be in this kind of position you need to know what their particular moral views are (see §6.1–2).[21] This is an interesting piece of the argument to push on but it might be that we add to ideal conditions the condition that you know the moral views of those with whom you disagree in ideal conditions, and you take their views to not be radically implausible. If we add this condition to the ideal conditions, it may still seem to many that there would be disagreement in such ideal conditions. For instance, it might be that I share enough background moral agreement with libertarians and classical liberals, such as

Gaus and Nozick, to be in a position where I should judge them to be my epistemic peers about moral and political topics (see §6.1–2). But it might also be that our disagreement about distributive justice would survive in ideal conditions.

11.3.2. WHERE DOES THIS LEAVE US METAETHICALLY?

If the argument from a lack of moral convergence undermines realism as much as constructivism where does this leave us? One idea is that this argument favours framework relativism or the moral error theory. Suppose that so much moral disagreement would survive in moral ideal conditions that realism and constructivism would entail that there are few moral truths. We might think that this yields a version of the moral error theory: we think that there are, and are committed to there being truths about many moral topics but in fact there are not. Alternatively, we might think this renders realism and constructivism less plausible that framework relativism. Framework relativists may be able to deny one of the key premises in the argument that I've been discussing, namely

> No convergence, no access. If there would be disagreement about the moral status of φ-ing in idealised conditions, then no one has access to the moral status of φ-ing.

One of the premises in the argument for this claim was that agents in moral ideal conditions would have to suspend moral belief if they found themselves in moral disagreements. Relativists can deny this. For relativists may be able to hold that if in moral ideal conditions A holds that φ-ing is wrong and B holds that it is not, then A and B just have different moral standards or frameworks. There are no standard-independent moral truths. And the fact that A judges that φ-ing is wrong-relative-to-her(A's)-framework should not lead B to suspend judgment or revise her believe that φ-ing is not-wrong-relative-to-her(B's)-framework if these frameworks are distinct. This argument can support relativism or the error theory even if moral dissensus is only a salient possibility (see Rowland, 2017b, pp. 816–821).

Why not think that the argument from moral convergence just favours non-objectivist views generally since it undermines objectivist views. One reason for worrying about this is that, as we discussed in §3.2, many non-objectivist non-cognitivists want to be quasi-realists who say almost everything that realists say about first-order moral and normative claims. But the argument from a lack of moral convergence against objectivism didn't rely on any claims that quasi-realists would reject and mostly depended on first-order normative claims. In this case, the argument from a lack of moral convergence might cut against quasi-realism as much as it cuts against realism and constructivism (see Rowland, 2017b, pp. 816–821).

11.4 DEBUNKING AND DISAGREEMENT

Evolutionary debunking arguments in metaethics aim to undermine robust realism and are widely held to provide a challenge for robust realism. The final way in which the epistemological implications of moral disagreement have been brought to bear on metaethics is in combination with evolutionary considerations.

Very briefly, and somewhat crudely, the challenge that evolutionary debunking arguments present for realism is the following: we have the capacity for forming moral judgments that we have due to evolution and we have the particular kinds of moral beliefs that we have due to evolution. This means that we make moral judgments—and we make the kinds of moral judgments that we make such as that it is wrong to assault and kill others and to break one's agreements—because our doing so promoted the survival of our genes. But according to robust moral realism, facts about what's right and wrong are entirely independent of us and what would promote the survival of our genes. In this case, realism seems to imply that our moral beliefs are entirely disconnected from the moral facts and truths: our beliefs are caused by evolutionary process, but these evolutionary processes are not sensitive to the mind- and gene-survival-independent moral truths.

There is an asymmetry here between evolution's insensitivity to mind-independent moral truths and its sensitivity to other truths. *Evolution would have selected us to make moral judgments so that we didn't kill our family members and kept agreements to one another even if there were no robustly real moral truths* (or even if the moral truths were very different). This is because our making these moral judgments made us able to be part of prosperous cooperative communities that would be more likely to survive than beings that didn't make these moral judgments—or didn't make any moral judgments at all. Making moral judgments (like these) promoted the survival of our genes. But it is not the case that evolution would have selected us to believe that, for instance, $2 + 2 = 4$ even if $2 + 2 = 4$. Believing that $2 + 2 = 4$—or having the critical capacities that enabled us to believe this would only help our genes to survive if $2 + 2 = 4$.[22] So, if robust realism is true, then our moral beliefs are entirely disconnected from the moral truths. In this case, moral realism would seem to imply that we have no moral knowledge and justified beliefs (for discussion see §2.2.3). But, as we discussed in Chapter 2, a view in metaethics that ensures that we have far less moral knowledge and justified beliefs that we think we do is not very plausible. And this presents a special problem for moral realism, since it is motivated to save the moral appearances. And we think that we have some moral knowledge such as that slavery is wrong and that homosexuality is permissible.

There is a debate about exactly how evolutionary debunking arguments work.[23] Some, such as Bogardus (2016) and Mogensen (2016), have argued that we should believe that the influence of evolution on our moral beliefs undermines the justification of those beliefs because it shows that we are in counterfactual moral disagreement. That is, we are in disagreement with the hypothetical versions of ourselves who evolved in different ways. This thought is probably made most intuitive if we consider Darwin's (2004, p. 73) claim that

> If ... men were reared under precisely the same conditions as hive-bees, there can hardly be a doubt that our unmarried males would, like the worker-bees, think it a sacred duty to kill their brothers, and mothers would strive to kill their fertile daughters; and no one would think of interfering.

The versions of us who evolved more like bees would disagree with us about whether killing our brothers is wrong. And, according to this line of thought, this counterfactual disagreement destroys our justification. Bogardus (2016: pp. 557–658) argues that '[i]t is unclear whether we are in a better epistemic position than our many nearby counterfactual selves [such as Darwin's people with a bee-like moral system] who disagree with us'. And that this fact combined with a thesis along the lines of conciliationism (chapter 5–6), may show that we are not justified in our moral beliefs and do not have moral knowledge. We do not need to hold the view that the many counterfactual versions of ourselves who evolved differently are our epistemic peers in order to come to this conclusion, according to Bogardus, for the fact that it is unclear whether we are in a better epistemic position than the counterfactual versions of ourselves who disagree with us about the morality of assault, killing, and promise-keeping undermines the epistemic justification of our beliefs even if we are not justified in believing that these counterfactual people are our epistemic peers.

Proponents of this argument like Bogardus and Mogensen argue that evolutionary debunking arguments work only if the counterfactual disagreement that evolution reveals undermines our moral beliefs. We might challenge this; we might argue that an alternative epistemic principle such as the principle, *safety*, which we discussed in Chapter 2, can be used to make debunking arguments without appeal to counterfactual disagreement. Exploring this issue would take us too far away from moral disagreement, so instead we'll discuss different disagreement-related responses.[24]

We might respond to this argument by arguing that only disagreement with actually existing people undermines the justification of our beliefs. The fact that an epistemic peer *could* or *would* disagree with you doesn't make a difference to what you ought to believe. However, as we discussed in §6.2.8, we must accept that sometimes the fact that some people *would* disagree with you if they were around does undermine the justification of our beliefs: suppose that no epistemic peers currently disagree with you about whether *p* because you slaughtered all your peers so that no peers disagree with you. The fact that you would find yourself in a peer disagreement had you not slaughtered your peers undermines the justification of your belief that p. Obviously, some merely counterfactual disagreements are not as epistemically important as actual peer disagreements. But some argue that the disagreements we have with counterfactual versions of ourselves who evolved differently are epistemically important. For instance, Mogensen (2016, esp. p. 268) argues that a merely counterfactual disagreement about whether p is epistemically significant when the fact that the person with whom you disagree about whether p is not around is not related to the truth of whether p. And that the fact that the counterfactual versions of ourselves who would have evolved differently and had different moral beliefs are not around is not relevant to the truth of our moral beliefs rather than theirs. (In contrast, the fact that there are no beings around who believe that $2 + 2 = 5$ is relevant to the truth of this matter; for the reason why they are not around is that holding false mathematical beliefs impedes one's ability to survive.)[25]

A different response is to argue that

(1) The counterfactual disagreement that evolution reveals is epistemically significant only if it is disagreement with others whom we should believe to be our approximate epistemic peers (or superiors); but
(2) To the extent that the disagreement evolution reveals is with our approximate epistemic peers it does not undermine robust realism
(3) So, the counterfactual disagreement that evolution reveals does not undermine robust realism.

(1) is explicitly denied by Bogardus, as discussed above. But we might argue that we should accept (1) because if we have no good reason to believe that another's epistemic credentials regarding p are approximately close to—or better than—our own, then the fact that they disagree with us about whether p gives us no disagreement-based reason to revise our view about p and cannot itself undermine the justification of our belief about whether p (§5.1).[26] I, like others, don't quite see how such disagreement with people whom we should not believe to be our epistemic peers could itself be very epistemically troubling. If we don't know that we're in a better epistemic position than very strange possible people whose epistemic credentials we have no reason to think to be any good, then there is a serious problem with our moral epistemology, but it's not a disagreement-based problem. For this serious problem seems to be that we just don't have any good reason to trust our own moral beliefs. Think of it this way: I know that if right-libertarians kidnapped me and brainwashed me (via some forceful conditioning and torture programme) I would have libertarian beliefs. But if I don't have good reason to hold my political beliefs rather than the possible right-libertarian-me's beliefs, this isn't

due to the epistemic significance of their disagreement with me. If I have any reason to hold my egalitarian beliefs, I should be able to hold that beliefs formed through such a brainwashing procedure are unreliable, and not justified. So, if I cannot hold that I'm in a better position than this possible right-libertarian-me, then that's a problem, but their disagreement with me has nothing to do with it. This would just show that the justification of my egalitarian beliefs was always built on sand: that I never had good justification for my moral beliefs to begin with. Similarly, if we have no good reason to believe that we are in a better epistemic position than counterfactual versions of ourselves who evolved to believe that killing their siblings is right, this points to a general problem with our moral epistemology rather than to a disagreement-related problem.[27]

So, let's presume (1) for the time being. Should we accept (2)?

2   To the extent that the disagreement evolution reveals is with our approximate epistemic peers it does not undermine robust realism.

Michael Klenk (2018) makes an argument for (2). He argues that

i   the counterfactual disagreement that the evolutionary causes of our beliefs reveals is either disagreement in nearby or non-nearby scenarios;
ii   in non-nearby scenarios, there will be disagreement, but not with epistemic peers;
iii   in nearby scenarios, there will not be moral disagreement about basic moral platitudes; and
iv   evolutionary debunking arguments only undermine robust realism if they undermine the justification of basic moral platitudes.

(i–iv) entails (2). Nearby scenarios are those in which we evolved similarly to how we actually evolved but not in exactly the same way. More specifically, Klenk (2018, p. 120) understands these scenarios as ones in which 'our counterfactual selves resemble the embers of human societies on the ethnographic record'. Non-nearby remote scenarios are those in which we evolved to be very different beings morally speaking—so we do not resemble the embers of human societies on the ethnographic record. Darwin's scenario in which we evolved to have a hive-bee-like moral system is one such remote scenario. (i) is trivially true. (ii)—the claim that in non-nearby scenarios, there will be disagreement, but not with epistemic peers—seems plausible. The counterfactual versions of ourselves that have a bee-like morality are so different to us that we would not be justified in believing them to be our epistemic peers. Since, as we discussed in Chapter 6 we seem to need a general background of moral agreement with another in order to be justified in believing that they are our epistemic peers about some moral issue. Klenk argues that we will lack this background in all remote scenarios—and not just the bee-persons scenario.

Basic moral platitudes are claims such as 'survival and reproductive success is at least somewhat good', 'pleasure is usually good, and pain is usually bad' and 'we have rights because we are reflective beings'. Anthropologists have argued, on the basis of large anthropological datasets, that platitudes like these have been accepted by all human societies.[28] If this is right, then (iii) holds. But in this case, the counterfactual moral disagreement in nearby scenarios revealed by evolution will not undermine the justification of basic moral platitudes like these. But evolutionary debunking arguments against robust realism need to show that we are disconnected from the moral truths about these moral platitudes in order to show that robust realism leaves us radically disconnected from the moral truths. If the arguments do not show that we are disconnected from the basic moral platitudes such that we lack justification in our platitudinous moral beliefs, then robust moral realism does not leave us radically disconnected from moral truths with no justified moral beliefs. So, (iv) holds. So, there is a good case that, *contra* some philosophers, the counterfactual moral disagreements that evolution reveals do not undermine robust realism. (Though such evolutionary debunking arguments might work in other ways.)

SUMMARY

The epistemic implications of moral disagreement have been argued to have metaethical implications. Some have argued that evolutionary debunking arguments against objectivist realism rely on the epistemic significance of counterfactual moral disagreement. But if such debunking arguments do rely on the epistemic significance of such disagreement it does not seem that they succeed. Some argue that the epistemic upshot of moral disagreement shows that objectivism is implausible if there would be a large amount of moral disagreement in ideal conditions. And some have argued that there would be such a large amount of disagreement in ideal conditions. It is unclear that there would be such a large amount of disagreement in ideal conditions, but the fact that there might be such disagreement does appear to somewhat undermine objectivist views—and perhaps some non-objectivist views—as well as supporting relativism. Some argue that the epistemic upshot of moral disagreement supports non-cognitivism or relativism because only these views can explain why intransigence is reasonable in light of moral disagreement or why certain moral disagreements are faultless. These arguments do not seem to succeed but it may be that non-cognitivism fits better than cognitivism with the fact that moral intransigence in light of peer disagreement is intelligible—even if it is not reasonable.

FURTHER READING

Tersman (2017) makes a different argument against realism that combines arguments from evolutionary debunking and moral disagreement. Vavova (2015), Street (2006), Joyce (2006), and Sauer (2018) are good first places to go when starting to think about evolutionary debunking arguments. Sampson (2019) defends realism from arguments like my own (in Rowland, 2017) by arguing that all epistemic arguments from disagreement against realism are self-defeating. Risberg and Tersman (2019) and Bennigson (1996) make further arguments against moral realism based on the epistemic consequences of moral disagreement.

NOTES

1   For discussion see Wright (2001), Kölbel (2004), and Hills (2013).
2   See Kölbel (2004) and Hills (2013, p. 411). A keen reader might realise that this case is exactly the kind of case that objectivists are willing to admit there is no objective truth about; instead they are willing to say that in this kind of case it is indeterminate whether we owe 10% or 11% (see §2.3.4). Some, including objectivists, have claimed that we have similar intuitions about other cases where this move is not so easily made—e.g. about the moral status of animals; see Hills (2013).
3   Wedgwood (2010) and Hills (2013) adopt this kind of response.
4   See Shah (2006, p. 481). See also Williams (1973, p. 148), Moran (1988, p. 146), and Foley (1993, p. 16).
5   See, for instance, Kelly (2010) and Christensen (2011).
6   See Scanlon (2003) (2014, lecture 2, lecture 4) and Daniels (2003). A moral reflective equilibrium's consistency with the best reasoning in other domains (e.g. economics, biology, sociology, epistemology) makes it a wide rather than natural reflective equilibrium.
7   See Leiter (2014).
8   See Doris and Plakias (2008b).
9   See also Pleasants (2009)
10 For more on deliberative polls see Fishkin (2011). The only ways in which our event differed from several deliberative polls that have been conducted without representative samples is that we used pictures in our questions and did not ask questions in the same form as those that are asked in deliberative polls.
11 This study was intended as a pilot. Deliberative polls are very costly, accordingly many pilot deliberative polls have a similarly small sample size.
12 See Rowland and Killoren (2020). Surprisingly, although we found that 39% of participants changed their view, there was no push towards convergence at all: the people who changed their view from one option to another were entirely cancelled out by those who changed in the opposite direction (for every option).
13 See Rowland (2017b, pp. 821–823).
14 And would also seem to clash with a charitable interpretation of many of our moral disagreements; see Chapter 4.
15 For other ways facts can pay such a normative role see Dancy (2004).
16 For a case for (i) see Rowland (2017b, pp. 809–812).
17 It could be argued that an accessibility requirement is plausible for non-moral facts but not for moral principles and values. The only reasons for holding this view that I'm aware of, however, are those reasons discussed in §7.2 for rejecting perspectivalism$^{moral\&nonmoral}$.

18 See Rowland (2017b, pp. 812–816).

19 Alternatively, one might hold that if the accessibility requirement is true, then realism is false because robust realism entails the falsity of this requirement. In this case, the argument that I've been elaborating (from peer disagreement in moral ideal conditions) in this section straightforwardly implies the falsity of realism.

20 Setiya (2012) also holds this position.

21 Thanks to David Killoren for raising a similar worry to me.

22 See the further readings at the end of this chapter. On the issue about mathematical facts and debunking cf. Joyce (2006) and Clarke-Doane (2012).

23 Part of this debate is about whether epistemic principles like *safety* (§2.2.3) are at work and can plausibly be used in debunking arguments. Bogardus (2016) argues that *safety* cannot be so used for instance.

24 Bogardus (2016) plausibly argues that if debunking arguments succeed, they must use a principle other than *safety*. However, as I show in Rowland (2019c, §2), other epistemic principles can be used to plausibly make debunking arguments that avoid some of the problems that Bogardus points out.

25 Things are slightly more complicated here: cf. Joyce (2006) and Clarke-Doane (2012).

26 For more on this kind of view see Vavova (2014).

27 Exactly what could the supposed alternative problem with our moral beliefs here be? I'm agnostic on whether there is any such problem. But here's one idea: our beliefs and those of the counterfactual versions of ourselves that evolved differently are both formed in the same kind of way, via reflective equilibrium reasoning. So, our counterfactual selves are just people who have different inputs in their reflective equilibria. But we have no reason to believe that the inputs of our reflective equilibria are better than other possible inputs (see §11.2.3 above). If this is right, we have no reason to believe that our beliefs that are the result of this reflective equilibrium process are more reliable or likely to be true than theirs. But the problem here is with moral justification via moral reflective equilibrium reasoning generally not with the moral disagreement that this generates.

28 See Curry et al. (forthcoming) and Klenk (2018, p. 123).

12

CONCLUSION

This book has shown that moral disagreement is metaethically, epistemologically, politically, and ethically significant. Metaethically, there are a variety of arguments that have been made against various forms of cognitivist realism including the explaining moral disagreement argument, the interpretation argument, the moral convergence argument, and the intelligibility of intransigence argument. This is a guidebook, and I haven't tried to show that these problems are insurmountable, but they do produce challenges for forms of cognitivist realism, as well as for other forms of objectivism such as constructivism. Non-cognitivism on the other hand seems to do quite well from moral disagreement. It faces a problem—the making room for disagreement problem—but contemporary expressivist non-cognitivists have developed a plausible way of overcoming this problem, and several arguments from moral disagreement favour non-cognitivism. The relationship between relativism and moral disagreement is less clear. Some arguments from moral disagreement such as the explaining moral disagreement and moral convergence problems seem to simultaneously undermine robust realism and provide strong support to relativism. And relativism may explain experimental data regarding how we respond to moral disagreement (§4.3). But relativism also faces more of a challenge to make room for moral disagreement than non-cognitivism and several arguments that favour non-cognitivism, such as the interpretation argument (§4.1) and the intelligibility of intransigence argument (§11.1) may seem to cut against it. Still moral disagreement provides more of a challenge for realism than alternatives. But it is an open question whether overall these problems for realism and virtues of alternatives show that we should reject realism; this will be affected by

DOI: 10.4324/9780429491375-16

how strong the arguments for and against robust realism elsewhere are. But *contra* what certain realists have argued, these arguments do seem to present serious challenges for realism.[1]

Epistemologically, moral disagreement does have important implications. But these implications do not produce moral scepticism; in fact they instead have very practical implications for what we should believe and do. Figuring out exactly what these implications are can be tricky. But it does seem that moral disagreement implies that we must moderate our views about the moral status of actions and practices that there is a significant amount of disagreement about among those with whom we otherwise agree morally. And this might mean that we, at least, have to give a little more to charity and eat less meat. Disagreement implies that we should act with greater moral caution that we otherwise would. Moral disagreement also seems to have implications in political philosophy for what laws and states are legitimate. It is not clear that considerations regarding moral disagreement show that only democracies are legitimate, though if these considerations do not show this, this is only because certain forms of deliberative democratic/epistocratic procedures may also be legitimate. But there is a relatively good case that legitimate states must only adopt laws that can be justified to all of those whom they coerce and must adopt such laws in a way that to some extent appeals to reasons that can be shared by all and not which there is moral disagreement about. There is also a good case that, in light of moral disagreement, we should, at least in principle, adopt political policies that amount to moral compromises.

Although I've shown that moral disagreement is important in moral philosophy in many different ways, and that the debates about its importance in moral epistemology and normative ethics, political philosophy, and metaethics are interlinked, there are still many issues regarding moral disagreement that have not been fully explored. The most salient to me are those issues surrounding the upshot of moral disagreement for normative ethical theorising and applied ethics. As may have been clear from the discussions in Chapters 6–8 moral disagreements' implications regarding what we practically ought to do are not fully explored. One particular area that might merit investigation here concerns whether we can be morally justified in taking action against a practice that we strongly believe to be unjust but which, due to moral disagreement (with our epistemic peers), we cannot justifiably believe to be unjust (e.g. if you believe that factory farming is unjust, but peer disagreement means you should not believe this can you be morally justified in breaking the law to protest it).[2] The implications of moral disagreement for normative ethical theory are also relatively under-explored.[3] Do the disagreements about what moral theory is true or about which reasons we have yield implications for the moral theory that we should accept, or for what moral reasons we should hold that there are. As discussed briefly in Chapter 1, many think that there are moral reasons to be loyal for its own sake: should moral theories explain this fact? Other things equal, should moral theories imply that there are such reasons? (In the same way that, other things equal, they should imply that there are generally reasons for us to keep our promises.) If not, why not? Is it because this intuition is not sufficiently widely shared? But how widely shared is sufficiently widely shared? Not everyone shares W. D. Ross's (1930, p. 138) intuition that a world in which people with morally bad characters are punished is better in itself than a world that is entirely the same except that those with good characters are punished. Not everyone shares G. E. Moore's (1903) intuitions that beauty and friendship are good in themselves, nor some egalitarians' intuitions that equality requires that we waste resources that will do good but exacerbate inequality (see Temkin, 2003). But do these intuitions support ethical theories? If they do, why do these intuitions support them but the intuitions of others that we have reasons to be loyal for itself do not? I hope that this book will give some the resources, and inspiration, to explore under-explored issues about moral disagreement like these.

NOTES

1　See e.g. Enoch (2009), McGrath (2010), Shafer-Landau (2003, 2006).
2　For thoughts on this see Rowland (2020).
3　Exceptions are Arvan (2016, ch. 1) and Sidgwick (1981); cf. de Lazari-Radek and Singer (2012).

GLOSSARY

Access entails immunity to defeat. The view that A has epistemic access to p at time T only if there is a justification R that A can justifiably believe p on the basis of at that time that is such that A's belief that p on the basis of R would not be defeated in more ideal or ideal conditions. (Where one way in which a belief can have its justification defeated is by its justification being defeated via peer disagreement defeating it).

Accessibility requirement. The view that if φ-ing has a moral status, then the moral status of φ-ing is accessible to some possible agent.

Approximate epistemic peer. For A to judge another to be her approximate epistemic peer about whether p is for A to either (a) judge them to be her peer about whether p or (b) judge that they are either her peer, or just her superior, or just her inferior about whether p, she doesn't know which.

Background agreement is sufficient for peerhood. If we should believe that another shares a background of general agreement with us about many propositions in domain D, then we should believe that they are our epistemic peer about (all) propositions in domain D. (Not to be confused with **great background agreement is sufficient for peerhood.**)

Beliefs track perceived evidence. The view that if one gains what one believes to be new evidence that bears on whether p, and one's judgment regarding p (whether p) is a belief, then either (i) one adjusts one's judgment regarding p in light of and in line with this evidence or (ii) one adjusts one's judgment that what one gained was in fact evidence bearing on whether *p*.

Borderline case. For some thing X to be a borderline case of some kind of thing K is for X to be neither clearly a K nor clearly not a K. For instance, a balding but not entirely bald man may be a borderline case of a bald man.

Burdens of judgment. See **reasonable persons**.

Causal theory of reference. According to a causal theory of reference for term T, the meaning and referent of sentences involving T is determined by whatever causally regulates the use of T. For instance, two terms T (e.g. water) both mean the same thing if they are both regulated by the same thing (e.g. H_2O).

Charitable interpretation. Providing an interpretation of someone's view or claim that makes it more likely to be true, or which takes account of a greater range of the things that they say and/or do.

Classical liberalism. A classical liberal state is one that secures basic civil rights and liberties for all (freedom of thought, conscience, assembly, etc.), protects its citizens from violence, attacks, and theft (via a police and army), and secures strong private property rights. But a classical liberal state does not engage in redistributive taxation for the purpose of reducing inequalities or for other purposes such as in order to fund museums and art galleries.

Cognitivism. The view that moral judgments are belief-like states. For instance, that to judge that stealing is wrong is to believe that stealing is wrong rather than to just disapprove of it or plan not to steal.

Compulsory pro-choice contributions. The view that abortions should be funded by the mandatory taxation contributions of only pro-choice taxpayers.

Conceptual role semantics. A view about meaning according to which two terms T1 and T2 have the same meaning if they play the same conceptual rule. For instance, according to Wedgwood's conceptual role semantics for moral and evaluative terms: A sentence S in some language other than English, which involves X-ing and Y-ing, means the same as the sentence 'X-ing is (all things considered) a better thing for A to do than Y-ing' iff accepting S commits one to have a preference for X-ing rather than Y-ing. This is because accepting the sentence 'X-ing is (all things considered) a better thing for A to do than Y-ing' commits one to having a preference for X-ing rather than Y-ing.

Conciliationism. The view that if we should believe that there is a substantial division of opinion among our (approximate) epistemic peers regarding whether p, then, other things equal (e.g. unless we have disagreement-independent reason to believe their views to be mistaken or to downgrade their status as our peer), we should suspend belief about whether p or significantly lower our confidence about whether p.

Constituency of public reason. The set of people whom a law must be justified to in order for that law to be legitimate (e.g. reasonable persons or normal persons) according to Public Reason views.

Constructivism. The view that moral facts and truths are constituted by the views about right, wrong, and justice that we would come to if we engaged in the best reasoning process about these topics. (See the further readings for chapter 2 for more information).

Cultural relativism. The view that the attitudes of our societies ground what's right, wrong, just, and unjust.

Deliberative restraint. The view that when deliberating and voting about particular issues citizens may only invoke, appeal to, and act on public reasons. Public reasons are reasons that other reasonable persons (in the Rawlsian sense) can see to be reasons. There are three more specific versions of deliberative restraint:

> *Strong restraint.* Citizens may only invoke, appeal to, and act on public reasons when deliberating about political issues.
> *Moderate restraint.* Certain citizens, such as legislators and judges, may only invoke, appeal to, and act on public reasons when deliberating about political issues. Other citizens must appeal to public reasons when deliberating about political issues but may also invoke and act on non-public reasons.
> *Weak restraint.* Citizens must appeal to public reasons when deliberating about political issues but may also invoke and act on non-public reasons.

Democratic legitimacy condition. The view that laws (or certain kinds of laws) are legitimate only if they are agreed to by a majority of those in the jurisdiction where that law applies or are agreed to by their legitimately elected representatives.

Disagreement in moral principles or values. A moral disagreement that is not the result of a disagreement about empirical economic or sociological facts such as about which policies would make things go better for some group. For instance, disagreements about what we should do in trolley case are disagreements in moral principles or values.

Epistemic peer. Someone is your epistemic peer about an issue if they are your epistemic equal regarding that issue. For instance, those with whom we took high school math classes and who were about as good as we were at mental math in these classes are our epistemic peers when it comes to mental math questions. We might see those with whom we went to, or are at, grad school with in philosophy as our epistemic peers about any randomly chosen question about contemporary philosophy or the history of philosophy. And most people that we talk to in person are our epistemic peers about whether the sun is shining where we are when we talk to them. For more specific accounts of epistemic peerhood in terms of likelihood and epistemic virtues see **epistemic virtues account of epistemic peerhood** and **likelihood view of epistemic peerhood**.

Epistemic superior. Someone is your epistemic superior about some matter if they have greater epistemic virtues than you regarding that matter or are more likely to be right about it than you are. See **epistemic virtues account of epistemic peerhood** and **likelihood view of epistemic peerhood.** For instance, nuclear physicists are the epistemic superiors of those who are not nuclear physicists about matters of nuclear physics.

Epistemic virtues account of epistemic peerhood. According to this view, A is our epistemic peer about p if and only if A has been exposed to the same evidence and arguments regarding whether p as we have, has the same relevant background knowledge as we have, and possesses general epistemic virtues (e.g. intelligence, freedom from bias, reasoning skill) to the same degree that we do.

Epistocracy. A form of government that involves rule by those who are epistemically best equipped to rule. However, some forms of epistocracy can involve rule by a random weighted sample of the population who have had their epistemic competence built or whose epistemic competence otherwise has been shown to pass a certain threshold.

Evolutionary debunking argument. A type of argument in ethics and metaethics that aims to show that all our moral beliefs, or a set of our moral beliefs, are not justified or do not constitute knowledge because they were caused by an evolutionary process. The most common evolutionary debunking arguments are arguments in metaethics that try to undermine robust realism. They aim to do this by aiming to show that if robust realism is true, then we lack justified moral beliefs or moral knowledge.

Explaining moral disagreement argument. An argument, crystallised in J.L. Mackie's work, that holds that non-objectivism in metaethics best explains widespread moral disagreement.

Expressivism. A particular form of non-cognitivism that holds that moral sentences are conventional devices for expressing pro and con attitudes towards their objects. We can also think of expressivism as non-cognitivism + an expressivist account of meaning for moral terms.

Expressivist account of meaning. The view that the meanings of sentences are determined by the states of mind that sentences can be used to express.

Faultless disagreement. There are several different senses in which a disagreement can be faultless:

i A disagreement is faultless if neither of the parties (who have inconsistent beliefs) has made a mistake.
ii A disagreement is faultless if both of the parties have exactly the views they ought to have and neither party would improve their beliefs by adopting new ones.
iii A disagreement is faultless if neither party is in error and further investigation by either party is not called for.
iv A disagreement is faultless if each party is blameless for having their differing beliefs.

Fetishism (moral fetishism or fetishistic motivation argument). The idea that a view is committed to moral fetishism is normally the idea that a view implies that we ought to be motivated to not perform an action just because it would be wrong and/or to perform an action just because it would be right. The idea here is that such motivation fetishises morality. This is because moral agents are concerned to perform/not-perform actions in virtue of particular morally relevant properties they have—that an action would involve keeping a promise, that it would involve benefitting/harming another, lying to another—rather than for the reason that the action would be right/wrong.

Framework relativism. The view that there is no such thing as an action being simply morally wrong or being simply good. Rather there are only actions that are wrong-relative to particular moral standards or frameworks and good for particular people and from particular perspectives. One can hold framework relativism as a view about our judgments: we only make judgments relative to particular moral judgments or standards. One can also hold it as a metaphysical view: there are only facts about what is right or wrong relative to particular standards are frameworks; there are no non-framework-relative moral facts.

Gausian public reason. A version of **public reason** according to which 'normal' rather than 'reasonable' people form the constituency of public reason. And the reasons that the constituency can have for accepting a law or state may differ rather than being the same. E.g. according to Gausian public reason a law can be legitimate because A would accept it for reason 1 but not for reason 2 and because B would accept it for reason 2 but not for reason 1. Cf. **Rawlsian public reason**.

Great background agreement is sufficient for peerhood. The view that if we should believe that another agrees with us about *pretty much all propositions in domain D*, then, other things equal, we should believe that they are our epistemic peer about (all) propositions in domain D.

Independence. The view that we should believe that another is our epistemic peer about whether p if and only if setting aside our disagreement with them regarding whether p we should believe that they are our epistemic peer about whether p.

Indeterminacy. For it to be indeterminate that X is F is for it to be neither true nor false that X is F.

Individualist relativism. The view that facts about right and wrong are grounded by our attitudes, what we judge to be right or wrong or the non-cognitive attitudes that we have. This view should not be confused with framework relativism, which is the most popular view referred to as relativism in contemporary metaethics.

Instrumental justification of democracy. The view that only democratic states are legitimate and that what makes this the case is the good instrumental consequences of having a democracy or democratic decision making.

Interpretation argument. An argument in metaethics, made by non-cognitivist expressivists, according to which in order to interpret many moral disagreements as genuine disagreements while charitably interpreting parties to these disagreements, we must accept non-cognitivist expressivism.

Intransigence. To be intransigent is to be unwilling to change one's view about something.

Intrinsic justification of democracy. The view that only democratic states are legitimate and that what makes this the case are intrinsic features of democracy or democratic decision-making.

Justified uncertainty. One is in a condition of justified uncertainty about proposition p if one is uncertain and justifiably uncertain about whether p (for instance, if one could not be justifiably certain that p or that not-p).

Legitimacy. A state or law is legitimate if we have a political obligation to obey it, for the reason that it is the law. A law or state may be legitimate even if it is not just.

Likelihood view of epistemic peerhood. According to this view, A is our epistemic peer about whether p if and only if A is as likely as we are to be right about whether p.

Making room for disagreement problem. A problem for non-objectivist metaethical views. The problem is to ensure that many moral disagreements are in fact disagreements rather than cases in which people are talking past one another or just have conflicting wants.

Maximise expected value (MEV). The view that in conditions of justified uncertainty about moral principles, we ought to maximise expected moral value.

Metaethics. Metaethics involves theories about the metaphysical status of moral facts, such as objectivism and non-objectivism, theories of the nature of morality, as well as theories of the nature of our moral thought and talk such as cognitivism and non-cognitivism.

Moral caution. The view that having considered the moral status of doing action A in context C, if due to her epistemic circumstances regarding moral principles and values, (i) subject S (epistemically) should believe or suspend judgment that doing A in C is a serious moral wrong, while (ii) S knows that refraining from doing A in C is not morally wrong, then S (morally) should not do A in C.

Moral caution*. The view that having considered the moral status of doing action A in context C, if due to her epistemic circumstances regarding moral principles or values, (i) subject S (epistemically) should believe or suspend judgment that doing A in C is a serious moral wrong, while (ii) S knows that refraining from doing A in C is not morally wrong, and *(iii) S cannot justifiably believe that it is likely that her not doing A would make her significantly worse-off than she otherwise would have been*, then S (morally) should not do A in C.

Moral deference. Deferring to the moral view of someone else.

Moral error theory. The view that all our moral judgments are false. No actions are right, wrong, or permissible. The view is normally that if there were moral facts or correct moral claims, then objectivism would have to be true, or there would have to be some metaphysically mysterious type of properties such as categorical or irreducibly normative reasons. But objectivism is not true, or there are no such metaphysically mysterious properties.

Moral ideal conditions. Conditions in which agents are fully informed of all the relevant empirical non-moral facts, are fully rational, are unaffected by cognitive biases, don't hold any conflicting beliefs, and have engaged in the best reasoning process about morality.

Moral twin earth. A thought experiment that poses a problem for forms of moral realism that adopt a causal theory of reference. In this thought experiment those on a twin earth are exactly the same as us in all relevant ways except that Kantian properties direct and regulate our use of 'is wrong' and utilitarian properties direct and regulate our use of 'is wrong'. We and twin earthers seem to disagree about which actions are wrong but the causal theory of reference implies that we cannot so disagree.

No convergence, no access. The view that if there would be disagreement about the moral status of φ-ing in moral idealised conditions, then no one has access to the moral status of φ-ing.

No convergence, no moral facts. The view that if there would be disagreement about the moral status of φ-ing in ideal conditions, then φ-ing does not have a moral status.

Non-cognitivism. The view that moral judgments consist in desire-like states such as approvals/disapprovals or plans rather than belief-like states. For instance, to judge that stealing is wrong is to disapprove of it in a certain way or to plan not to steal.

Non-moral agreement is sufficient for peerhood. The view that if we should believe that A agrees with us about non-normative, non-moral topics, and is just as generally intelligent and socially developed as we are, then we should believe that A is our epistemic peer about moral issues.

Non-objectivism. The view that objectivism in metaethics is false. According to this view, there are facts about what's right relative to us and our society, but no objective moral facts beyond this.

Non-purely-pragmatic reason to compromise. A reason to adopt a compromise provided straightforwardly by, and just by, the benefits of adopting this compromise.

Normal persons (or normal moral agents). These are the people whom Gaus believes fall within the constituency of (his form of) Public Reason. Normal moral agents have conceptions of the right, the good, and the just within 'the common human horizon' of such conceptions. Libertarians, socialists, Marxists, and anarchists have conceptions that are within this common human horizon, as do those with religious conceptions of the right, the just, and the good. Normal persons need not be reasonable persons in the Rawlsian sense.

Objectivism (metaethics). The view that facts and truths about what's right and wrong outstrip what we or our community or culture judge to be right or wrong. For instance, according to this view, even though we or our culture currently believe that it is permissible to eat animal products we could be wrong about this.

Objectivism about moral obligation. The view that our evidence or epistemic perspective does not affect what we ought to do or are morally obligated to do. For instance, if your pressing a light switch would severely harm someone even though you have no evidence at all that this is the case, objectivism holds that you may not press the light switch.

Paternalism. Paternalistic actions are actions that try to improve the well-being of particular people motivated by a negative judgment about these people's ability to manage their own well-being. For example, a mother who pays her daughter to do her homework acts paternalistically because she does not believe that she will make a responsible choice on her own.

Perspectivalism. The view that what we morally ought to do is affected by our evidential situation. For instance, if you cannot justifiably believe that a substance in a jar is arsenic rather than sugar, then you ought not put the substance in a cake to give to your guests even if the substance is in fact sugar.

Perspectivalism$^{moral\&nonmoral}$. The view that what we morally ought to do is affected by our evidential situation regarding moral principles and values as well as empirical non-moral facts.

Perspectivalism^{nonmoral}. The view that what we morally ought to do is affected by our evidential situation regarding empirical non-moral facts.

Public reason (account of legitimacy). The view that a law (or set of laws) L is legitimate iff it can be (publicly) justified to all those who fall into the constituency of public reason (e.g. reasonable or normal citizens depending on the account) who are citizens (or residents) in the jurisdiction that L is proposed in.

Public reasons. Reasons that other reasonable persons (in the Rawlsian sense) can see to be reasons; these are referred to as public reasons. Religious reasons, as well as other controversial metaphysical and epistemological claims are not public reasons. However, settled scientific theories and standards of evidence that are generally accepted by the relevant experts in the relevant fields do constitute public reasons. And values shared by all reasonable persons such as freedom and equality (for all), fairness, economic efficiency, equality of political and civil liberty, equality of opportunity, economic reciprocity, and the common good are liberal public values and so are public reasons; for all reasonable persons (in the Rawlsian sense) hold these values.

Pure moral disagreement. A moral disagreement that is not the result of a disagreement about empirical non-moral facts (i.e. is a disagreement in moral principles and values) and is not the result of a religious, non-moral-philosophical, or metaphysical disagreement. For instance, disagreements about what we ought to do in trolley cases are probably for the most part pure moral disagreements (see chapter 1).

Pure moral fact. Pure moral facts correspond to who is right in pure moral disagreements. For instance, if utilitarians are right about the footbridge trolley case, then it is a pure moral fact that we ought to push one person off the bridge to save the five in that case.

Rawlsian public reason (PR). A version of **public reason** according to which 'reasonable' rather than 'normal' people form the constituency of public reason. And the reasons that the constituency can have for accepting a law or state must be the same rather than being different. E.g. suppose that A and B are reasonable persons and that law L can be justified to A on the basis of reason 1 but not reason 2 and L can be justified to B on the basis of reason 2 but not reason 1. In this case Rawlsian public reason holds that this law is not legitimate but it would be if it could be justified to A and B (and all other reasonable persons) on the basis of the same reason. Cf. **Gausian public reason**.

Reasonable persons. Rawlsian reasonable persons are people who are morally motivated, are willing and able to reason sincerely with others about what is good, right, just, and true, and accept that society is a cooperative venture between free and equal persons. They are people who accept what Rawls calls the 'burdens of judgment'. That, is they accept that it is very difficult to come to the correct views about the right and the good because of the complexity of the evidence, conceptual vagueness, and influence of diverse life experiences on the normal functioning of the cognitive faculties of morally motivated people (at least within relatively free liberal societies). In this case if we accept the burdens of judgment we accept that:

i   moral judgment is difficult in virtue of these features of our epistemic situation; and

ii   in virtue of (i), people who are minimally reasonable will quite understandably and through no fault of their own come to different moral views and views of the good life; but

iii   such reasonable people with different moral views must still be cooperated with politically for the purpose of establishing legitimate laws.

Rawlsian reasonable persons can hold a wide range of substantive views of what is right and good. For instance, liberal Muslims, utilitarians, and Catholics can all continue to hold, with full certainty, their view of what is right, good, and just, while still holding that for the purposes of assessing whether a law is legitimately authoritative more must be taken into account than their own conceptions of the right, the good, and the just.

Reflective equilibrium. When we engage in wide reflective equilibrium reasoning we take the moral intuitions and judgments that we are greatly confident in and which persist over time (e.g. that slavery is wrong, homosexuality is permissible, it is often wrong to break promises, etc.) and we try to find moral principles that explain these intuitions and judgments. For instance, the Kantian view that an action is wrong iff it involves harmfully using someone as a mere means to yours or others, ends could explain why slavery is wrong—for slavery uses people in such a way—and why homosexuality is permissible, for it does not. In a search for wide reflective equilibrium we consider modifying these principles in line with any of our stable considered judgments with which they clash and modifying any judgments with which these principles clash to fit with more general and simple principles. We try to refine our intuitions and the principles that explain them until we have a strong consistency, or equilibrium, between these principles and judgments. In wide reflective equilibrium we also we try to ensure that these principles and judgments mesh with the best theorising in other domains such as sociology, economics, epistemology, etc.

Relativism. See **framework relativism**. In Chapter 2 'relativism' is sometimes used as synonymous with **non-objectivism**.

Robust realism. The view that there are truths and facts about right, wrong, good and bad, and what we morally ought to do. And these facts are not constituted by or grounded in what we, or our society do or would believe in any particular circumstances. On this view, moral truths are 'mind-independent'.

Safety principle. The view that if *S* knows that (or is justified in believing that) *p*, then in nearly all nearby possible worlds in which *S* forms the belief that *p* in the same way as she forms her belief in the actual world, *S* only believes *p* when *p* is true.

Self-defeat and arguments that views are self-defeating. If a view is self-defeating, then by accepting it we are committed to rejecting it. Views that are self-defeating are views that, if true, call for their own rejection.

Significant or substantial division of opinion. The way that these terms are used in this book, there is a substantial or significant division of opinion about whether *p* if there is approximately between a 40/60 and a 60/40 split about whether *p*.

Steadfast view. The opposite to (and competitor to) a conciliatory view regarding the epistemology of peer disagreement. According to this view, we typically should not revise our judgments about whether *p* when we find out that there is a significant division of opinion among those whom we should judge to be our epistemic peers about whether *p*.

Toy view. A toy view is a simplified version of a view used in order to get clear on a general kind of view or issue without getting into contextually irrelevant or unhelpful complexity.

Tradition & bias. A principle about when we can justifiably downgrade another's status as our epistemic peer about an issue. According to this principle, we can justifiably downgrade someone's status as our epistemic peer about whether *p* if:

(a) their view about whether *p* is the status quo or traditional view (and our view is a non-traditional view that is gaining popularity);
(b) we have some reason to believe that their view regarding whether *p* is driven or sustained by cognitive biases; and
(c) our view regarding whether *p* is not a traditional or status quo-based view and we have good reason to believe that our view regarding whether *p* is not driven or sustained by cognitive biases.

Trolley case. A case in which we must decide whether it is permissible to kill one person (or significantly harm them) in order to save a greater number of lives (or save a greater number of others from harm).

Truth relativism. The view that whether our moral claims are true or false is determined by the particular moral standards that we hold; this can be true even if the moral judgments that we make are not all made relative to particular standards or frameworks.

Voluntary pro-choice contributions. The view that abortions should be funded only via voluntary contributions made by only pro-choice taxpayers.

REFERENCES

Anderson, E. (1999). What is the Point of Equality? *Ethics*, 109, 287–337.

Andale, C. (2019). Charitable Interpretation Examples. YouTube, 15 March. Retrieved from www.youtube.com/watch?v=m_8sx_BVoCc.

Appiah, K. A. (2011). *The Honor Code: How Moral Revolutions Happen.* New York: W. W. Norton & Company.

Arvan, M. (2016). *Rightness as Fairness: A Moral and Political Theory.* Basingstoke: Palgrave.

Ayer, A. J. (2001). *Language, Truth and Logic.* London: Penguin.

Bächtiger, A., Dryzek, J. S., Mansbridge, J. & Warren, M. E. (eds) (2018). *The Oxford Handbook of Deliberative Democracy.* Oxford: Oxford University Press.

Bagnoli, C. (2017). Constructivism in Metaethics. In E. Zalta (ed.), *The Stanford Encyclopedia of Philosophy.* Retrieved from https://plato.stanford.edu/archives/sum2020/entries/constructivism-metaethics.

Ballantyne, N. (2014). Counterfactual Philosophers. *Philosophy and Phenomenological Research*, 88(2), 368–387.

Barrett, H. C., Bolyanatz, A., Crittenden, A. N., Fessler, D. M., Fitzpatrick, S., Gurven, M., ... Pisor, A. (2016). Small-scale Societies Exhibit Fundamental Variation in the Role of Intentions in Moral Judgment. *Proceedings of the National Academy of Sciences*, 113(17), 4688–4693.

Barnett, Z. (2019a). Belief Dependence: How Do the Numbers Count? *Philosophical Studies* 176(2), 297–319.

Barnett, Z. (2019b). Philosophy Without Belief. *Mind*, 128(509), 109–138.

Barry, C. & Tomlin, P. (2016). Moral Uncertainty and Permissibility: Evaluating Option Sets. *Canadian Journal of Philosophy*, 46(6), 898–923.

BBC. (2019). America's Gun Culture in Charts. BBC News, 5 August. Retrieved from www.bbc.co.uk/news/world-us-canada-41488081.

Bennigson, T. (1996). Irresolvable Disagreement and the Case against Moral Realism. *Southern Journal of Philosophy*, 34(4), 411–437.

Blackburn, S. (1984). *Spreading the Word.* Oxford: Clarendon.

Blackburn, S. (1993). *Essays in Quasi-Realism.* Oxford: Oxford University Press.

Blackburn, S. (1998). *Ruling Passions.* Oxford: Oxford University Press.

Blackburn, S. (1999). Is Objective Moral Justification Possible on a Quasi-Realist Foundation? *Inquiry*, 42(2), 213–227.

Bolinger, R. (2017). Reasonable Mistakes and Regulative Norms: Racial Bias in Defensive Harm. *Journal of Political Philosophy*, 25(1), 196–217.

Bogardus, T. (2016). Only All Naturalists Should Worry about Only One Evolutionary Debunking Argument. *Ethics*, 126(3), 636–661.

Bostrom, N. & Ord, T. (2006). The Reversal Test: Eliminating Status Quo Bias in Applied Ethics. *Ethics*, 116, 656–679.

Bourget, D. & Chalmers, D. (2014). What Do Philosophers Believe? *Philosophical Studies*, 170(3), 465–500.

Boyd, R. (1988). How to Be a Moral Realist. In G. Sayre-McCord (ed.), *Essays on Moral Realism* (pp. 181–228). Ithaca, NY: Cornell University Press.

Brandt, R. (1954). *Hopi Ethics: A Theoretical Analysis.* Chicago, IL: University of Chicago Press.

Bregman, R. (2020). *Humankind: A Hopeful History.* London: Bloomsbury.

Brennan, J. (2017). *Against Democracy.* Princeton, NJ: Princeton University Press.

Brightstorm. (2010). Relativity in Motion. Retrieved from www.youtube.com/watch?v=PKBXNVzpCJY.

Brink, D. (1989). *Moral Realism and the Foundations of Ethics*. Cambridge: Cambridge University Press.

Bykvist, K. (2017). Moral Uncertainty. *Philosophy Compass*, 12(3), 1–8..

Carter, J. A. (2018). On Behalf of Controversial View Agnosticism. *European Journal of Philosophy*, 26(4), 1358–1370.

Caviola, L., Everett, J. A. C. & Faber, N. S. (2019). The Moral Standing of Animals: Towards a Psychology of Speciesism. *Journal of Personality and Social Psychology*, 116(6), 1011–1029.

Chagnon, N. (2000). *Yanomamö: The Last Days of Eden*. San Diego, CA: Harvest Books.

Christensen, D. (2007). Epistemology of Disagreement: The Good News. *Philosophical Review*, 116, 187–218.

Christensen, D. (2009). Disagreement as Evidence: The Epistemology of Controversy. *Philosophy Compass*, 4(5), 756–767.

Christensen, D. (2011). Disagreement, Question-Begging, and Epistemic Self-criticism. *Philosophers Imprint*, 11(6), 1–22.

Christensen, D. (2013). Epistemic Modesty Defended. In D. Christensen & J. Lackey (eds), *The Epistemology of Disagreement*. Oxford: Oxford University Press.

Christensen, D. & Lackey, J. (2013). *The Epistemology of Disagreement*. Oxford: Oxford University Press.

Christiano, T. (2008). *The Constitution of Equality: Democratic Authority and its Limits*. Oxford: Oxford University Press.

Clarke, R. (2013). Belief is Credence One (in Context). *Philosophers Imprint*, 13(11), 1–18.

Clarke-Doane, J. (2012). Morality and Mathematics: The Evolutionary Challenge. *Ethics* 122(2), 313–340.

Cohen, G. A. (1989). On the Currency of Egalitarian Justice. *Ethics*, 99(4), 906–944.

Crisp, R. (2003). Equality, Priority, and Compassion. *Ethics*, 113(4), 745–763.

Cuneo, T. (2007). *The Normative Web: An Argument for Moral Realism*. Oxford: Oxford University Press.

Curry, O. S., Austin Mullins, D. & Whitehouse, H. (forthcoming). Is It Good to Cooperate? Testing the Theory of Morality-as-Cooperation in 60 Societies. *Current Anthropology*.

Dancy, J. (2000). Should We Pass the Buck? *Royal Institute of Philosophy Supplements*, 47, 159–173.

Dancy, J. (2004). *Ethics without Principles*. Oxford: Oxford University Press.

Daniels, N. (2003). Reflective Equilibrium. In E. Zalta (ed.), *The Stanford Encyclopedia of Philosophy*. Retrieved from https://plato.stanford.edu/archives/sum2020/entries/reflective-equilibrium.

Darwin, C. (2004). *The Descent of Man: Selection in Relation to Sex*. London: Penguin.

Davidson, D. (2001). *Inquiries into Truth and Interpretation: Philosophical Essays* (Vol. 2). Oxford: Oxford University Press.

De Cruz, H. (2018). *Religious Disagreement*. Cambridge: Cambridge University Press.

de Lazari-Radek, K. & Singer, P. (2012). The Objectivity of Ethics and the Unity of Practical Reason. *Ethics*, 123(1), 9–31.

Decker, J. (2014). Conciliation and Self-Incrimination. *Erkenntnis*, 79(5), 1099–1134.

Decker, J. & Groll, D. (2013). On the (in) Significance of Moral Disagreement for Moral Knowledge. *Oxford Studies in Metaethics*, 8, 140–167.

Doris, J. & Plakias, A. (2008a). How to Argue about Disagreement: Evaluative Diversity and Moral Realism. In W.Sinnott-Armstrong (ed.), *Moral Psychology, Vol. 2. The Cognitive Science of Morality: Intuition and Diversity* (pp. 303–331). Cambridge, MA: MIT Press.

Doris, J. & Plakias, A. (2008b). How to Find a Disagreement: Philosophical Diversity and Moral Realism. In W.Sinnott-Armstrong (ed.), *Moral Psychology, Vol. 2. The Cognitive Science of Morality: Intuition and Diversity* (pp. 345–354). Cambridge, MA: MIT Press.

Dowell, J. (2016). The Metaethical Insignificance of Moral Twin Earth. *Oxford Studies in Metaethics*, 11, 1–27.

Dreier, J. (2002). Meta-ethics and Normative Commitment. *Philosophical Issues*, 12, 241–263.

Dreier, J. (2009). Relativism (and Expressivism) and the Problem of Disagreement. *Philosophical Perspectives*, 23(1), 79–110.

Dunaway, B. (forthcoming). *Reality and Morality*. Oxford: Oxford University Press..

Dunaway, B. & McPherson, T. (2016). Reference Magnetism as a Solution to the Moral Twin Earth Problem. *Ergo, an Open Access Journal of Philosophy*, 3.

Dworkin, R. (2002). *Sovereign Virtue*. Cambridge, MA: Harvard University Press.

Edmonds, D. (2010). Matters of Life and Death. *Prospect*, 7 October. Retrieved from www.prospect magazine.co.uk/magazine/ethics-trolley-problem.

Eklund, M. (2011). What Are Thick Concepts? *Canadian Journal of Philosophy*, 41(1), 25–49.

Elga, A. (2007). Reflection and Disagreement. *Nous*, 41(3), 478–502.

Elga, A. (2010). *How to Disagree about How to Disagree*. In R. Feldman & T. A. Warfield (eds), *Disagreement*. Oxford: Oxford University Press.

Elstein, D. & Hurka, T. (2009). From Thick to Thin: Two Moral Reduction Plans. *Canadian Journal of Philosophy*, 39(4), 515–535.

Enoch, D. (2009). How Is Moral Disagreement a Problem for Realism? *The Journal of Ethics*, 13(1), 15–50.

Enoch, D. (2010). Not Just a Truthometer: Taking Oneself Seriously (but Not Too Seriously) in Cases of Peer Disagreement. *Mind*, 119(476), 953–997.

Enoch, D. (2011). *Taking Morality Seriously: A Defense of Robust Realism*. Oxford: Oxford University Press.

Enoch, D. (2013). The Disorder of Public Reason. *Ethics*, 124(1), 141–176.

Enoch, D. (2014). A Defense of Moral Deference. *The Journal of Philosophy*, 111(5), 229–258.

Enoch, D. (2015). Against Public Reason. *Oxford Studies in Political Philosophy*, 1, 112–142.

Enoch, D. (2017). Political Philosophy and Epistemology. *Oxford Studies in Political Philosophy*, 3, 132–165.

Estlund, D. (ed.) (2001a). *Democracy*. Oxford: Wiley-Blackwell.

Estlund, D. (2001b). Introduction. In D. Eslund (ed.), *Democracy*. Oxford: Wiley-Blackwell.

Estlund, D. M. (2009). *Democratic Authority: A Philosophical Framework*. Princeton, NJ:Princeton University Press.

Estlund, D. & Landemore, H. (2018). The Epistemic Value of Democratic Deliberation. In A. Bächtiger, J. S. Dryzek, J. Mansbridge & M. E. Warren (eds), *The Oxford Handbook of Deliberative Democracy*. Oxford: Oxford University Press.

Fearon, J. (1998). Deliberation as Discussion. In J. Elster (ed.), *Deliberative Democracy* (Vol. 1). Cambridge: Cambridge University Press.

Feldman, R. &. Warfield , T. (eds) (2010). *Disagreement*. Oxford: Oxford University Press.

Feser, E. (2003). Hayek on Tradition. *Journal of Libertarian Studies*, 17(1), 17–56.

Finlay, S. (2008). The Error in the Error Theory. *Australasian Journal of Philosophy*, 86(3), 347–369.

Finlay, S. (2014). *Confusion of Tongues: A Theory of Normative Language*. Oxford: Oxford University Press.

Finlay, S. (2017). Disagreement Lost and Found. *Oxford Studies in Metaethics*, 12, 187–205.

Finlay, S. & Schroeder, M. (2017). Reasons for Action: Internal vs. External. In E. Zalta (ed.), *The Stanford Encyclopedia of Philosophy*. Retrieved from https://plato.stanford.edu/archives/fa ll2017/entries/reasons-internal-external.

Fishkin, J. S. (2011). *When the People Speak: Deliberative Democracy and Public Consultation*. Oxford: Oxford University Press.

Fitzpatrick, S. (2014). Moral Realism, Moral Disagreement, and Moral Psychology. *Philosophical Papers*, 43(2), 161–190.

Fletcher, G. (2016). Moral Testimony. *Oxford Studies in Metaethics*, 11.

Foley, R. (1993). *Working without a Net*. Oxford: Oxford University Press.

Frances, B. (2010). The Reflective Epistemic Renegade. *Philosophy and Phenomenological Research*, 81(2), 419–463.

Frances, B. (2014). *Disagreement*. Chichester: John Wiley & Sons.

Frances, B. & Matheson , J. (2018). Disagreement. In E. Zalta (ed.), *The Stanford Encyclopedia of Philosophy*. Retrieved from https://plato.stanford.edu/archives/sum2020/entries/disagreement.

Fraser, B. & Hauser, M. (2010). The Argument from Disagreement and the Role of Cross Cultural Empirical Data. *Mind & Language*, 25(5), 541–560. doi:10.1111/j.1468-0017.2010.01400.x

Freeman, S. (2000). Deliberative Democracy: A Sympathetic Comment. *Philosophy & Public Affairs*, 29(4), 371–418.

Freeman, S. (2007). *Rawls*. New York: Routledge.

Fried, B. (2012). What Does Matter? The Case for Killing the Trolly Problem (Or Letting it Die). *Philosophical Quarterly*, 62(248), 505–529.

Fritz, J. (2018a). Conciliationism and Moral Spinelessness. *Episteme*, 15(1), 101–118.

Fritz, J. (2018b). What Pessimism about Moral Deference Means for Disagreement. *Ethical Theory and Moral Practice*, 21(1), 121–136.

Fritz, J. & McPherson, T. (2019). Moral Steadfastness and Meta-ethics. *American Philosophical Quarterly*, 56(1), 43–56.

Gander, K. (2017). A Satanist on Why Everything you Think you Know about His Religion Is Wrong. *The Independent*, 2 June. Retrieved from www.independent.co.uk/life-style/satanist-reverend-religions-everything-know-facts-devil-worship-church-ashley-s-palmer-a7767641.html.

Gaus, G. (2011). *The Order of Public Reason: A Theory of Freedom and Morality in a Diverse and Bounded World*. Cambridge: Cambridge University Press.

Gaus, G. (2015). On Dissing Public Reason: A Reply to Enoch. *Ethics*, 125(4), 1078–1095.

Gaus, G. & Vallier, K. (2009). The Roles of Religion Conviction in a Publicly Justified Polity: The Implications for Convergence, Asymmetry and Political Institutions. *Philosophy and Social Criticism*, 35(1–2), 51–76.

Gibbard, A. (1990). *Wise Choices, Apt Feelings*. Oxford: Clarendon Press.

Gibbard, A. (2003). *Thinking How to Live*. Cambridge, MA: Harvard University Press.

Goodin, R. E. (2008). *Innovating Democracy: Democratic Theory and Practice after the Deliberative Turn*. Oxford: Oxford University Press.

Goodwin, G. P. & Darley, J. M. (2008). The Psychology of Meta-Ethics: Exploring Objectivism. *Cognition*, 106(3), 1339–1366.

Graham, J., Haidt, J. & Nosek, B. A. (2009). Liberals and Conservatives Rely on Different Sets of Moral Foundations. *Journal of Personality and Social Psychology*, 96(5), 1029–1046. doi:10.1037/a0015141

Graham, P. A. (2010). In Defense of Objectivism about Moral Obligation. *Ethics*, 121(1), 88–115.

Greenhalgh, T., Schmid, M. B., Czypionka, T., Bassler, D. & Gruer, L. (2020). Face Masks for the Public during the Covid-19 Crisis. *British Medical Journal*, 369(1435), 1–4.

Gruen, L. (2017). The Moral Status of Animals. In E. Zalta (ed.), *The Stanford Encyclopedia of Philosophy*. Retrieved from https://plato.stanford.edu/archives/fall2017/entries/moral-animal.

Gruenbaum, E. (2001). *The Female Circumcision Controversy: An Anthropological Perspective*. Philadelphia, PA: University of Pennsylvania Press.

Gutmann, A. & Thompson, D. F. (1998). *Democracy and Disagreement*. Cambridge, MA: Harvard University Press.

Gutmann, A. & Thompson, D. F. (2014). *The Spirit of Compromise: Why Governing Demands It and Campaigning Undermines It*. Princeton, NJ:Princeton University Press.

Haidt, J. (2012). *The Righteous Mind: Why Good People Are Divided by Politics and Religion*. New York: Vintage.

Halsanger, S. (2000). Gender and Race: (What) Are They? (What) Do We Want Them To Be? *Noûs*, 34(1), 31–55.

Haltzman, S. (2013). The Morality of Infidelity. *Huffington Post*, 31 July. Retrieved from www.huffpost.com/entry/gallup-poll-infidelity_b_3367769?guccounter=1.

Hansard. (2014). *Hansard* HC, 5 February. Retrieved from https://publications.parliament.uk/pa/cm201314/cmhansrd/cm140205/text/140205w0002.htm#140205w0002.htm_wqn16

Hare, R. M. (1952). *The Language of Morals*. Oxford: Oxford University Press.

Harman, E. (2015). The Irrelevance of Moral Uncertainty. *Oxford Studies in Metaethics*, 10, 53–79.

Harman, G. (1975). Moral Relativism Defended. *Philosophical Review*, 84(1), 3–22.

Harman, G. (1996). Moral Relativism. In G. Harman & J. J. Thomson, *Moral Relativism and Moral Objectivism*. Oxford: Blackwell.

Harman, G. & Thomson, J. J. (1995). *Moral Relativism and Moral Objectivity*. Oxford: Blackwell.

Haslanger, S. (2000). Gender and Race: (What) Are They? (What) Do We Want Them to Be? *Noûs*, 34(1), 31–55.

Hauser, M., Cushman, F., Young, L., Jin, R. K. X. & Mikhail, J. (2007). A Dissociation between Moral Judgments and Justifications. *Mind & Language*, 22(1), 1–21.

Hawthorne, J. P. (2004). *Knowledge and Lotteries*. Oxford: Oxford University Press.

Hedden, B. (2016). Does MITE Make Right. On Decision-Making under Normative Uncertainty. *Oxford Studies in Metaethics*, 11.

Helm, B. (2005). Friendship. In E. Zalta (ed.), *The Stanford Encyclopedia of Philosophy*. Retrieved from https://plato.stanford.edu/archives/sum2020/entries/friendship.

Hicks, A. (2018). Moral Uncertainty and Value Comparison. *Oxford Studies in Metaethics*, 13.

Hills, A. (2009). Moral Testimony and Moral Epistemology. *Ethics*, 120(1), 94–127.

Hills, A. (2013). Moral Testimony. *Philosophy Compass*, 8(6), 552–559.

Hills, A. (2013). Faultless Moral Disagreement. *Ratio* (new series), 26(4), 410–427.

Hong, L. & Page, S. E. (2004). Groups of Diverse Problem Solvers Can Outperform Groups of High-ability Problem Solvers. *Proceedings of the National Academy of Sciences*, 101(46), 16385–16389.

Horgan, T. & Timmons, M. (1991). New Wave Moral Realism Meets Moral Twin Earth. *Journal of Philosophical Research*, 16, 447–465.

Horgan, T. & Timmons, M. (2009). Analytical Moral Functionalism Meets Moral Twin Earth. In I. Ravenscroft (ed.), *Minds, Ethics, and Conditionals: Themes from the Philosophy of Frank Jackson*. Oxford: Oxford University Press.

Huemer, M. (2007). *Ethical Intuitionism*. New York: Springer.

Huemer, M.(2013). *The Problem of Political Authority*. Basingstoke: Palgrave.

Jackson, F. (1991). Decision-Theoretic Consequentialism and the Nearest and Dearest Objection. *Ethics*, 101(3), 461–482.

Jackson, F. (1998). *From Metaphysics to Ethics*. Oxford: Oxford University Press.

Jones, K. (1999). Second-hand Moral Knowledge. *The Journal of Philosophy*, 96(2), 55–78.

Joyce, R. (2002). *The Myth of Morality*. Cambridge: Cambridge University Press.

Joyce, R. (2006). *The Evolution of Morality*. Cambridge, MA: MIT Press.

Kagan, S. (2016). What's Wrong with Speciesism? Society for Applied Philosophy Annual Lecture 2015. *Journal of Applied Philosophy*, 33(1), 1–21.

Kahane, G. (2011). Evolutionary Debunking Arguments. *Nous*, 45(1), 103–125.

Kalderon, M. E. (2005). *Moral Fictionalism*. Oxford: Oxford University Press.

Kalf, W. (2018). *Moral Error Theory*. Basingstoke: Palgrave.

Kappel, K. (2012). The Problem of Deep Disagreement. *Discipline Filosofiche*, 22(2), 7–25.

Kappel, K. (2018a). There is no Middle Ground for Deep Disagreements about Facts. Aeon. Retrieved from https://aeon.co/ideas/there-is-no-middle-ground-for-deep-disagreements-about-facts

Kappel, K. (2018b). Higher Order Evidence and Deep Disagreement. *Topoi*, 1–12.

Kappel, K. (2018c). How Moral Disagreement May Ground Principled Moral Compromise. *Politics, Philosophy & Economics*, 17(1), 75–96.

Kelly, T. (2005). The Epistemic Significance of Disagreement. In T. Gendler & J. Hawthorne (eds), *Oxford Studies in Epistemology*, vol. 1. Oxford: Oxford University Press.

Kelly, T. (2010). Peer Disagreement and Higher-Order Evidence. In R. Feldman & T. Warfield (eds), *Disagreement* (pp. 111–174). Oxford: Oxford University Press.

Kelly, T. (2019). The Epistemic Significance of Disagreement. In E. Sosa, J. Fantl & M. McGrath (eds), *Contemporary Epistemology: An Anthology* (pp. 249–264). Oxford: Wiley Blackwell.

Kelly, T. & McGrath, S. (2010). Is Reflective Equilibrium Enough? *Philosophical Perspectives*, 24, 325–359.

Kelman, M. & Kreps, T. A. (2014). Playing with Trolleys: Intuitions About the Permissibility of Aggregation. *Journal of Empirical Legal Studies*, 11(2), 197–226. doi:10.1111/jels.12039.

Khoo, J. & Knobe, J. (2018). Moral Disagreement and Moral Semantics. *Noûs*, 52(1), 109–143.

Kiesewetter, B. (2017). *The Normativity of Rationality*. Oxford: Oxford University Press.

Killoren, D. (2009). Moral Intuitions, Reliability, and Disagreement. *Journal of Ethics and Social Philosophy*, 4(1), 1–36.

Kim, K. R., Kang, J. S. & Yun, S. (2012). Moral Intuitions and Political Orientation: Similarities and Differences between South Korea and the United States. *Psychological Reports*, 111(1), 173–185.

King, N. L. (2011). Rejoinder to McGrath. *Journal of Philosophical Research*, 36, 243–246.

Klenk, M. (2018). Evolution and Disagreement. *Journal of Ethics and Social Philosophy*, 14(2), 112–142.

Köhler, S. (2014). Expressivism and Mind-Dependence: Distinct Existences. *Journal of Moral Philosophy*, 11(6), 750–764.

Kölbel, M. (2004). Faultless Disagreement. *Proceedings of the Aristotelian Society*, 104(1), 53–73.

Kornblith, H. (2010). Belief in the Face of Controversy. *Disagreement*, 29, 52.

Korsgaard, C. (1995). *The Sources of Normativity*. Cambridge: Cambridge University Press.

Korsgaard, C. (2018). *Fellow Creatures: Our Obligations to the Other Animals*. Oxford: Oxford University Press.

Kramer, M. H. (2009). *Moral Realism as a Moral Doctrine*. (Vol. 3). Chichester: John Wiley & Sons.

Lackey, J. (2010). A Justificationist View of Disagreement's Epistemic Significance. In A. M. A. Haddock & D. Pritchard (ed.), *Social Epistemology*. Oxford: Oxford University Press.

Lackey, J. (2013). Disagreement and Belief Dependence: Why Numbers Matter. In D. Christensen & J. Lackey (eds), *The Epistemology of Disagreement*. Oxford: Oxford University Press.

Landemore, H. (2017). *Democratic Reason: Politics, Collective Intelligence, and the Rule of the Many*. Princeton, NJ: Princeton University Press.

Lane, P. (dir.) (2019). *Hail Satan?* New York: Magnolia Pictures.

Lefeber, Y. & Voorhoeve, H. W. (1998). *Indigenous Customs in Childbirth and Child Care*. Assen: Uitgeverij Van Gorcum.

Leiter, B. (2014). Moral Skepticism and Moral Disagreement in Nietzsche. In Russ Shafer-Landau (ed.), *Oxford Studies in Metaethics*, 9 Oxford: Oxford University Press.

Leiter, B. (2012). Philosophers, Eating, Ethics—a Discussion of the Poll Results. Leiter Reports, 10 October. Retrieved from https://leiterreports.typepad.com/blog/2012/10/philosophers-eating-ethics-a-discussion-of-the-poll-results.html

Leland, R. & van Wietmarschen, H. (2012). Reasonableness, Intellectual Modesty, and Reciprocity in Political Justification. *Ethics*, 122(4), 721–747.

Lenman, J. & Shemmer, Y. (2012). *Constructivism in Practical Philosophy*. Oxford: Oxford University Press.

Lister, A. (2016). *Public Reason and Political Community*. London: Bloomsbury Publishing.

Lockhart, T. (2000). *Moral Uncertainty and its Consequences*. Oxford: Oxford University Press.

Loeb, D. (1998). Moral Realism and the Argument from Disagreement. *Philosophical Studies*, 90(3), 281–303.

López-Guerra, C. (2014). *Democracy and Disenfranchisement: The Morality of Electoral Exclusions*. New York: Oxford University Press.

Lord, E. (2015). Acting for the Right Reasons, Abilities, and Obligation. In Russ Shafer-Landau (ed.), *Oxford Studies in Metaethics*, 10, 26–52. Oxford: Oxford University Press.

MacAskill, W. (2014). *Normative Uncertainty*. PhD dissertation, University of Oxford 2014. Retrieved from: http://www.williammacaskill.com/research

MacAskill, W. (2016). Normative Uncertainty as a Voting Problem. *Mind*, 125(500), 967–1004.

MacFarlane, J. (2007). Relativism and Disagreement. *Philosophical Studies*, 132(1), 17–31.

Mackie, J. (1977). *Ethics: Inventing Right and Wrong*. London: Penguin.

Margalit, A. (2009). *On Compromise and Rotten Compromises*. Princeton, NJ: Princeton University Press.

Matheson, J. (2015a). Disagreement and Epistemic Peers. Oxford Handbooks Online. Retrieved from www.oxfordhandbooks.com/view/10.1093/oxfordhb/9780199935314.001.0001/oxfordhb-9780199935314-e-13.

Matheson, J. (2015b). *The Epistemic Significance of Disagreement*. New York: Springer.

Matheson, J. (2016). Moral Caution and the Epistemology of Disagreement. *Journal of Social Philosophy*, 47(2), 120–141.

May, S. C. (2005). Principled Compromise and the Abortion Controversy. *Philosophy and Public Affairs*, 33(4), 317–348.

May, S. C. (2011). Moral Compromise, Civic Friendship, and Political Reconciliation. *Critical Review of International Social and Political Philosophy*, 14(5), 581–602.

May, S. C. (2013). Compromise. *International Encyclopedia of Ethics*. Retrieved from https://onlinelibrary.wiley.com/doi/10.1002/9781444367072.wbiee565.pub2

McCarthy, J. (2014). Same-Sex Marriage Support Reaches New High at 55%. Gallup.com May 21, 2014. Retrieved from www.gallup.com/poll/169640/sex-marriage-support-reaches-new-high.aspx.

McCarthy, N. (2017). The World Is Divided on the Use of Torture. Forbes 26 January 2017. Retrieved from www.forbes.com/sites/niallmccarthy/2017/01/26/the-world-is-divided-on-the-use-of-torture-infographic/#4d3c58e55ac6

McCarthy, N. (2018). Who Are America's Vegans and Vegetarians? Forbes 6 August 2018. Retrieved from www.forbes.com/sites/niallmccarthy/2018/08/06/who-are-americas-vegans-and-vegetarians-infographic/#16f33170211c

McGrath, S. (2008). Moral Disagreement and Moral Expertise. In Russ Shafer-Landau (ed.), *Oxford Studies in Metaethics*, 3(87). Oxford: Oxford University Press.

McGrath, S. (2010). Moral Realism without Convergence. *Philosophical Topics*, 38(2), 59–90.

McGrath, S. (2011). Skepticism About Moral Expertise as a Puzzle for Moral Realism. *Journal of Philosophy*, 108(3), 111–137.

McGrath, S. (2011). Reply to King. *Journal of Philosophical Research*, 36, 235–241.

McGrath, S. (2014). Relax? Don't Do it! Why Moral Realism Won't Come Cheap. In Russ Shafer-Landau (ed.), *Oxford Studies in Metaethics*, 9. Oxford: Oxford University Press, 186–214.

McGrath, S. (2020). Philosophical Methodology and Levels of Generality. *Philosophical Perspectives*, early view.

McGraw, C. (2008). The Realism/Anti-Realism Debate in Religion. *Philosophy Compass*, 3(1), 254–272.

McKenna, R. (2019). Irrelevant Cultural Influences on Belief. *Journal of Applied Philosophy* 36(5), 755–768.

McKinnon, C. (2007). *Toleration: A Critical Introduction*. Abingdon: Routledge.

McNaughton, D. (1996). An Unconnected Heap of Duties? *The Philosophical Quarterly*, 46(185), 433–447.

Mendelberg, T. (2002). The Deliberative Citizen: Theory and Evidence. *Political Decision Making, Deliberation and Participation*, 6(1), 151–193.

Merli, D. (2002). Return to Moral Twin Earth. *Canadian Journal of Philosophy*, 32(2), 207–240.

Michaelson, E. & Reimer, M. (2019). Reference. In E. Zalta (ed.), *The Stanford Encyclopedia of Philosophy*. Retrieved from https://plato.stanford.edu/archives/spr2019/entries/reference.

Mill, J. S. (1978). *On Liberty*. Indianapolis, IN: Hackett.

Miller, A. (2003). *An Introduction to Contemporary Metaethics*. Cambridge: Polity Press.

Mogensen, A. (2016). Contingency Anxiety and the Epistemology of Disagreement. *Pacific Philosophical Quarterly*, 97(4), 590–611.

Mogensen, A. (2017). Disagreements in Moral Intuitions as Defeaters. *Philosophical Quarterly*, 67(267), 282–302.

Moore, G. E. (1903). *Principia Ethica*. Cambridge: Cambridge University Press.

Moran, R. (1988). Making Up Your Mind: Self-interpretation and Self Constitution. *Ratio*, 1, 135–151.

More Perfect. (2017). Mr Graham and the Reasonable Man. More Perfect, 30 Novemberc 2017. WNYC Studios. Podcast retrieved from www.wnycstudios.org/podcasts/radiolabmoreperfect/episodes/mr-graham-and-reasonable-man radiolab

Morgan, R. (2016). The Slow but Steady Rise of Vegetarianism in Australia. Retrieved from www.roymorgan.com/findings/vegetarianisms-slow-but-steady-rise-in-australia-201608151105

Morgan-Knapp, C. (2015). Nonconsequentialist Precaution. *Ethical Theory and Moral Practice*, 18(4), 785–797.

Nisbett, R. E. & Cohen, D. (1996). *Culture of Honor: The Psychology of Violence in the South*. Boulder, CO: Westview.

Nozick, R. (1974). *Anarchy, State and Utopia*. Oxford: Basil Blackwell.

Nguyen, C. T. (2010). Autonomy, Understanding, and Moral Disagreement. *Philosophical Topics*, 38(2), 111–129.

Nguyen, C. T. (2018). Cognitive Islands and Runaway Echo Chambers: Problems for Epistemic Dependence on Experts. *Synthese*, 197, 2803–2821.

Olson, J. (2010). The Freshman Objection to Expressivism and What to Make of it. *Ratio*, 23(1), 87–101.

Olson, J. (2014). *Moral Error Theory: History, Critique, Defence*. Oxford: Oxford University Press.

Otsuka, M. (2003). *Libertarianism without Inequality*. Oxford: Clarendon Press.

Parfit, D. (2011a). *On What Matters*, Vol. 1. Oxford: Oxford University Press.

Parfit, D. (2011b). *On What Matters* Vol. 2. Oxford: Oxford University Press.

Peter, F. (2007). *Democratic Legitimacy*. Abingdon: Routledge.

Pianalto, M. (2011). Moral Conviction. *Journal of Applied Philosophy*, 28(4), 381–395.

Pittard, J. (2015). Resolute Conciliationism. *The Philosophical Quarterly*, 65(260), 442–463.

Pleasants, N. (2009). Wittgenstein and Basic Moral Certainty. *Philosophia*, 37(4), 669.

Plunkett, D. & Sundell, T. (2013). Disagreement and the Semantics of Normative and Evaluative Terms. *Philosophers Imprint*, 13(23), 1–37.

Polletta, F. & Gardner, B. G. (2017). The Forms of Deliberative Communication. In A. Bächtiger, J. S. Dryzek, J. Mansbridge & M. E. Warren (eds), *The Oxford Handbook of Deliberative Democracy*. Oxford: Oxford University Press.

Portmore, D. W. (2011). *Commonsense Consequentialism: Wherein Morality Meets Rationality* (Vol. 2). New York: Oxford University Press.

Pritchard, D. (2005). *Epistemic Luck*. Oxford: Clarendon Press.

Pryor, J. (2000). The Skeptic and the Dogmatist. *Nous*, 34(4), 517–549.

Pölzler, T. & Wright, J. C. (2019). Empirical Research on Folk Moral Objectivism. *Philosophy Compass*, 14(5), 1–15.

Quong, J. (2011). *Liberalism without Perfection*. Oxford: Oxford University Press.

Quong, J. (2013). Public Reason. In E. Zalta (ed.), *The Stanford Encyclopedia of Philosophy*. Retrieved from https://plato.stanford.edu/archives/sum2020/entries/public-reason.

Rabinowitz, D. (2011). The Safety Condition for Knowledge. *Internet Encyclopedia of Philosophy*. Retrieved from https://iep.utm.edu/safety-c.

Radiolab. (2019). The Good Samaritan. Radiolab, 24 May 2019. WNYC Studios. Podcast retrieved from www.wnycstudios.org/podcasts/radiolab/articles/good-samaritan.

Rawls, J. (1971). *A Theory of Justice*. Cambridge, MA: Harvard University Press.

Rawls, J. (1996). *Political Liberalism*. New York: Columbia University Press.

Rawls, J. (1999). *Collected Papers* (ed. S. Freeman). Cambridge, MA: Harvard University Press.

Rawls, J. (1974). The Independence of Moral Theory. Proceedings and Addresses of the American Philosophical Association, vol. 48, 1974, 5–22.

Rawls, J. (1980). Kantian Constructivism in Moral Theory. Journal of Philosophy, 77, 515–572.

Raz, J. (1998). Disagreement in Politics. American Journal of Jurispridence, 43, 25.

Reply All. (2020). #158: The Case of the Missing Hit. Reply All, 5 March 2020, Gimlet Media. Podcast retrieved from https://gimletmedia.com/shows/reply-all/o2h8bx.

Rini, R. (2015). How Not to Test for Philosophical Expertise. Synthese, 192(2), 431–452.

Risberg, O. & Tersman, F. (2019). A New Route from Moral Disagreement to Moral Skepticism. Journal of the American Philosophical Association, 5(2), 189–207.

Roberts, D. (2011). Shapelessness and the Thick. Ethics, 121(3), 489–520.

Robin, C. (2011). The Reactionary Mind: Conservatism from Edmund Burke to Sarah Palin. Oxford: Oxford University Press.

Ross, W. D. (1930). The Right and the Good. Oxford: Oxford University Press.

Rowland, R. (2013). Moral Error Theory and the Argument from Epistemic Reasons. Journal of Ethics and Social Philosophy, 7(1), 1–24.

Rowland, R. (2017a). The Epistemology of Moral Disagreement. Philosophy Compass, 12(2), 1–16.

Rowland, R. (2017b). The Significance of Significant Fundamental Moral Disagreement. Noûs, 51(4), 802–831.

Rowland, R. (2018). The Intelligibility of Moral Intransigence: A Dilemma for Cognitivism about Moral Judgment. Analysis, 78(2), 266–275.

Rowland, R. (2019a). The Normative and the Evaluative: The Buck-Passing Account of Value. Oxford: Oxford University Press.

Rowland, R. (2019b). Companions in Guilt Arguments in the Epistemology of Moral Disagreement. In C. Cowie & R. Rowland (ed.), Companions in Guilt Arguments in Metaethics. Abingdon: Routledge.

Rowland, R. (2020). Moral Conviction, Moral Spinelessness, and the Practical Implications of Conciliationism. Unpublished manuscript.

Rowland, R. (2019c). Local Evolutionary Debunking Arguments. Philosophical Perspectives 33, 2: 170–199.

Rowland, R. & Killoren, D. (2020) Moral Deliberation and Moral Judgment Shift. Unpublished manuscript.

Rowland, R. & Simpson, R. (2021). Permissivism and Reasonable Pluralism. In M. Hannon & J. de Ridder (eds.), The Routledge Handbook of Political Epistemology. Abingdon: Routledge.

Sampson, E. (2019). The Self-undermining Arguments from Disagreement. In Russ Shafer-Landau (ed.), Oxford Studies in Metaethics, 14. Oxford: Oxford University Press.

Sayre-McCord, G. (1997). 'Good' on Twin Earth. Philosophical Issues, 8, 267–292.

Sauer, H. (2018). Debunking Arguments in Ethics. Cambridge: Cambridge University Press.

Sauer, H. (2019). The Argument from Agreement: How Universal Values Undermine Moral Realism. Ratio, 32(4), 339–352.

Scanlon, T. M. (2003). Rawls on Justification. In S. Freeman (ed.), The Cambridge Companion to Rawls. Cambridge: Cambridge University Press.

Scanlon, T. M. (2014). Being Realistic about Reasons. Oxford: Oxford University Press.

Scheffler, S. (1994). The Rejection of Consequentialism: A Philosophical Investigation of the Considerations Underlying Rival Moral Conceptions. Oxford: Oxford University Press.

Schroeder, M. (2007). Slaves of the Passions. Oxford: Oxford University Press.

Schroeder, M. (2008). What is the Frege–Geach Problem? Philosophy Compass, 3(4), 703–720.

Schroeder, M. (2014). Does Expressivism Have Subjectivist Consequences? Philosophical Perspectives, 28(1), 278–290.

Schroeder, M. A. (2010). Noncognitivism in Ethics. New York: Routledge.

Sepielli, A. (2009). What to Do When You Don't Know What to Do. In Russ Shafer-Landau (ed.), Oxford Studies in Metaethics, 4. Oxford: Oxford University Press, 5–28.

Sepielli, A. (2013). Moral Uncertainty and the Principle of Equity among Moral Theories. *Philosophy and Phenomenological Research*, 86(3), 580–589.

Sepielli, A. (2016). Moral Uncertainty and Fetishistic Motivation. *Philosophical Studies*, 173(11), 2951–2968.

Setiya, K. (2012). *Knowing Right from Wrong*. Oxford: Oxford University Press.

Shafer-Landau, R. (1994). Ethical Disagreement, Ethical Objectivism and Moral Indeterminacy. *Philosophy and Phenomenological Research*, 54(2), 331–344.

Shafer-Landau, R. (2003). *Moral Realism: A Defence*. Oxford: Oxford University Press.

Shafer-Landau, R. (2006). A Defense of Ethical Nonnaturalism. In T. Horgan & M. Timmons (eds), *Metaethics after Moore*. Oxford: Oxford University Press.

Shafer-Landau, R. (2017). *The Fundamentals of Ethics*. Oxford: Oxford University Press.

Shah, N. (2006). A New Argument for Evidentialism. *The Philosophical Quarterly*, 56(225), 481–498.

Sher, G. (1981). Subsidized Abortion: Moral Rights and Moral Compromise. *Philosophy and Public Affairs*, 10(4), 361–372.

Sherman, B. (2014). Moral Disagreement and Epistemic Advantages: A Challenge to McGrath. *Journal of Ethics and Social Philosophy*, 8(3), 1–19.

Shields, L. (2018). *Just Enough*. Edinburgh: Edinburgh University Press.

Sidgwick, H. (1981). *The Methods of Ethics* (7th edition). Indianapolis, IN: Hackett Publishing. Silk, A. (2016). *Discourse Contextualism: A Framework for Contextualist Semantics and Pragmatics*. Oxford: Oxford University Press.

Silk, A. (2017). Normative Language in Context. In R. Shafer-Landau (ed.), *Oxford Studies in Metaethics*, vol. 12. Oxford: Oxford University Press.

Simmons, A. J. (1999). Justification and Legitimacy. *Ethics*, 109(4), 739–771.

Sliwa, P. (2012). In Defense of Moral Testimony. *Philosophical Studies*, 158(2), 175–195.

Smart, J. J. C & Williams, B. (1973). *Utilitarianism: For and Against*. Cambridge: Cambridge University Press.

Smith, M.. (1994). *The Moral Problem*. Oxford: Blackwell.

Sobel, D. (2016). *From Valuing to Value*. Oxford: Oxford University Press.

Sorensen, R. (1995). Unknowable Obligations. *Utilitas*, 7(2), 247–271.

Sosa, E. (1999). How to Defeat Opposition to Moore. *Noûs*, 33, 141–153.

Staffel, J. (2017). Accuracy for Believers. *Episteme*, 14(1), 39–48.

Stevenson, C. L. (1963). *Facts and Values: Studies in Ethical Analysis*. New Haven, CT: Yale University Press.

Stich, S. (2007). The Persistence of Moral Disagreement. Lecture series. Part 1 of 6 retrieved from www.youtube.com/watch?v=3EU5LiJAaCQ (other parts also available on YouTube).

Stout, J. (2009). *Democracy and Tradition*. Princeton, NJ:Princeton University Press.

Stratton-Lake, P. (2011). Recalcitrant Pluralism. *Ratio*, 24(4), 364–383.

Stratton-Lake, P. (2014). Intuitionism in Ethics. In E. Zalta (ed.), *The Stanford Encyclopedia of Philosophy*. Retrieved from https://plato.stanford.edu/entries/intuitionism-ethics.

Strawser, B. J. (2010). Moral Predators: The Duty to Employ Uninhabited Aerial Vehicles. *Journal of Military Ethics*, 9(4), 342–368.

Street, S. (2006). A Darwinian Dilemma for Realist Theories of Value. *Philosophical Studies*, 127, 109–166.

Street, S. (2010). What is Constructivism in Ethics and Metaethics? *Philosophy Compass*, 5(5), 363–384.

Streumer, B. (2011). Are Normative Properties Descriptive Properties? *Philosophical Studies*, 154(3), 325–348.

Streumer, B. (2013). Can We Believe the Error Theory? *The Journal of Philosophy*, 110(4), 194–212.

Streumer, B. (2017). *Unbelievable Errors: An Error Theory about All Normative Judgements*. Oxford: Oxford University Press.

Tarsney, C. (2018a). Intertheoretic Value Comparison: A Modest Proposal. *Journal of Moral Philosophy*, 15(3), 324–344.

Tarsney, C. (2018b). Moral Uncertainty for Deontologists. *Ethical Theory and Moral Practice*, 21(3), 505–520.

Temkin, L. (2003). Egalitarianism Defended. *Ethics*, 113(4), 764–782.

Tersman, F. (2006). *Moral Disagreement*. Cambridge: Cambridge University Press.

Tersman, F. (2017). Debunking and Disagreement. *Noûs*, 51(4), 754–774.

Thomson, J. J. (1990). *The Realm of Rights*. Cambridge, MA: Harvard University Press.

Timmerman, T. & Cohen, Y. (2019). Actualism and Possibilism in Ethics. In E. Zalta (ed.), *The Stanford Encyclopedia of Philosophy*. Retrieved from https://plato.stanford.edu/entries/actualism-possibilism-ethics.

Trustify. (2018). Infidelity Statistics 2018: Why, When, and How People Stray. Trustify, 11 October 2018. Retrieved from www.trustify.info/blog/infidelity-statistics-2018.

Vallier, K. (1996). Public Justification. In E. Zalta (ed.), *The Stanford Encyclopedia of Philosophy*. Retrieved from https://plato.stanford.edu/archives/sum2020/entries/justification-public.

Vallier, K. (2015). Public Justification versus Public Deliberation: The Case for Divorce. *Canadian Journal of Philosophy*, 45(2), 139–158.

Van Inwagen, P. (2010). We're Right. They're Wrong. In R. Feldman & T. A. Warfield (eds), *Disagreement*. Oxford: Oxford University Press.

Van Roojen, M. (2015). *Metaethics: A Contemporary Introduction*. Abingdon: Routledge.

Van Roojen, M. (2018). Moral Cognitivism vs. Non-Cognitivism. In E. Zalta (ed.), *The Stanford Encyclopedia of Philosophy*. Retrieved from https://plato.stanford.edu/archives/fall2018/entries/moral-cognitivism.

Van Wietmarschen, H. (2013). Peer Disagreement, Evidence, and Well-groundedness. *Philosophical Review*, 122(3), 395–425.

Van Wietmarschen, H. (2018). Reasonable Citizens and Epistemic Peers: A Skeptical Problem for Political Liberalism. *Journal of Political Philosophy*, 26(4), 486–507.

Vavova, K. (2014). Moral Disagreement and Moral Skepticism. *Philosophical Perspectives*, 28(1), 302–333.

Vavova, K. (2015). Evolutionary Debunking of Moral Realism. *Philosophy Compass*, 10(2), 104–116.

Vavova, K. (2018). Irrelevant Influences. *Philosophy and Phenomenological Research* 96, 1, 134–152.

Väyrynen, P. (2013). *The Lewd, the Rude and the Nasty: A Study of Thick Concepts in Ethics*. Oxford: Oxford University Press.

Väyrynen, P. (2018). A Simple Escape from Moral Twin Earth. *Thought: A Journal of Philosophy*, 7(2), 109–118.

Väyrynen, P. (2019). Thick Ethical Concepts. In E. Zalta (ed.), *The Stanford Encyclopedia of Philosophy*. Retrieved from https://plato.stanford.edu/archives/sum2019/entries/thick-ethical-concepts.

Waldron, J. (2001). The Constitutional Conception of Democracy. In D. Estlund (ed.), *Democracy* (pp. 282–312). Oxford: Wiley Blackwell.

Weatherson, B. (2007). Disagreeing about Disagreement. Retrieved from https://philpapers.org/rec/WEADAD-2.

Weatherson, B. J. (2013). Disagreements, Philosophical and Otherwise. In D. Christensen & J. Lackey (eds), *The Epistemology of Disagreement*. Oxford: Oxford University Press.

Weatherson, B. (2014). Running Risks Morally. *Philosophical Studies*, 167(1), 141–163.

Wedgwood, R. (2001). Conceptual Role Semantics for Moral Terms. *The Philosophical Review*, 110(1), 1–30.

Wedgwood, R. (2010). The Moral Evil Demons. In R. Feldman & T. A. Warfield (eds), *Disagreement* (pp. 216–246). Oxford: Oxford University Press.

Weijers, D., Unger, P. & Sytsma, J. (2019). Trolley Problems Reconsidered: Testing the Method of Several Options. Unpublished manuscript.

Weinstock, D. (2013). On the Possibility of Principled Moral Compromise. *Critical Review of International Social and Political Philosophy*, 16(4), 537–556.

Wendt, F. (2011). Compromising on Justice. Special issue of *Critical Review of International Social and Political Philosophy*.

Wendt, F. (2016). *Compromise, Peace and Public Justification: Political Morality beyond Justice.* New York: Springer.

Wiegmann, A. & Meyer, K. (2015). *When Killing the Heavy Man Seems Right: Making People Utilitarian by Simply Adding Options to Moral Dilemmas.* Paper presented at CogSci. Retrieved from www. psych.uni-goettingen.de/de/cognition/publikationen-dateien-wiegmann/in%20press__2015 WiegmannMeyer_When%20killing%20the%20heavy%20man%20seems%20right.pdf.

Wielenberg, E. J. (2010). On the Evolutionary Debunking of Morality. *Ethics*, 120(3), 441–464.

Wiens, D. (2015). Political Ideals and the Feasibility Frontier. *Economics & Philosophy*, 31(3), 447–477.

Wiland, E. (2017). Moral Testimony: Going on the Offensive. In Russ Shafer-Landau (ed.), *Oxford Studies in Metaethics*, 12. Oxford: Oxford University Press.

Williams, B. (1973). *Problems of the Self.* Cambridge: Cambridge University Press.

Williams, B. (1981). Internal and External Reasons. In B. Williams, *Moral Luck.* Cambridge: Cambridge University Press.

Williams, B. (2006). *Ethics and the Limits of Philosophy.* Abingdon: Routledge.

Wolff, J. (2012). *Ethics and Public Policy.* Abingdon: Routledge.

Wolff, J. (1996). *An Introduction to Political Philosophy.* Oxford: Oxford University Press.

Wolff, R. P. (1998). *In Defense of Anarchism.* Berkeley, CA: University of California Press.

Wong, D. B. (1984). *Moral Relativity.* Berkeley, CA: University of California Press.

Wong, D. (2011). Relativist Explanation of Interpersonal and Group Disagreement. In S. Hales (ed.), *A Companion to Relativism* (pp. 411–429). Malden, MA: Wiley-Blackwell.

Wright, C. (1995). Truth in Ethics. *Ratio* (new series), 8(3), 209–226.

Wright, C.(2001). On Being in a Quandary: Relativism Vagueness Logical Revisionism. *Mind*, 110(437), 45–98.

Zangwill, N. (2000). Against Analytic Moral Functionalism. *Ratio* (new series), 13(3), 275–286.

Zimmerman, M. (2014). *Ignorance and Moral Obligation.* Oxford: Oxford University Press.

INDEX

9781138589858